SPEAKING ILL OF THE DEAD:

Jerks in Georgia History

SPEAKING ILL OF THE DEAD:

Jerks in Georgia History

John McKay

Guilford, Connecticut

Text design: Sheryl P. Kober
Project editor: Lauren Brancato
Layout artist: Justin Marciano

Library of Congress Cataloging-in-Publication Data is available on file.

ISBN 978-0-7627-7881-2

Printed in the United States of America

10 9 8 7 6 5 4 3 2 1

Contents

CONTENTS

Acknowledgments

In addition to the staffs of the Atlanta Historical Society, the Georgia Department of Archives and History, the Library of Congress, the National Archives and Records Administration, and a number of libraries, genealogical groups, and historical societies around the state of Georgia, who maintain very useful online and physical archives, there are several people I would like to thank by name, who lent great assistance and marvelous support to the stories of the sometimes difficult, sometimes embarrassing, and almost always highly controversial people who are written about in this book.

I am most grateful to Anne Amerson and Jimmy Anderson of the Lumpkin County Historical Society, for their assistance with uncovering some new material on Harrison Riley. Darinda Stafford of *Georgia Backroads* magazine was a great help in obtaining some material that appeared in long-unavailable copies of the magazine.

Mark Hickman of the Pegasus Archive and Dr. Jonathan F. Vance of the University of Western Ontario were most helpful in clearing up some misperceptions and pointing me in the right direction for finding a photo of George Harsh. Yvonne Oliver of the Imperial War Museum in London was equally as helpful in running down, at long last, the rare and difficult to locate image of Harsh that appears in this book.

Gerald Flinchum and Larry Stephens of Georgia Highlands College were of great help with both background and direct information about the Confederate guerilla John P. Gatewood.

Laron and Ruth Waite were exceptionally helpful and most kind in their assistance and permission to use some of the material from their own work, in relation to their ancestor Charles Blacker; I only wish that I could have related his story in a more positive light!

Marian Presswood is exactly the kind of archivist and researcher whom any historian would love to collaborate with; she went far above and beyond the call of her entirely volunteer duties to help run down every available scrap of information on both William Fain and John Gatewood. I can honestly say that I have never in all my years of research and writing had any such archival help provide me with the exact GPS coordinates of something I was looking for in the field, much less the location of the obscure, abandoned, and nearly forgotten grave of what was a peripheral character in the story! She is a marvel and jewel in the field of historical research and genealogy, and I treasured both meeting her and touring the facility she put together for such work in Benton, Tennessee.

Gail Miller DeLoach of the Georgia Archives was another archivist who went far above and beyond what would be expected in locating information about several different people who appear in this book.

I also want to extend my thanks to Lynn Garwood, Mary Lou Jordan, and Erica Rohlfs of the Dawson County Library, all of whom lent their kind assistance on a particularly difficult research case.

My mother, Peggy Carden McKay, father James Edward McKay, and sister, Phyllis Ann McKay, were all very helpful with both oral stories and written materials related to parts of the John Wallace story, especially about the eccentric character Mayhayley Lancaster in Heard County.

As always, I am most grateful to my chief proofreader, partner on research trips, primary critic and most steadfast champion, the dearest love of my life and my wife, Bonnie Kathleen McKay. I have so enjoyed our adventures thus far, and look forward to what the Lord has in store for us next!

Introduction

In many ways, this is a difficult book to research, to write, and to read. Those of us who live in Georgia, especially those fortunate (relative) few who were born and raised here, see this state as the epitome of all that is good and right about the South. It has beautiful rural countryside and gleaming new cities, gracious and honestly friendly people, weather that is temperate yet has some swings both hot and cold enough to keep things interesting, and fascinating nuggets of history tucked away in all sorts of odd corners and places. It is this last bit, though, that causes such concern on closer examination, for our home is also the site of so many painful, embarrassing, and horrifying incidents caused and perpetuated by some of our families, friends, and neighbors. And this is the picture we look at directly in this book, the dark and negative side of Georgia history.

Georgia was founded, in part, to serve as a religious refuge and a new home for imprisoned debtors back in England, a place where they and other groups could carve out a new and better home in the middle of what was considered a blank wilderness. Even in the very beginning, though, there were signs of things to come. The pirate Edward Teach, better known as Blackbeard, a very real historical figure, showed up on the coast to raid and plunder like the worst of commercial businesses would do in our cities hundreds of years later. John Wesley showed up as a newly frocked minister of the Gospel, but soon fell prey to temptations of the flesh, ruining his reputation and ministry, just as legions of later preachers would succumb to the same enticements. Wars would produce heroes and villains in near equal measure, sometimes within the same persons. Reputations would be honestly earned and earnestly protected in some, while others hid behind their own good public faces to commit demonically inspired crimes.

One aspect that affects the retelling of these sorts of stories is the natural reluctance of so many born and bred Southerners to "air their dirty laundry" in public. This book as originally planned had two more chapters concerning men who had very different public and private lives, the effects of which resulted in murder, mayhem, death, destruction, and the courts. In both of these cases not enough material could be gathered to create anything resembling an even-handed study of these men's lives, despite the abundance of inflammatory headlines about them in newspapers of their day. In several other cases of people who are included in this book, historical society archivists, research librarians, local historians, or genealogists were reluctant or downright refused to lend any research assistance to their stories, most doing so very politely, but declining to involve themselves in the tales of former residents in their areas who had committed horrific atrocities, even many decades previously.

However, to fully retell the stories of these criminals, rogues, and miscreants, it is necessary to look at the full picture of their lives. An old Southern expression is "bless their hearts," used when talking about people who fall short in one area or another, when gossiping about them and their affairs, meaning that everyone has some good in them somewhere, and the same approach is used here in most cases. It is difficult, if not impossible, to find a good and honest side to Edward Teach, but in other cases, the bad people did is tempered with other parts of their lives whenever possible, leading to a more complete and fleshed-out portrait of that person. George Harsh, for one example, was an archetypical "spoiled rich brat" who killed at least one man pretty much just for the thrill of killing him. To end his story when he was bundled off to jail to serve out the rest of his presumably worthless life would be to miss a truly glorious and marvelous tale, not of his redemption, but of his moving on to a better life while never letting go of what he had done. One field research visit yielded something in this line that was startling and somewhat disturbing—one of the people written about here had murdered at least four men by his own confession, and absolutely ruled his small part of Georgia by using equal parts Southern gregariousness and outright terror. His tombstone, however, had a large array of fresh flowers on it, not connected to his birthday or any other reason discernable, sixty-one years after his execution in Georgia's electric chair.

This is the dark side of what we consider God's own home, the South. These stories are meant to enlighten, expose, and examine the truth of what happened, as accurately and objectively as possible. No condemnation or undue criticism is meant against any of them, despite the occasional tone of what has been produced by a highly opinionated and somewhat curmudgeonly historian. May God rest their souls, each and every one, as they, like all of us, await his final judgment.

CHAPTER I

Edward Teach, aka "Blackbeard":
Pirate on the Georgia Coast

Along Georgia's coastline is a broken series of long, narrow, low-slung islands amid a maze of marshes, glens, and inlets, seemingly tailor-made for hiding out from authorities and as bases for conducting raids in the just-offshore sea lanes. In the early part of the eighteenth century, this is precisely what the coastline was used for, by no less than the most famed, feared, and notorious pirate of all who sailed the Caribbean waters, Edward Teach, better known as Blackbeard. And it was from one island in particular, what is today called Blackbeard Island, that the near-mythical figure swooped out upon passing Spanish merchant ships; this island is also where he reportedly buried his load of stolen treasure.

The 5,618-acre island, really a semidetached northeastern corner of Sapelo Island south of Savannah and north of Brunswick, has been a federally administered National Wildlife Refuge since 1924. It is roughly half-covered with a maritime forest, the other half consisting of salt marshes and open beaches, and is uninhabited and unconnected to the mainland or any other island. "Blackbeard's Island" appeared on maps of the area as early as 1760, although the stories of hidden treasure on it predate even that, going back to the time of the notorious pirate himself.

After a century of pirate movies featuring various fanciful incarnations of the legendary Blackbeard, it is somewhat startling to find out not only that he actually existed, but also that some of the more outlandish stories about him are actually true. Nothing is recorded about Teach's early life, but it is generally believed that he was born around 1680 in Bristol, England. Even his real name is up for debate, as there are no birth or other contemporary records for him, and several documents from around the time of his piracy period have multiple variations of his last name. "Thatch"

B. Cole sculp.

Blackbeard the Pirate.

Illustration from A General History of the Robberies and Murders of the most notorious Pyrates, *written by Captain Charles Johnson, 1724*

and variations of the name are the most prominent alternatives, but one contemporary record holds that Blackbeard was in fact a Drummond. It is tempting to suppose that he was born into a poor or working-class family, as a seagoing career was very common for their offspring at the time, but it is known that he was able to read and write, unusual for the lower classes, and one historian has even proposed that his parents were in the English peerage.

One fact that is little disputed about Teach is that he crewed at least one British Royal Navy auxiliary ship in the Caribbean during Queen Anne's War, the American part of the larger War of Spanish Secession, in the first years of the eighteenth century. He probably crewed lesser merchant ships, possibly slave ships crossing the Atlantic, and first appeared in historical records as an officer of a vessel around the time he was thirty-seven. Because of this known and documented ranking, it is safe to assume that Teach had gone to sea at least twenty years earlier, possibly as much as twenty-eight or more years earlier, as a cabin-boy and powder monkey. Teach first shows up in documented logs in 1716, as second in command of the privateer *Mary Anne*, under Captain Benjamin Hornigold.

There is some confusion today about the difference between pirates and privateers; simply put, privateers are legal pirates. During the four-hundred-year period between the discovery of the New World and the end of the Age of Exploration, not one fledgling navy had the full capacity to both protect its country's colonial outposts and attack other countries' maritime resources on the high seas. In the early days of this period, there were no true navies in the modern sense whatsoever, military operations on the open seas being a new concept. The laws of economics in a free market holding that a supply will be created to meet any demand, it was not long before independent mariners offered their services and were subsequently commissioned to put pressure on other nations' merchant fleets. These commissions were called "letters of marque," and most outlined whom the privateer might attack, and for what length of time. So long as they were operating under these letters, the privateers were considered legal combatants flying the national flag at sea. It is somewhat startling to realize that the US Constitution still has an active clause authorizing Congress to "grant letters of marque and reprisal"; the last time Congress did so was in 1942, when it issued a letter of marque to the Goodyear Tire Company, using its blimp *Resolute* as an armed antisubmarine platform off the California coast.

After the conclusion of the official hostilities of Queen Anne's War in 1713, Hornigold continued his raids and seizures, albeit without official sanctioning by the British Crown. He scrupulously kept to the other terms of his letter of marque, refusing to attack any British flagged vessel, maintaining a veneer of legitimacy by claiming that he was continuing to participate in the related but already concluded European War of Spanish Secession. Hornigold had started this part of his postwar privateer career with a single-masted, eight-gun sloop, the *Mary Anne,* which probably featured Teach among the crew even before he was given a command status. By 1717 Hornigold had moved up to the *Ranger,* described as a thirty-gun (possibly thirty-six, with fore and aft chasers and twin swivel guns), fast and highly maneuverable sloop with a 140-man crew, probably better described as a small frigate, roughly the size of today's 90-meter offshore racing yachts. By far the most powerful ship in the Caribbean basin in that day, the *Ranger* allowed him to raid and seize Spanish ships with little difficulty. For comparison, the fictional *Black Pearl* in the *Pirates of the Caribbean* movies is a very similar style of ship, a highly modified heavy merchantman turned into a three-masted, single-gundecked frigate carrying thirty-two twelve-pounder canons, with half mounted on the main deck, probably close to the same arrangement of the main batteries used on the *Ranger*. It had been strictly an economic war at sea, with little actual combat. Captured ships and cargos were distributed as prizes among the crews, leading to their natural reluctance to give up the life of relatively easy profit. Captain Hornigold had the additional problem of keeping his crews satisfied with their lot, as his own position depended upon it.

A commonly held misconception about most pirate ships is that they were exclusively captained by the most ruthless and bloodthirsty of the lot, who held their positions through fear, intimidation, and the sword. To understand the nature of most pirates, it helps to look at them for what they were: seagoing highway robbers. Most turned to piracy for both easy profits and a relatively easy lifestyle, since the various navies and merchant fleets required their sailors to submit themselves to more structure and discipline. Most crews were the purest of democracies; anyone could join with the consent of the rest of the crew, anyone could leave pretty much any time he wished, the plunder was painstakingly divided up evenly, and most pirate captains stood for election by the rest of the crew. On top of that, such captains were subject to "recall votes" and could be replaced if the crew lost confidence in their leadership abilities. Needless to say, these "recall elections" could turn deadly at times!

The victims of most pirate attacks also were not treated as popular novels and movies usually portray. The bottom line was the bottom line, and so long as the captured merchantman did not try to escape, its crew did not resist, and the ship itself was not better, more desirable, or just needed more by the pirate crew, the valuable cargo would be taken, "volunteers" to join the pirate crew would be accepted, and the ship would then be let go in as short order as possible. By the mid-1720s, pirate-hunting privateers and even formal naval forces were becoming more widespread and feared, and hanging out in the neighborhood of such a seaborne mugging was not advisable. If anything went the other way, though, all bets were off, and there were few limits to the subsequent levels of violence that would occur. Pirate ships were outfitted in such a way to make these sorts of "swooping" attacks most efficiently: Most were shallow-draft sloops or small frigates, and their cannons were loaded with bar-shot, grapeshot, or rough equivalents, which would kill or maim the crew and damage the rigging and sails, while leaving the hull and masts intact. The speed of attacks was aimed at increasing the terror and intimidation levels of their victims, while leaving their ships dead in the water but relatively easy to rapidly fix, in case the ship itself could serve as a juicy prize.

When seen in this light, pirates come across like particularly ruthless businessmen pressing hard on their deals; in fact, legitimate capitalists today are often given the epithet of "pirate." In the real world of the seventeenth- and eighteenth-century Caribbean and other pirate hotspots, however, the reality was far from what Walt Disney, or even his current namesakes and company executives, would find acceptable as family entertainment. An Internet joke circulating a few years ago held that a "pirate PDA" consisted of writing "Rape, pillage, *then* burn" on their palms, to make sure that they got the sequence correct. This is morbidly amusing, as it hits very close to the truth: Pirates as a lot were drawn from the ranks of sociopaths, professional criminals, the semifunctional, the aggressive mentally ill, and a host of others who, in current polite society, one normally sees only behind bars. In short, they were a bunch of smelly and rather manic drunken jerks, all in all.

Efforts at increasing the terror level of victims were reflected in the famous "pirate flags" as well. Flag colors and insignias were more or less standard, even in that early day of developing navies, with the various national flags flown by privateers, solid black flags flown showing the intent of that ship to engage in combat, and solid red flags, the actual *jolie rouge* ("pretty red"), indicating that the crew would give no quarter in the ensuing battle, meaning that prisoners would not be taken and it would be a no-holds-barred fight to the death. The very first documented "skull and crossbones" was displayed by a French crew on a red flag in December 1687, ironically during a land-based fight, though it is obvious the intent and meaning was well known by that time; the 1567 ship's equipment list of the English forty-seven-gun galleon *Bonaventure* contained at least one "bluddey flagge." By the golden age of piracy, many such crews had settled on black flags with various symbols on them to indicate their respective commands, though all did carry and would raise the *jolie rouge* when the mood struck them. These symbols were not always unique, as was the case in traditional European heraldry symbols. The very familiar skull and crossbones on a black flag was flown by several notorious pirates, including Edward England, John Taylor, Sam Bellamy, and John Martel. Interestingly, the well-known flag shown in the *Pirates of the Caribbean* movies, the skull and crossed cutlasses on a black flag, identified primarily with the pirate Jack Rackham, seems to be entirely fictional (at least in the age of pirates; it is now used as a symbol of the US Navy SEAL teams).

Hornigold and Teach began their joint pirate command by raiding the West Indies sea lanes, and within a few weeks, Teach had taken command of one of the prize ships, the *Adventure*, a six-gun sloop with a seventy-man crew. Hornigold and Teach continued raiding for a short while as "consorts," or as a small fleet of pirates under a single command structure, capturing several large merchant ships with valuable cargoes of flour and Madeira wine. In September 1717, they ran into one of the most famous of the Golden Age pirates in Nassau, Stede Bonnet. Formerly a wealthy landowner in Barbados, Bonnet had turned to piracy earlier that year to escape an unhappy marriage, purchasing a twelve-gun sloop he named the *Revenge*, and raiding along the eastern North American coast with his 150-man paid crew, highly unusual if not unique for that time. An inexperienced sailor at best, and a disaster as a combat commander, Bonnet was recovering in Nassau from injuries he suffered following an ill-considered, unsuccessful attack on a much larger armed Spanish frigate. He and Teach struck up a friendship of sorts, and with the blessings (and undoubtedly relief) of Bonnet's crew, Teach took over command of the *Revenge* while giving control of the *Adventure* to an unknown subordinate. The three took to sea again with their three-ship consort fleet, this time raiding shipping along the English and Spanish colonies of the eastern and southeastern North American coastline, basing their operations for a time around Georgia's barrier island and marshland network, through the fall of 1717.

It was during this period that Teach, a natural born leader, began to eclipse his mentor and master Hornigold. After a raid in the Bay of Delaware on October 12, the master of one captured ship did not report the presence of Hornigold, by far the best-known pirate at the time, but reported on the new guy, "Tatch," who was accompanied by the also well-known but still visibly unwell Bonnet, who "walks about in his morning-gown." Hornigold and Teach had apparently amicably separated by this time, both briefly returning to raiding the eastern Caribbean in the late fall of 1717, before Hornigold sailed separately for Nassau and retired from the life, accepting a king's pardon the following June. After parting with Hornigold, Teach's two-ship flotilla captured a French guineaman (a moderately sized naval warship converted to a heavy merchantman) named *La Concorde* off the coast of Saint Vincent, carrying a cargo of slaves. Teach sold the slaves, possibly allowing a few to join his crew, overhauled the ship, increased its armament to forty guns, and renamed it the *Queen Anne's Revenge*. With its crew of over three hundred, it was one of the largest and best-armed pirate ships of all times, the equivalent size of one of the smaller ships of the line in the regular navies, known there as a "fifth-rate" warship.

With a few notable exceptions, the historical record of the remainder of Teach's career is spotty, conflicting in its documentation, and exaggerated to the point of making it all seem like a bad novel. Teach himself helped in no small part in all of this; he had a natural motivation to conceal his true movements, while letting rumors fly all around the Caribbean as to his whereabouts. Teach personally cut quite a figure in his heyday, no doubt to reinforce the terrible image he already had, cowing any potential victims even further and making his plundering that much easier. A vivid, if entirely second- or third-hand description of Teach was given by Captain Charles Johnson in his 1724 book, *A General History of the Robberies and Murders of the most notorious Pyrates*:

> *Captain Teach assumed the cognomen of Black-beard, from that large quantity of hair, which, like a frightful meteor,*

covered his whole face, and frightened America more than any comet that has appeared there a long time.

This beard was black, which he suffered to grow of an extravagant length; as to breadth, it came up to his eyes; he was accustomed to twist it with ribbons, in small tails, after the manner of our Ramilies wigs, and turn them about his ears; in time of action, he wore a sling over his shoulders, with three brace of pistols, hanging in holsters like bandoliers; and stuck lighted matches under his hat, which appearing on each side of his face, his eye naturally looking fierce and wild, made him altogether such a figure, that imagination cannot form an idea of a fury, from Hell, to look more frightful.

Although a bit far-fetched, Johnson's vivid description is reinforced in part by similar written descriptions by two of Teach's foes: Henry Bostock of the *Margaret* wrote in 1717, "the Captain by the name (as he thinks) of Capt. Tach . . . was tall Spare Man with a very black beard which he wore very long"; and Lieutenant Robert Maynard, the one who finally defeated Teach in battle, later wrote to a friend an even more sparse but consistent description, "[Captain Teach] went by the name of Blackbeard, because he let his beard grow, and tied it up in black ribbons."

Other than these eyewitness descriptions, there is little known about Teach's personal life. One source repeats a rumor that Teach had "a wife and children in London," but no documents exist that support this claim; if it were true, he would have been one of the few known married pirates of that age. The idea of a real-life "pirate father," much less the dread pirate Blackbeard himself, is almost too bizarre to contemplate in any case! Another, less reliable source claims that Teach had at least fifteen wives in various ports, going on to claim in lascivious detail the sodden outrages to which he purportedly exposed some of them.

Teach's encounters with his victims have equally wild tales surrounding them, most noting his hulking, ferocious appearance and flying red and black flags; later reports were embroidered with all sorts of bloodthirsty outrages in which he purportedly engaged during his raids. However, the few available records seem to indicate otherwise, most victims reporting that their ships' cargoes were ransacked but that the crews and shipmasters were not molested, unless they made the mistake of attempting to resist their capture. After seizing what cargoes he pleased, Teach seemed to simply let the crews go in their ships; or if he seized their ship, as in the *La Concorde* situation, he gave them one of his other, smaller prize vessels to take to shore. All of this does not dilute, however, the fact that he was a pirate, possibly the most notorious and bloodthirsty criminal wretch of all of that sordid community. Those who made the grave error of resisting Teach's raping, pillaging, and plundering of their property were either cut down with a flurry of cutlasses, shot down immediately, or worse, marooned without supplies on the nearest deserted beach.

Very little is known about Teach's movements between December 1717 and January 1718, but he did strike at several places around the eastern and western Caribbean, seizing six more ships with full loads of crew to add to his flotilla. In February or early March 1718, he returned to the northern Caribbean, raiding again along the Florida and Georgia coasts, and it is believed that he once again set up his base of operations for a time around what is today Blackbeard Island. Awarding himself the grand title of Commodore, and commanding the largest and most capable pirate fleet at the time, he decided to hit a richer target in a more spectacular way. He also desperately needed medication for his numerous sick crewmen, as a yellow fever epidemic was laying waste to the large number of men he needed to man his ships. Arrogant with power and desperate for these supplies, he took his fleet to the port of Charleston in May 1718, blocking off the entrance to the harbor. For six days he held the city in siege, demanding medicines from the residents, some of his men swaggering drunkenly around town, while his sloop commanders stopped and looted every ship that came into the harbor. It was an odd siege, and although Teach seemed to enjoy the power and terror he spread during the ordeal, he eventually acquired medicines worth only about four hundred pounds, while all of the other booty was worth about an extra sixteen hundred pounds, along with some really nice clothing he literally took from the backs of the wealthier citizens and ship captains. This was during a period when Teach and his men had a combined net worth of roughly 250,000 pounds, a height of power that quickly ended.

The Royal Navy and other pirate hunters were increasing in force in the Caribbean and the American colonies by this time, and doubtlessly Teach felt the heat. His flagship was big and powerful, but also ponderously slow and less maneuverable than the classic pirate sloops. It also required an exceptionally large crew, which would share in all the potential booty. Sailing north from Charleston, Teach deliberately grounded the *Queen Anne's Revenge* and one of his other sloops, the *Adventure*, at Topsail Inlet on the North Carolina coast. In a well-planned deception, he left most of his men to try to refloat the two ships, while he and a select few others grabbed as much loot as they could handle, and fled in his two remaining ships. Setting up operations in Bath and on nearby Ocracoke Island, North Carolina, Teach used his influence to convince the governor to grant him a pardon in June 1718, which carried little weight outside of the state boundaries. He did allegedly marry a local planter's daughter, Mary Ormond (also allegedly his fourteenth or fifteenth wife), and bought his way into a life of gentry leisure in the wealthy agricultural community.

That interlude lasted a whole month, the siren call of crime on the high seas proving irresistible. By August he had returned to sea and his pirate ways, joined again by his faithful and utterly ruthless first mate, Israel Hand, on board the refloated *Adventure*. This period also did not last long, ending on November 22, 1718, when a small Royal Navy task force under Lieutenant Robert Maynard invaded Teach's base at Ocracoke Island. In the ensuing bloody battle, featuring an epic hand-to-hand combat between Teach and Maynard on the deck of the *Adventure*, the much-feared pirate finally went down in defeat, "fell with five Shot in him, and 20 dismal Cuts in several Parts of his Body."

A near-demon in life, at least in reputation and actions, Teach was treated accordingly in death. Maynard ordered his head cut off and suspended under the bowsprit of his own ship, the *Jane*, while Teach's body was simply thrown overboard. The legends did not end there: Stories abound that Teach's headless body "swam several times around" the *Jane* before sinking into the depths of the Atlantic Ocean.

Teach was known to have amassed a rather sizable fortune from his plundering, but all that could be located after his death amounted to just a couple of thousand pounds' worth. He had allegedly told some of his fellow pirate captains that he had "banked" most of it in a remote location. From the hints that he dropped, it was entirely possible that he was talking about his temporary raiding base on the Georgia coast. Local legends abound that the specific location was in the forests of what is today Blackbeard Island, though many search attempts, including a large and well-funded search in 1934, have yielded no sign whatsoever of the dread pirate's treasure. Yet.

CHAPTER 2

John Wesley:
Jilted Fugitive from the Savannah Colony

I t is no surprise to learn that a person held in high regard in some circles is not viewed as highly in others; for any late-breaking examples, we always have Congress. It is, however, surprising to find out that a person credited with helping to found a major denominational branch of the Christian church would have a history of crime and moral turpitude not from a wayward youth, but during his missionary efforts, leading to a trial and his fleeing from justice. That honor, however, does belong to none other than John Wesley, who is credited with the establishment of the Methodist Church.

Wesley was born in June 1703 in Epworth, England, as the fifteenth of nineteen children of Samuel Wesley, a somewhat controversial and unsuccessful Anglican rector, better known as a noted poet and literary contemporary of Daniel DeFoe. John, one of ten siblings who survived to adulthood, was rescued from a fire in his father's rectory at the age of five, a dramatic scene that deeply impressed him and led him to a life in the ministry. He frequently remarked on this incident later in life, commenting that he had been singled out by God to be saved for his eventual missionary work, frequently quoting the last phrase of Zechariah 3:2, "And the LORD said unto Satan, The LORD rebuke thee, O Satan; even the LORD that hath chosen Jerusalem rebuke thee: is not this a brand plucked out of the fire?"

Wesley's formal Christian education began at the age of eleven, when he was sent to the Charterhouse School in London, where he studied primarily under the scholar and pastor John King, a devotee of the writings of Thomas à Kempis. King's teachings mirrored those of Kempis, whose c.1420 book, *De Imitatione Christi*

John Wesley's monument in Savannah's Reynolds Square
PHOTO BY JOHN MCKAY

(*The Imitation of Christ*) called for a life reenergized and refocused on Christ himself, one of monkish piety, withdrawal from worldly concerns and distractions, and internal self-examination in the light of the gospels, as opposed to the standard external displays of official poverty and corporate praise and worship the church practiced. Wesley later said that this work, which was one of the earliest writings that laid the foundations for evangelical concepts of rebirth in the Spirit, was one of the greatest influences on his conviction and subsequent conversion. Wesley also was enthusiastic about William Law's *A Serious Call to a Devout and Holy Life*, published later in his scholarly life, with its similar call to a life spent in worship and adoration of God, to the exclusion of mindless attention to earthly matters.

John later graduated from Christ College at Oxford, was ordained as an Anglican priest in 1728, and the following year formed and became the leader of the Oxford Holy Club, whose members were sneeringly referred to as "methodists" for their unusually regimented and ordered prayer and devotional life. In 1735, John accepted an invitation from the Trustees of the Colony of Georgia to become the minister for the newly established parish church in Savannah, officially as part of a mission from the Society for the Propagation of the Gospel. He boarded the sailing ship *The Simmonds* on October 14, along with his brother Charles, who had accepted a post as Georgia trustee and founder James Oglethorpe's personal secretary, and a small group of German Moravian missionaries, also bound for Christian work in the new colony. During the voyage, John and Charles both became friends with the Moravians, frequently discussing deep issues of theology and ecclesiology, practical ways of how a member of the church was to function in the world while living a life of pious devotion. John became deeply influenced by the Moravian approach to missionary work, seeing how it dovetailed with and fleshed out his own personal worldview.

Despite Martin Luther's widespread recognition for leading a reform effort against the excesses of the medieval Church, he was not the first to do so. One group that preceded him by no less than a century was the Hussites, followers of the reform teaching of Jan Hus, a Czech devotee of the fourteenth-century English dissident John Wycliffe. After Hus was burned at the stake in Constance in 1415 (in what is today the Czech Republic), the pope, along with the various Holy Roman emperors (leaders of the Holy Roman Empire, who ruled in what is today Germany, Austria, Hungary, and the Czech Republic) led a series of five crusades against his followers, known as the Hussite Wars, resulting in a succession of Hussite victories and a final but limited peace settlement with Rome in 1434. This movement in the numerous small states of the Holy Roman Empire was constantly under attack by later Holy Roman emperors and popes, but survived in small groups and pockets, partially influencing Martin Luther's more widely successful reforms nearly a century later. One small group of Hussites in Moravia (a region of the eastern Czech Republic) started one of the first formal Protestant churches, the Unity of the Brethren, which ended up as loosely affiliated, heavily persecuted, small splinter groups, but survived the subsequent Thirty Years War and other attempts at stamping out the reform movements. Some of survivors of these Bohemian splinter groups gathered in what is today Saxony, Germany, in the 1720s, formally establishing a new Protestant denominational church, the Moravians. In short order it became the first large-scale evangelical Protestant missionary movement, sending out its first missionaries before the church numbered more than three hundred members. One of these early missionary efforts came in February 1735, when a group of ten Moravians went as a "First Company," to establish a foothold mission in the new colony of Georgia. A "Second Company" of forty-one Moravians followed in October, led by August Gottlieb Spangenberg and David Nitschmann, including twelve ministers and evangelists, the very group that sailed to Georgia along with the Wesley brothers.

The English colony of Georgia was created primarily to serve as a buffer colony between the rich colonial properties in Virginia and the Carolinas, and the hostile Spanish colonies to the south in Florida. A secondary purpose for the colony was to provide a refuge and avenue of compensation for the staggeringly high number of debtors who were imprisoned until they could pay off their debts; even at this time, imprisonment was considered by many to be a badly-thought-out method of handling the problem. A third potential goal for the colony was to provide a haven for oppressed Protestants from other American colonies. An unstated goal was put forth by Thomas Bray and his Society for the Propagation of the Gospel, which was to bring the good news of the Gospel of Jesus Christ to the African immigrants (not slaves, since slavery was not yet allowed in Georgia) and Native Americans of this southernmost colony, a goal heartily endorsed by his friend and colonial founder James Oglethorpe, who also forbade the institution of slavery in the new colony. George II, the second of the "German" British kings, and the first to be able to speak English, granted Oglethorpe and a board of twenty-two trustees a proprietary (corporate) charter for the colony in 1732. On February 12 of the following year, Oglethorpe and a selected group of 116 men and women established the first Georgia settlement, at Yamacraw Bluff on the Savannah River, on the north side of what is now downtown Savannah.

No debtors came in the first group of settlers, and despite Oglethorpe's heartfelt desire for Georgia to become a haven for them, few ever settled there. Alcohol was banned and the first settlers were limited to just five hundred acres of individually owned land, but the colony almost immediately began attracting a large number of middle-class English tradesmen, as well as persecuted Protestants from western Europe, and a surprisingly high number of Jewish immigrants. The largest block of immigrants by far, though, was the Scots, persecuted and driven from their homeland by new English landlords. The numbers of these, especially Highlanders, radically increased following the failure of the last Scottish rebellion in 1746. The Jews tended to remain cloistered in their religious establishments, but the Scots and other European Protestants brought a strong flavor of evangelical missionary fervor, especially the Moravians and their new friends, John and Charles Wesley.

Oglethorpe's original pastor was the Anglican Rev. Henry Herbert, who performed the first formal church service in the new colony. Herbert unfortunately made little impression on the new community; he fell seriously ill after just a few weeks and sailed back to England, passing away on the voyage. Rev. Samuel Quincey (or Quincy) of Boston applied to the Trustees to fill his position and was accepted in May 1733. He also proved to be inadequate for the task in the harsh frontier climate, being chronically ill and frequently having to rely on pulpit-filling pastors from South Carolina, arguing with colonial authorities, and refusing to report to the Trustees about his activities and expenses. His license to preach was revoked on October 10, 1735, and he was essentially fired from his position. Oglethorpe accepted the Society's recommendation of John Wesley to fill the position. This appointment was one that seemed destined to fail from the very beginning, though, as Oglethorpe was seeking a regular parish priest to oversee the spiritual needs of his new colony, while Wesley was simply on fire to evangelize the Native Americans, and had little interest in holding a staid, routine church office.

Even during the voyage across the Atlantic, Wesley's Holy Club "methodism" was reflected in his daily routine:

> Our common way of living was this: From four in the morning till five, each of us used private prayer. From five to seven we read the Bible together, carefully comparing it (that we might not lean to our own understanding) with the writings of the earliest ages. At seven we breakfasted. At eight were the public prayers. From nine to twelve I usually learned German and Mr. Delamotte Greek. My brother writ sermons, and Mr. Ingham instructed the children. At twelve we met to give an account to one another what we had done since our last meeting, and what we designed to do before our next.

About one we dined. The time from dinner to four, we spent in reading to those whom each of us had taken in charge, or in speaking to them severally, as need required. At four were the Evening Prayers; when either the Second Lesson was explained (as it always was in the morning,) or the children were catechised, and instructed before the congregation. From five to six we again used private prayer. From six to seven I read in our cabin to two or three of the passengers, (of whom there were about eighty English on board), and each of my brethren to a few more in theirs. At seven I joined with the Germans in their public service; while Mr. Ingham was reading between the decks to as many as desired to hear. At eight we met again, to exhort and instruct one another. Between nine and ten we went to bed, where neither the roaring of the sea, nor the motion of the ship, could take away the refreshing sleep which God gave us. (Fries, Ch. 4)

Quincey remained in the parish house for some time after his dismissal, before moving to another, more successful assignment in the Carolinas. Wesley stayed aboard ship for a few more nights after arriving in Savannah, and then moved in with the Moravians at their invitation. Deeply and sincerely influenced by their evangelical work, Wesley made clear to Oglethorpe in their first meeting that his heart was in the missionary field, but the colonial leader convinced him that the time was not yet right for such work. Oglethorpe told him that the necessity of first establishing a firm basis for the colony was paramount and that he really needed Wesley to see first to the needs of Savannah itself. Accepting Oglethorpe's counsel, at least for the time being, Wesley ascended to the office of rector of Christ Church in Savannah in February 1736, where to all reports he threw himself into his new office with great diligence and energy. With the enthusiasm of most young and inexperienced church leaders, he sought not only to bring the formal traditions of Anglican Church life to the new parish, but also to establish his newly discovered devotional disciplines in his parishioners, influenced by his encounter with the Moravians. Even from the beginning of his duties, though, he began evangelical missionary work first among the "non-churched" settlers in and around Savannah, and then among the Native Americans in the area, expanding within a few weeks to efforts to evangelize the black slave population on plantations in nearby South Carolina. Wesley saw these missionary efforts as perhaps even more important than his church leadership duties, remarking that he undertook them "to save my own life."

Wesley gave his first sermon on March 7 from his new pulpit at Christ Church, which then met in the courthouse. From that first day he established a personal habit of preaching the morning and afternoon services, and then going in the evening to visit the Moravian services, where he helped translate some of their hymns and materials into English. The rest of his week was just as filled, with visitations, prayer meetings, and missionary work, and soon Wesley was confiding to his friends that he was simply exhausted. It is very probable that this overreaching effort led to a series of disastrous errors in judgment. Like the first two colonial priests, Wesley was soon embroiled in controversy and friction among the colonists. In view of his later breakaway and establishment of the Methodist Church, it is ironic that his earliest conflicts arose when he was accused of adhering too strictly to the "high church" doctrinal requirements, without giving due concern to the somewhat raw conditions in this frontier settlement. His increasingly frequent and public outreach efforts to the local Native Americans earned him a series of warnings from Oglethorpe and others that his attention was straying too far from his assigned duties, and his efforts to convert the slave populations across the Savannah River in South Carolina earned him the enmity of their owners. Oglethorpe had led the effort to ban slavery from the new Georgia colony, but he was in no mood to create any friction between the neighboring colonies, and was distinctly displeased with Wesley's violation of the South Carolina law against converting slaves. Wesley further alienated himself from some of his congregants by meddling in political affairs, giving unneeded, unnecessary, and divisive verbal support to some malcontent factions that were attempting to overthrow some or all of the rules of the Trustees, who were his employers. In light of this, it is a wonder that Wesley held on to his position as long as he did!

While John Wesley was having his own problems in Savannah, his brother Charles found himself in the middle of similar disputes farther south. Oglethorpe had assigned him to administrative duties at Fort Frederica on Saint Simons Island, and sent Rev. Benjamin Ingham along as the first parish priest for the area. Ingham was a former Oxford Holy Club member himself, and had sailed for Georgia along with the Wesley brothers. Charles expanded his own duties without authority of the colonial officials to include exhortations to piety and a self-examined, disciplined prayer life among the colonists, who did not appreciate his efforts, to say the very least. Saint Simons Island was the southernmost English outpost, literally standing guard against Spanish incursions from Florida, and attracted the rough-and-tumble sort accustomed to such harsh living conditions. The somewhat delicate and sickly Charles was soon subject to a serious backlash from the settlers, including a vicious gossip attack started by two of the post's women, and was even reproached by Oglethorpe himself for "stirring dissention" in the frontier post. To Charles's great relief, Oglethorpe soon removed him from Fort Frederica and sent him back to England to handle some administrative chores related to the colony. After Charles was removed, John traveled to Saint Simons Island, in an ill-advised and unauthorized move, to see the situation for himself, and tried to affect the spiritual state of the outpost in a manner similar to his brother, to the same bitter end. One of the gossips, Beata Hawkins, even tried to shoot John, and after missing, tried to stab him with her scissors before she was subdued. Deeply shaken, he left after this visit, never to return.

In addition to the difficulties Wesley had in his ministry efforts, he allowed himself to become embroiled in a serious scandal with one Sophia Hopkey, who had sailed on the same ship bringing Wesley and the Moravians to Georgia. They had conversed occasionally on the trip over, and over the first year of his parish ministry he met with her daily for breakfast and spiritual instruction at the home of her uncle and Georgia Chief Magistrate under the Trustees, Thomas Causton. The thirty-three-year-old Wesley was quite smitten with the eighteen-year-old "Miss Sophy," frequently courting her at her home in the evenings as well, but he was concerned that a marriage would negatively impact his ministry work; his first concern was to establish a network of missions among the Native Americans before he did anything about his personal life. To all accounts, Hopkey returned his affections in kind, at least verbally, and dropped not a few hints that she would welcome such an invitation to marriage. Wesley's Moravian friends also advised him against the marriage, as it would distract him from his full attention on the Kingdom of God. Hopkey expressed her desire to marry Wesley, repeatedly and frequently, but through her subsequent actions seemed to want to be married more than she was particular who the groom would be, and in March 1737 told Wesley that if he would not marry her, she was going to marry someone else. Wesley decided to cast lots to decide whether to marry the young woman, and seemed satisfied when his chosen lot was not to do so. He let her know this in their last courting meeting and agreed that she could marry another, if she so chose. It is not recorded what Hopkey's reaction to this decision was after wasting so much time trying to persuade Wesley into marriage, but one can easily presume she did not take it gracefully. Wesley responded in what seems to be his own awkward, selfish, and socially inept style, writing in his journal about this last meeting. It probably was even more awkward than his description:

> *This was indeed an hour of trial. Her words, her air, her eyes, her every motion and gesture, were full of such softness and sweetness. I know not what might have been the consequence had I then but touched her hand! And how I avoided it I know not. Surely God is over all.*

Even so, he seemed quite shocked when, shortly afterward, she announced that she was to wed a Mr. William Williamson, a wedding that was to be presided over by none other than Wesley himself. Wesley performed the ceremony, but was almost maddened in his grief over the loss of his one true love, even drawing up his will in the throes of despair.

Compounding his series of bad decisions, he attempted to serve as the newlyweds' pastor and spiritual confessor; not surprisingly, this came to a bad end. Four months after their wedding, Wesley somewhat arrogantly refused Sophia communion one Sunday at the altar of Christ Church, on the feeble grounds that she had not previously notified him of her intent to accept it. On her husband and uncle's protest, Wesley doubled down on his series of bad decisions, and changed his stated reason for refusing her communion, claiming that he knew she had "unconfessed sin in her life." The Williamson's immediately filed a one-thousand-pound civil suit against him for defamation of character, which split the church into mutually supporting factions. Sophia's uncle Causton also misused his office as Chief Magistrate as a weapon against Wesley, directing the grand jury to investigate the matter and other related charges against Wesley as a criminal case.

The grand jury, allegedly filled with Causton's friends and others opposed to Wesley, returned a "true bill" on ten criminal counts against him. Welsey countered that nine of the counts were purely ecclesiastical, and therefore out of the court's purview, but demanded an immediate trial on the one remaining criminal charge, that he had written Sophia without her husband's consent. The courts were reluctant to step into this mess, refusing an immediate trial, and postponing trial six more times at later hearings. Wesley was quite vocal about the case, even from his pulpit, and the details were widely reported all across the colonies. Realizing that the entire affair was making his missionary efforts impossible, he appealed to the courts to release him from his bond, allow him to travel back to England, and clear his name before the Board of Trustees. They refused to drop the bond and allow him to leave, but didn't seem to make much of an effort to prevent his departure, either. On the night of December 2, 1737, he sneaked across the Savannah River in a boat to South Carolina, and then quietly made his way to Charles-Town, boarding a ship back to England after what he described as an epic flight through "jungle-like" terrain in the coastal lowlands. He was allowed to make his case before the Trustees, on February 22, 1738, while both the Williamsons and Causton filed formal regrets with the board for their part in the whole scandal. The Trustees did not make a ruling either way, but with the acknowledgment that his witness was permanently damaged in Georgia, Wesley was allowed to resign his position on April 26.

Wesley seemed less than introspective about his time in Georgia and the scandal in which he became embroiled; his autobiographical *Journal* pretty much skips over the details of the various charges against him, at least his own views of them, and hammers away at the fact that he was brought up on civil charges for what he saw as a purely ecclesiastical issue. Though it is entirely safe to say that John Wesley's immature efforts in Georgia were feeble at best and absolutely counterproductive at worst, and it is clear that he acted rashly and foolishly throughout most of his Georgia ministry, and absolutely like a jerk over the entire court affair, it is also necessary to point out that his contact and relations with the Moravians during this time affected his own devotional theology deeply. As a result, a humbled, more mature Wesley later in life played no small part in the development of one of America's largest Protestant denominations.

CHAPTER 3

Thomas Brown:
Loyalist Guerilla Fighter during the Revolution

Thomas Brown never set out to become a notorious guerilla fighter and accused (if never tried) war criminal, much less an international fugitive expelled from multiple countries, his name a synonym for the worst among traitors and thieves. All he wanted, at first, was to live the quiet life of a gentleman planter, in a town he founded and grew all on his own in the rich hill country outside of Augusta, Georgia. That dream ended, nearly permanently, with the actions of a maddened mob in 1775.

Thomas Brown was born to a prosperous family in the port town of Whitby, in Yorkshire, England, on May 27, 1750, the great-grandson of Isaac Newton. His father was a well-respected businessman who owned a shipping company with a regular trade route to Charlestown in South Carolina, crewed by men from the Orkney Islands in the far north of Scotland. As expected for the son of such moneyed gentry, Thomas attended a school in town with a classic educational curriculum, where he learned French, Latin, ancient Greek, and Roman history and literature. One of his seagoing neighbors, Commander James Cook, returned to Whitby for a visit to the town the same month Brown left to see the world and conduct his father's business, December 1771.

Working in commercial ports all up and down the Atlantic seaboard and through the British-held Caribbean, Brown became deeply intrigued with the freedoms and possibilities that the American colonies held, and decided to settle there permanently, in the newly ceded raw frontier backcountry of Georgia. Brown first tried to obtain a comfortable government position, but failing that, decided in 1774 to become a gentleman planter. He recruited families in Yorkshire and in Scotland to join him on his stake, which Georgia Royal Governor James Wright would increase by two hundred acres per family and fifty acres per person who immigrated. Brown was in turn to pay the royal governor five pounds sterling for every hundred acres granted him, with a later "improvements" assay of up to five shillings an acre. His first group of twenty-nine immigrants sailed from Whitby on August 12, onboard the *Marlborough*, bound for the Orkney Islands to pick up additional immigrants, and then on for the port of Savannah.

Brown and his first group of settlers arrived in Savannah in November 1774, and Governor Wright was quickly taken by the twenty-four-year-old Brown, whom he called a "young Gentleman," and immediately arranged a political office of magistrate for him. Wright wanted to settle this new land with a "better class" of people: not the rough-and-tumble frontiersmen who were so hard to control, but the genteel businessmen and planters with whom Wright was more accustomed to dealing back in England. What Brown didn't know was that while the plots he was ceded to establish his own township were in fact quite rich in forestry and other resources, the governor deliberately failed to tell him of the dangers that lurked there. His original stake was 5,600 acres north of the Little River, in the interior countryside west of Augusta, in some of the newly acquired territory in the colony.

A few months before Brown landed, Wright had obtained this territory from the Cherokee, with the agreement that the sale of the land would recoup the large debt the tribe owed to traders in Augusta. The problem with this plan was that the Creek nation had a competing, and better, claim for some of this same land. After several Creek attacks on white outposts, and a subsequent refusal by whites to trade with the Creek, the Cherokee and Creek chiefs finally agreed to the land cession, but passions were still running very high among the illegal settlers and their Indian adversaries in the area.

At the same time, news of political uprisings in Boston had reached Georgia, and passions against the Crown were starting to heat up, with a fight brewing over the Intolerable Acts. Savannah merchants opposed these harsh measures, of course, but somewhat surprisingly, the backcountry settlers still tended to support the Crown in this case. In January 1775, Governor Wright had permitted an unofficial Provincial Congress to meet instead of the colony's official assembly. It was badly split in the political opinions of its members, but agreed to support the anti-Crown American Association being called for by some of the other colonies. Petitions were drawn up showing support or opposition to these Parliamentary measures. In addition, names were taken of those who refused to join the Association, officially for shunning them economically and socially; as a result, hard lines were being drawn between factions in the coming war.

There are a number of unfortunate misconceptions about the American Revolutionary War; possibly the worst is that it occurred wholly, primarily, or even most importantly in New England and Virginia. Another is that it was a "gentlemen's war," one where customs and rules of warfare were habitually followed, a genteel affair between the conventional armed forces of Great Britain, France, and the American colonies. Nothing could be further from the truth in nearly every regard.

The war started on April 19, 1775, of course, just outside of Boston, when a group of Lexington Colonial militiamen drew up in formation on their square as a British regular army reinforced patrol moved through toward a suspected arms cache at Concord. Tensions were running very high, and although the militia did begin dispersing on the British commander's order, shots were exchanged, and eight Americans were killed, only one British regular was slightly wounded. At Concord, the British patrol found most of the cache already removed, but faced off again with another group of Colonial militia, this time retreating in some disarray from the fight at the Old North Bridge. Their retreat back to Boston should have sent a signal as to how the coming war would be fought; thousands of Colonial militia rushed to the scene, setting up multiple ambushes and harassment actions as the

British repeatedly broke their rank-and-file discipline in their near-panicked rush back east. The British suffered three hundred casualties against "farmers and common rabble," who themselves only suffered the wounding and loss of ninety-three.

It didn't take long, though, for the war to be turned over to the professionals, at least in the North. The Continental Congress realized that the British Crown would never recognize the independence of a nation based on the combat actions of irregulars and guerillas, whom they viewed then how we view terrorists today. The land combat in North America shifted to the South in 1780, as yet another attempt was made to subdue Colonial militia forces with British regulars. The use of this mistaken tactic on the part of the British contributed to the Americans' ability to win the war, and also provided a theater in which it turned to complete savagery.

The Southern American colonies had been inhabited and built by a very different group of people than their neighbors to the north. The Northern colonies were first settled by gold-seeking Englishmen, but very rapidly the region attracted fewer get-rich-quick sorts and more religious dissenters, middle-class tradesmen, and northern Europeans fleeing poverty, war, and persecutions of various natures. The Southern colonies were initially settled as proprietary colonies by groups of investors and as buffer states against the dangerously aggressive Spanish colonies to the south and west. The region's abundant rice, indigo, and timber eventually attracted a relative handful of wealthy planters, as well as a significant number of Scots, Scots-Irish, Irish, and lower-class English, who were comfortable in the harsh frontier region, along with a scattering of missionaries, Catholics, Jews, and others religiously or politically persecuted in their home countries.

While the Northern colonies largely settled into tightly bound township communities with outlying small-plot farms closely clustered around, the Southern colonies featured large commercial plantations, mostly near the coastlines, with widely scattered small-plot and subsistence farms ranging deep into the interior. Indians were viewed almost universally in the North as dangerous pests, while in the South there were great distinctions made between savage and "civilized tribes," with strong missionary activity and commercial trade engaged in with the nations presumed friendly.

For the first 140 years, there was little in the way of dissension between Britain and its American colonies, but this changed during the French and Indian War. There was some friction between the professional British army officers and their American militia counterparts during the war, which led to some later antipathies, but more importantly, due to the nature of that war and the necessity for the colonists to shoulder a great deal of responsibility for their own safety from the French and their allied Indian nations, a great spirit of independence was sparked. With the end of the war in 1763, compromises negotiated between Britain and France caused the American frontier to shrink significantly; no longer were colonists allowed to settle anywhere west of the Appalachian Mountains, now French and Spanish territory. On top of that, both sides in the war had allied with and used extensively the warriors of various Native American nations, dividing loyalties, disrupting the trade and commerce between them that had been established over the previous century, and most significantly, reigniting a vicious, low-intensity war along the frontier regions between the opposing Spanish, French, and their allied Indian tribes, and the American colonists and their respective allied Indian tribes. This warfare, plus the political movement for independence that had been sparked primarily in the Northern colonies, combined with the exhaustion of the British treasury and its need to refill its coffers, preferably with American taxes, grew into a serious level of dissension between the Americans and the British over the next decade.

It has been noted frequently that by 1773 the Americans were deeply divided over their support for separation from Great Britain, with roughly a third supporting the Crown, known as Loyalists or Tories, another third supporting the independence movement, known as Patriots or Whigs, and the rest simply wanting to be left alone and out of the political mess, at least up until the time of the tea parties and the so-called "Boston Massacre." The Scots and Irish who had been hounded off their land by the English, especially when the Scottish Highlands were cleared after the failure of its last rebellion against its English overlords in 1745–46, populated a significant percentage of the Southern colonies, and in turn, would seem to favor the Patriot cause. Surprisingly, a not insignificant number of these families ended up supporting the Crown as Loyalists; they had seen firsthand the terrible atrocities wrought against them by English lords given free hand by the Crown, and feared the wealthy and powerful men leading the Patriot cause in the North would eventually turn on them as well. Not surprisingly, given the rough-and-tumble nature of both the land and the people living in the South, passions ran very high on both sides, with things turning ugly even before the open combat started at Lexington and Concord, and independence was subsequently formally declared. By 1774, lines between the two sides were clearly being drawn up.

Brown arrived in the middle of this whole mess, and although he originally had deeds to land north of the Little River, it was far too dangerous to settle any of that land immediately, with the still-hostile band of Creek warriors roaming about. He ended up establishing his settlement, Brownsborough, about thirty miles northwest of Augusta, in a good fertile valley between the Big and Little Kiokee Creeks, just west of the Savannah River. While his settlers were building up and clearing the area, Brown himself took up a fine home in Augusta, moving in sometime in February or April of 1775. Close by Brown's in-town home, at the fork of the roads leading into Cherokee and Creek territories, was a trading post in a large Georgian building owned by Robert MacKay, who quickly befriended and welcomed the wealthy young man into the Augusta social circles.

News of the exchange of gunfire at Lexington and Concord reached Savannah in late May, but Governor Wright decided it would be imprudent and inflammatory to request that British troops be sent to guard critical locations. It was a poor decision— the powder house was broken into and a large quantity of arms and ammunition was stolen on May 11. The following week the Savannah Committee (or Council) of Safety, a nascent Patriot organization, was announced and their first organizational meeting called for on June 21. Brown, not a little impetuous and rash himself, publicly declared that he would use his magistrative office to support the Crown in every way, and in July set about organizing a "loyal association" to oppose the Georgia Provincial Congress and the Councils of Safety in the state, immediately making him a marked man to the Whigs. A group of "Liberty Boys," a local chapter of the Sons of Liberty, which quite frankly were little more than thuggish mobs in the model of the Boston group headed by Samuel Adams, decided to pay Brown a visit and make an example out of him.

Headed by Captain Robert Hamilton, Thomas Graham, and Chesley Bostick, the mob "visited" a number of Augusta-area Loyalists before they found Brown at his friend James Gordon's Augusta home, New Richmond, on August 2. Brown stood his ground on the porch of Gordon's home as Hamilton's mob loudly demanded he repudiate his loyalist stances, accompany them to Augusta, and sign an oath of allegiance to the Association. Brown argued that he could not do so, as he was already under oath as a magistrate, and that he did not wish to take up arms against the Crown, but at the same time he did not wish to take up arms against his new neighbors, either. He also argued, apparently quite effectively, that they could not strip him of the privilege of his own opinions, and that if they in fact did value public liberty, they should respect his private liberties. With that effective argument, roughly half the mob left, but shortly afterward, Brown was physically attacked by some of the others, led by an inflamed Bostick. He tried to defend himself with sword and pistols, but after a few minutes of fighting, was struck from behind with the butt of a pistol, which fractured his skull and briefly knocked him out.

Brown was carried off as the mob ransacked his friend's home. He was scalped, tarred and feathered, then tied to a tree and a pile of wood under his feet set on fire. The mob laughed and jeered at his screams of agony. Before he died from the torture, the fire was extinguished, Brown was cut down from the tree, strapped to a rail atop a cart, and paraded around parts of Augusta. He was finally released to another friend's care, Martin Weatherford, who obtained proper medical care for him. His head wound never completely healed, he suffered serious headaches the rest of his life, he lost two toes, and he spent weeks regaining the ability to walk on his burned legs. As soon as he was able to mount a horse, though, he left the state, bound for a Loyalist stronghold in Ninety-Six, South Carolina, vowing to return with "blood and fire" for his torturers. Jubilant Whigs promptly nicknamed him "Burnfoot" Brown, a name that followed him for many years after the war.

While he was still recuperating at Ninety-Six from his grievous injuries, the revenge-minded Brown not only continued his anti-Association activities, but also started actively recruiting "loyal men" to defend the king's cause in the Georgia and South Carolina backcountry, swearing all the while that he would pay back his Augusta tormentors in spades. Whig publications that had made light of his torture and subsequent appearance took on a different tone later in the summer of 1775, dropping their light-hearted mockery of Brown and stating a dire warning that he was attempting to stir up the Indians against the backcountry settlers. This was a common theme of both sides throughout the era, when memories of fearsome battles and merciless raids by French-allied Indians during the earlier war were still very fresh. Instead, political infighting among those loyal to the king in upstate South Carolina ended up destroying any chance of forming a strong Loyalist military force there.

Some of the leaders who had housed Brown formally surrendered to the Charlestown Associators, while Brown returned to Savannah to deal with his settlement business. There, his last load of settlers came in from Scotland aboard the *Marlborough*, many sick and some already dead from smallpox, only to find their master Brown still recovering from his tortures and about to be exiled from the colony. They, too, had to choose sides almost as soon as they landed. Brown and Royal Governor Wright left for the then British-held Saint Augustine colony aboard the HMS *Hinchinbrook* on January 18, 1776.

In St. Augustine, Brown presented a plan to Florida Royal Governor Patrick Tonyn to do exactly what the Whigs had accused him of plotting to do: travel through the north Florida and western Georgia backcountries recruiting and equipping the various Indian tribes and nations to fight against the nascent Patriot rebels. Unbeknownst to Brown, the decision to use Indians in the coming fight had already been made by General Thomas Gage, initial overall commander of the British forces in America, and supported by General Sir Henry Clinton, newly in charge of the Southern theater. Brown's intent was to raise a white-led Indian force in the Georgia and South Carolina backcountry, supply it from the base at Saint Augustine, and attack and seize Augusta as soon as possible, supported by regular British army troops moving north from Charlestown under Clinton. His plan quickly approved, Brown was given a commission as a provincial lieutenant colonel, and moved north in late March 1776, with a small force of recruits and a wagon train of gunpowder and arms. He entered Georgia just west of the Okefenokee Swamp, moving farther north along the Flint and Chattahoochee river basins, through the Creek Nations.

Once in the backcountry, Brown discovered that he was not the only one trying to recruit Indians to fight for his cause—Patriot George Galphin had already begun the same process to build a white-led Indian force to attack the Loyalists in the backcountry. Unfortunately for Galphin, there had already been too many incidents in which white settlers had killed Creek, and he was unable to overcome their animosity. He sent a letter to the Patriot commander of the Southern theater, Major General Charles Lee, suggesting that efforts to persuade the Indians would lead to nothing, and the preferable course of action would be to use some of their military force to destroy and drive them out of Georgia instead. This was approved, and the backcountry Patriot militias of both Georgia and South Carolina spent much of the late summer of 1776 fighting with elements of the Cherokee nation, mostly the western Chickamauga band under their war chief Dragging Canoe, clearing them from most of the territory north and west of Augusta.

Brown lived among the Creek for the rest of 1776, and was able to gain their trust, loyalty, and support of his recruitment efforts. He attempted the same with the Chickamauga Cherokee, but as they were on the "warpath" with the Patriot militias, they were in no mood to distinguish between whites, and he was not able to form any lasting alliances with them. Brown also found out in the fall that his settlement of Brownsborough and his friends' homes in Augusta had been ransacked by these same Patriot militias. He returned to Saint Augustine in January 1777, and was immediately given command of the East Florida Rangers, a mixed force of white Loyalists and Indians that was intended to work alongside and support a regular British force under Lieutenant Colonel Lewis Valentine Fuser, a somewhat arrogant and disdainful officer of His Majesty's Sixteenth Regiment of Foot Infantry. Tonyn had personally asked Brown to play nice with the regular British officer, but while their subsequent expeditions into south Georgia and northeast Florida were successful, it was very clear that the fast-moving guerilla tactics used by Brown and the slow, plodding, heavy infantry tactics employed by Fuser were a bad mix. An attack on a mounted Georgia Patriot militia near the St. Johns River resulted in Brown's Indians attacking and killing twenty-four Georgians, allegedly after they had surrendered. There were several different accounts of this event, but in the end Brown's reputation as a vicious, unmerciful leader of a bloodthirsty guerilla band was made in the minds of both the Patriots and the regular British commanders.

By the winter of 1777–78, Brown commanded four companies of Rangers, with looser command over several hundred Creek war parties, all scattered throughout northeastern Florida, and southern and western Georgia. His own headquarters was at Fort Tonyn on the Saint Mary's River, near present-day Jacksonville. His men roamed nearly at will all across Georgia, even passing through

Augusta and taking Fort Frederica on Saint Simons Island with relatively little difficulty. Despite Brown's less-than-sterling reputation among the regular British officers—given his refusal to join their ranks and be under their direct authority—his men carefully chose their battles and very rarely lost a fight. After attacking and taking a major Patriot fortification along the Altamaha River, Fort Howe, Brown was sent north into South Carolina to rally and organize Loyalist militias. One reason for this mission was that he had become a thorn in the side of the regular British command, who saw him as rash, unpredictable, and not under any serious military discipline, faults in their minds not necessarily supported by any battlefield performances, which could complicate measures in the political aspects of the war. With him out of the picture, however briefly, it was hoped that they could persuade Governor Tonyn to disband his command.

Instead, a determined Brown was able to identify, organize, and send to Florida large numbers of Loyalists willing to fight, as well as set up an extensive and effective intelligence and scouting network all across the region. This had the end effect of increasing the efforts of the regular British officers to strip him of his command, who saw his increasingly successful battlefield efforts as underlining their own relative lack of any real success, and therefore, making them appear weak and ineffectual. However, when Tonyn reluctantly asked his fiery militia commander to agree to serve under the direct command of the regulars, the rebelliously independent Brown offered his resignation instead. Before any action could be taken, a Continental army invasion of south Georgia and northeast Florida kicked off, led by General Robert Howe, with six hundred South Carolina Continentals under Colonel Charles Pinckney and five hundred Georgia Continentals under Georgia Governor John Houstoun. Brown was forced to withdraw from and burn his fort, and then turn to his usual guerilla tactics of hiding in the swamps and conducting hit-and-run attacks. Even while the regular British forces were engaged in fighting back this American invasion, they kept up pressure on Governor Tonyn to eliminate Brown's command or bring it in under their own discipline. This same animosity extended into December 1778, when another large regular British force, this time under Lieutenant Colonel Archibald Campbell, attacked and took Savannah, with Brown's Rangers working in a supporting role. Campbell's opinion of Brown did rise significantly, however, when he played a major role in helping to plan and execute a successful raid and capture of Augusta in January 1779. Brown remained in Georgia for the next year and a half, working alongside regular British forces in a series of actions, including the initially unsuccessful attempt to capture Charlestown.

In June 1779, while commanding a small outpost at Ebenezer with his Ranger force, the exiled Georgia Royal Governor, James Wright, offered Brown a new command. Eager to get out from under the thumb of Fuser and the other Florida-based British regulars and assume command of his own corps, Brown reorganized and regrouped his scattered former command. Renamed the King's Rangers, they were outfitted with their first formal uniforms of the war, green jackets with red collars and cuffs. At some point they were taught regular infantry tactics of the day, including the use of the bayonet, which they put to good service in the defense of Savannah from a French-led invasion in October. The following May, Charlestown finally fell to the British, and Brown once again moved his force north, to seize and hold Augusta. Brown immediately set about pacifying the countryside, which involved equal parts diplomacy with the Whigs who had held sway for so many months, and savage small battles between Loyalist and Patriot militias. One of the most effective and notorious in the latter was one of Brown's subordinates, Captain Daniel McGirth, who commanded a group of Carolina Loyalists and Indians. Like Brown, McGirth had also been måltreated by Patriots early on in the struggle. Also like Brown, McGirth became widely notorious as a "banditti," an outright terrorist under very loose if any military discipline, well known for plundering farms and homes of those not loyal to the Crown. His reputation for savagery and lack of any quarter given in battle was at least equal to—if not exceeding—that of Brown himself.

However, the single action that set Brown's reputation once and for all took place on September 14, 1780, at his friend Robert MacKay's trading post in Augusta. Back in February of that year, a large group of Carolina Loyalist militia, over six hundred men commanded by Colonel James Boyd, was traveling through the north Georgia backcountry heading to rendezvous with British forces in Augusta. They made camp on the morning of February 14 at Kettle Creek near Wrightsborough, about eight miles from present-day Washington, which was the site of several combat actions during the war. Boyd had endured several small harassment actions from some Patriot militias along the way, but was unaware that he was being tracked by a larger irregular force, led by a trio of Georgia and Carolina Patriot commanders: Colonel Andrew Pickens, Colonel John Dooly, and Lieutenant Colonel Elijah Clarke. Clarke and Brown had crossed swords before, and seemed destined to do so again in this campaign, as Brown's Rangers were already en route from Augusta to meet and guide Boyd's force farther south to Savannah. Instead, the three Patriot militias launched a somewhat coordinated attack on Boyd's command before Brown could arrive, resulting in a confused skirmish in the hilly, forested terrain. Boyd was killed by a Patriot militiaman, who was part of a group that had gotten lost in the woods and happened to stumble into the middle of the Loyalist camp. With that, his command fled, only about 270 meeting up with Brown's Rangers a few days later. Somewhere between seventy and 150 Loyalists were captured, and roughly seventy more were killed in the action, while five more Loyalists were later hung by Pickens and Clark.

Several months later, Brown had returned to Augusta with his Rangers and roughly a thousand Creek warriors, taking back the town and command of several other Ranger companies and independent militias in the area. Clark was once again trying to pacify Georgia, a more urgent task by then with the Patriot loss and rout at Camden on August 16, giving the British a stronger hold in South Carolina. In early September, he led a Patriot militia force of roughly six hundred men south along the old Creek trading path toward Augusta, capturing a British officer along the way who revealed the presence of and disposition of Brown's commands. Standing directly in Clark's way was Robert MacKay's trading post, occupied and fortified by Loyalist Captain Andrew Johnston's Rangers, with most of the Creek Indians encamped nearby, and Brown's own Rangers along with another militia at Fort Grierson on the other side of the town.

Clark divided his force, and on the morning of September 14, his subordinate Major Samuel Taylor took one group into the Indian encampment, while another under Lieutenant Colonel James McCall struck from the east. Clark himself led the rest of his force down the Savannah Road straight into town, rapidly advancing to and taking the MacKay house. Johnston was killed in the quick, savage, close-quarters fight, while the rest of his command quickly surrendered. Before Clarke could consolidate his forces, Brown's Rangers and his Indian allies struck from the Augusta side of the road. Brown's men formed a line of battle in a nearby cultivated field, called Garden Hill, and deployed two small, one-pounder cannons that British General Cornwallis had given him. After a few volleys of cannon fire, the Rangers and Indians charged the house, pushing out the Patriot defenders with heavy losses. Clark reformed his command in the nearby woods, and assaulted the MacKay house again, this time with Brown's commands inside and in hastily dug entrenchments outside. The Rangers quickly tore out floorboards and brought up other materials from the basement, to strengthen the static defenses of the house, all while repulsing Clark's advances. Brown himself was shot through both thighs during the battle, but refused to be taken for treatment before collapsing from the pain. Clark held the house under heavy fire in siege for the next four days, unable to dig Brown out from the now strongly fortified outpost, before his own spies reported the approach of a British relief force.

As the relief troops approached the house from the east, Clark's men started bugging out, despite his orders for them to remain in place. Seeing the Patriot command dissolving, Brown ordered his Rangers and Indians to leave the house and pursue them. The Patriot retreat became a panicked rout, the Rangers capturing a number of prisoners, while the Creek warriors returned to their habitual savage slaughter of all the Patriots they encountered, once they were out of sight and out of direct control of Brown. Showing little mercy himself, Brown ordered thirteen of the prisoners to be hanged in the MacKay house stairwell, as he found they had violated their paroles from earlier encounters. At that time, prisoners who were released had to vow to abandon the war; those who returned to the fighting were considered by the enemy as in violation of their parole. No other prisoners were harmed, though McCall and Clark both later claimed that Brown had ordered the hangings of the prisoners "and other outrages" to settle his own bloodlust and to wreak vengeance for his own tortures. It took some time for the newly unleashed Creek warfare in the backcountry to be brought under control, spreading to civilian outposts and settlements that had only loose Patriot connections before it ended; Clark claimed that this, too, was the result of Brown's direct command of the Creek. He and McCall also spread a false rumor that the remaining prisoners were turned over to the Creek to be tortured to death, when in fact they were sent under guard to Savannah.

Brown kept and even expanded his militia commands through the rest of the war, but his reputation had already been ruined. Loyalist prisoners were hung after later battles, with the excuse that Brown had done it first. An 1887 history of Georgia by Charles Colcock Jones referred to Brown as a "devil incarnate," though officers and officials of both sides during and after the war raised no special objections to Brown's tactics or orders, even praising him for his honor and loyalty in command, including such luminaries as the great American officer General Henry "Light Horse Harry" Lee. This is not to give the impression that he wasn't a rogue personality at all; he did have quite a foul mouth against the American cause during the early years (which is why the Whigs tortured him nearly to death), and his tactics were distinctly aberrant from

Battle of Kettle Creek Monument, near Washington, Georgia
PHOTO BY JOHN MCKAY

the prevailing rules of war, which caused him no end of grief from both the Patriots and regular British officers. Since both sides used these tactics to greater degrees as the war progressed and deepened, however, both sides subsequently decided to let sleeping dogs lie and not discuss the nastier bits of the Southern guerilla war any further. After the war, Brown relocated to Saint Augustine with thousands of other displaced Loyalists, attempting once again to settle down to his dream of becoming a quiet planter. This second start, though, was doomed with the cession of Florida back to Spain in 1783. Brown appealed to the state of Georgia to allow him to return and resume his settlement at Brownsborough; his letter was not even answered.

After being expelled from both the nascent United States and the newly reacquired Spanish colony of Florida, Brown bounced around the Caribbean for several years, briefly returning home to his father's estate in Whitby before finally receiving a grant of land on the Caribbean island of Saint Vincent from the British government in 1799. He built another agricultural settlement there, Grand Sable Plantation, where he was finally able to take up the life of a gentleman planter before dying in 1825. His best-known legacy, regardless of its fairness or accuracy, remains that of being "Burnfoot" Brown, the maddened butcher of the Georgia backcountry and the mass murderer at the MacKay house.

CHAPTER 4

Major Ridge:
Cherokee Chief and Signer of the New Echota Treaty

One of the least glorious events in US history occurred in the winter of 1838–39, when most of the remaining Cherokee Indians east of the Mississippi were rounded up by army troops, held in concentration camps in Georgia and Tennessee until the hardest part of winter was nearly upon them, and then forced at bayonet point to walk from Georgia to reservations in Oklahoma, via the scenic route by way of Illinois. All of this was done in a perfectly legal manner by the US government, written permission given by none other than twenty-two of the leaders of the various Cherokee bands themselves, including Kahnungdatlageh, "The Man Who Walks on the Mountain Top," better known as Major Ridge.

The one event that led directly to the removal of Cherokee and other Indian bands, tribes, and nations from Georgia was the "discovery" of gold on Cherokee land in 1828. There had already been no small amount of friction between white settlers and Indians, reaching a peak during the backcountry guerilla skirmishes of the American Revolutionary War period. Some bands of the Cherokee had actively sided with the Loyalists during the Revolution, as did many of the Creek and other nations in the region, and as a result, lost many of their land holdings after the war. Though the Cherokee nation was seriously split between the Loyalist-allied warrior bands, primarily the Chickamaugan band under the war chief Tsi'yu-gunsini ("Dragging Canoe"), and those who either supported the Patriots or simply chose to be neutral, no attempt of any sort was made by the white governments to distinguish between the differing factions. A series of treaties was brokered between the US government, the state of Georgia gov-

*Major Ridge, a Cherokee chief. Printed and colored
by F. W. Greenough, c. 1838*
COURTESY OF THE LIBRARY OF CONGRESS

ernment, and the various Indian nations, that by the early part of the nineteenth century left only parts of northwestern Georgia as a Cherokee reserve, while other parts of the central and southern areas of the state were left in Creek hands, small fractions of the vast areas both had formerly controlled. As in many, if not most of the previous and subsequent Indian treaties, this land was "given over" to the Indians primarily because the white settlers saw little use for it at the time.

Out of this forced resettlement came a new group of tribal leaders, Major Ridge and Guwisguwi ("Rare Bird"), otherwise known as John Ross, being the most prominent. Ironically, these two leaders took power with the intent to stop any further cession of Cherokee lands. Most traditional Indians from the area, known as the Western Cherokee, had already moved to lands set aside for them in Arkansas by 1819, and to another set of land reservations in Oklahoma in 1828. These moves came primarily as a result of an 1806 treaty brokered by Chuquilatague ("Doublehead"), who as a result was labeled a traitor and assassinated by a group of warriors headed by Major Ridge.

Ross, who was elected as the principal chief in 1827, and Ridge built a different community for their Eastern Cherokee nation, hoping that by assimilating into white culture they could avoid being displaced and having their land seized. In a very short length of time, about thirty years, they completely changed their entire nation's way of living, adopting European-style clothing, mannerisms, culture, farming methods, and housing, and dropping their animistic religion and embracing Christianity as a nation. Showing complete disregard for long-standing traditions, Ridge ordered that ancient traditional bands and clans within the nation be broken up and replaced by elected tribal councils in 1817. A unique and formal capital of the Eastern Cherokee nation was set up in 1825 at New Echota, with a surrounding village of streets, factory, and warehouse buildings, and European-style residences. One of their members, Sequoyah, or George Gist, even invented a European-style syllabary and writing system in the 1810s and '20s, the only time in known human history that an illiterate people have accomplished such a feat. A Christian missionary in the Cherokee nation, Samuel Worchester, helped to develop a version of Sequoyah's new syllabary that could be used on a printing press, which he also purchased and used to print a newspaper in the language. This development also led to the drafting and adoption of a written constitution, based heavily on the US Constitution, in 1827.

While Ridge led all of this effort with the pragmatic hope of being able to settle into a new, American-style world, therefore avoiding the utter destruction that so many other Indian nations and tribes had endured—with himself as chief of the new nation, of course—it was accomplished with a heavy price. Ancient traditions, bonds, ceremonies, and customs were all swept away in the rush to assimilate, causing this nation to become something new and radically different in an astonishingly short amount of time. Ridge was a highly effective salesman, of the snake oil variety, and his "new and better" approach obliterated the more traditional leadership of Ross and other chiefs resistant to assimilation. One telling example of the depth of these radical changes is mentioned in James Mooney's 1900 work, *Myths of the Cherokee*, and concerns the name of their own nation: "Cherokee, the name by which they are commonly known, has no meaning in their own [reinvented] language, and seems to be of foreign origin."

The colonial-era leaders George Washington and Henry Knox had enjoyed good relationships with the Indian nations with which they had interacted, and proposed a six-point plan where all or most of the other Indian nations could be "civilized," and by doing so, gain acceptance in white society. The abandonment of the warpath, for the most part, and widespread adoption of "white" ways led to the *Tsa-la-gi* (Cherokee), *Tchakta* (Choctaw), *Muscogee* (Creek), *Chikashsha* (Chickasaw), and Seminole being referred to as the "Five Civilized Tribes," though only most of the Cherokee and about half the Creek really met the definition. Nevertheless, the erosion of Native American culture through assimilation into white society was not a welcome change to many targeted tribes, and created many negative repercussions. The Seminole, for example, later gained a quite different reputation, fighting successfully for their independence in three separate wars spread over forty years.

The political and cultural assimilation of the Cherokee with white society extended to forming military alliances with them; they refused to join Tecumseh's confederation in 1811 (which lost the Battle of Fallen Timbers against the US Army on November 7 of that year), refused to support the Red Stick Creek uprising in 1813, and sided with the United States in the subsequent Creek War of 1813–14. At one battle during that war, Horseshoe Bend in east central Alabama, Cherokee warriors fought directly alongside General Andrew Jackson, and allegedly saved his life from a band of Red Stick warriors who broke through the lines. The Red Sticks were a traditional, antiwhite band of Upper Creek warriors, and following their loss at Horseshoe Bend, abandoned their territory in Alabama and moved into Florida, assimilating with the Seminole. Many Lower Creek warriors fought alongside Jackson as well, and thought at first that they, as well as the Cherokee, would be treated as honored allies following the war.

Jackson was not one who would allow trivial concerns of personal gratitude and sacred honor disturb his quest to rid the east of Indians, though; at the Fort Jackson meeting that ended the war, he demanded not only that the hostile Upper Creek cede all of their land, but also that his allied Lower Creek and Cherokee give up huge chunks of their own land as well. They did so, but only very reluctantly and after years of negotiations and further treaties.

The Creek War and the Battle of Horseshoe Bend were quickly overlooked in the media by larger events during the contemporaneous War of 1812. Andrew Jackson's greatest fame from the period grew not from his Indian fighting, but from his successful defense of New Orleans, which ironically occurred three weeks after a peace treaty had been signed in Belgium. Another group of "civilized" Indians, the Choctaw, fought alongside Jackson in the trenches of Chalmette Plantation during that battle.

In the meantime, the state of Georgia was even more deter-mined than Jackson to rid itself of Indians, and repeatedly peti-tioned the federal government for help in doing so. In 1822 the state formally asked Congress to vacate an 1802 treaty with the Cherokee, and strip them of all land claims within the boundaries of the state. When that failed, a bill was passed to allocate thirty thousand dollars in state funds to buy the Cherokee's land from them; this, too, was refused. The Cherokee legislature passed its own bill that year calling for the death penalty for any individual who sold any Cherokee land to the whites.

The attempts to assimilate and live alongside the white world came to a complete end in 1828, when Jackson was elected Presi-dent, and almost simultaneously, major amounts of gold were discovered in Cherokee lands. Legend has it that a man named Benjamin Parks was hunting on Cherokee land in late 1828 near the present-day city of Dahlonega, when he literally tripped over a nugget of gold. The truth is that small gold-mining operations had already been in place in the area since 1826, but the publicity of Parks's later "find" and simultaneous discoveries of gold fields in other parts of the territory led to the Georgia Gold Rush of 1829, the first major gold rush in US history. The Cherokee were quickly overwhelmed by the sheer numbers of prospectors who rushed into their territory, an 1830 news report claiming that over four thousand miners were working just one creek in the territory, while the boom towns of Lick Log (later Dahlonega) and Auraria sprang up nearly overnight, topping off at populations of over fif-teen thousand at the height of the rush. Even the new vice presi-dent of the United States, John C. Calhoun, got in on the action, building a hotel in Auraria during the rush, while it was still offi-cially Cherokee land.

Ross and Ridge appealed to the state of Georgia for help in controlling the flood of miners and their supporters, which at first resulted in state militias being called out to bring some sort of order to the territory. Very quickly, though, any concern for the tribe's well-being was forgotten in the light of gold's allure, and these same militias were used against the Cherokee to keep them from enforcing their territorial rights on the trespassing hordes. Completely overwhelmed, with no chance of successfully using the warpath to defend themselves, the Cherokee leaders appealed to the federal government for help, asking it to enforce the treaties they had signed. Their appeals fell on deaf ears: Jackson was not likely to take the Indian side in any land dispute under the best of circumstances, and in the case of this massive gold rush, was even less likely to lift a finger to do anything to help the Cherokee.

Jackson not only did not move to help the appeal of the Cherokee, he had also introduced in Congress an Indian Removal Act in 1829, calling for the "voluntary" and total exclusion of the so-called "Five Civilized Tribes" from their lands. Two of Jackson's bitter political opponents, Senators Daniel Webster and Henry Clay, managed to hold up passage of the bill for a year, primarily because of political conflicts that had nothing to do with the Indians themselves. With overwhelming public support, though, Jackson signed the bill into law on May 28, 1830. Military, political, and diplomatic options exhausted, the Cherokee turned to the courts for relief. In the meantime, the state of Georgia simply extended its authority over this territory, officially a foreign country, divided up the entire area into land lots, and hosted two land lotteries in 1832 to give it away to non-Indian settlers.

Three cases brought by the Cherokee quickly wound their way up through the federal court system. Two ended up being decided against the Cherokee in lower courts and were refused Supreme Court review: *Georgia v. Tassels* (1830) and *Cherokee Nation v. Georgia* (1831). The third case, *Worchester v. Georgia* (1832), was finally taken up for review by the Supreme Court. The old Cherokee territory missionary, Samuel Worchester, had refused to follow a new Georgia law requiring him to register with the state and obtain a license to do missionary work in the territory. He believed, undoubtedly rightfully, that the state would simply refuse to issue him a license, and remove him from his influential supportive position in the Indian nation. He and six other missionaries were arrested, convicted, and sentenced to four years of hard labor, and then ordered to leave the state and Cherokee territory. He appealed his conviction in the federal court, basing his appeal on the point that the Cherokee territory was legally a separate sovereign nation, where the laws of Georgia did not apply and could not be enforced.

Chief Justice of the Supreme Court John Marshall and President Jackson were old and very bitter political rivals, and several popular histories have spread a tale that Marshall used this case to fire a political shot at Jackson. This tale also holds that Jackson ignored Marshall's explicit order to enforce the Cherokee treaties, and usually includes a marvelous bit of political infighting undermining the Constitution, in which Jackson presumably responded to Marshall's decision by saying, "John Marshall has made his decision, let his armies now enforce it." Marshall and Jackson were in fact political rivals, but all of the rest of this tale is false. The court's decision upheld Worchester's appeal, emphasizing in their opinion the central point that the Cherokee were a separate nation, and that the treaties between the United States and the Cherokee were the same as between foreign sovereign nations, but limited their court order to Worchester being freed from state custody. The clear implication was that the United States should enforce its treaties and that Georgia had no rights in the territory, but the court's decision did not include any mandate for Jackson to enforce such a finding, another bit of very careful political maneuvering on Marshall's part. Jackson could have easily used public opinion against this decision to destroy the integrity and authority of the court, just like he had previously undermined and destroyed the Bank of the United States, and Marshall knew this. As a further sign of political disdain and the relative weakness of the court, the state of Georgia kept Worchester in custody for several months after the decision before releasing him.

Shortly after the Worchester decision, a small delegation led by a desperate Ridge met with Jackson in the White House. Despite all the evidence to the contrary—particularly given Jackson's history of using Native Americans for personal gain and having no qualms at abandoning them once their usefulness to him was exhausted—Ridge held on to the hope that his attempts to pander to the whites by assimilating his tribe into the their culture would give him entrée with this powerful white leader. Ever consistent, Jackson assured the disillusioned Ridge that he most certainly would not use federal force to protect the Cherokee's treaty rights, and urged them to sign a new treaty and leave the state for reservations already set up in the west. Broken by the unflinching refusal, Ridge became convinced that he and his nation were rapidly approaching a pair of hard choices: leave or die. He and Ross agreed that their nation would be unable to fend off the actions of the state of Georgia, but even after the stern refusal of support from Jackson, they disagreed in how to go about solving the dilemma. Determined to maintain a strong stance for his people, as well as retain what little was left of their homeland (and pride), Ross wanted to find some way to force the US government to guarantee their treaty rights to the north Georgia territory. Meanwhile, Ridge believed this was impossible, given the political climate in Washington at the time, and thought the best solution was to negotiate a removal treaty. Rather than continue to fight and risk another defeat (or hope for anything better), Ridge was willing to surrender, effectively sanctioning the demise of the Cherokee nation.

A delegation led by a desperate but determined Ross went to Washington in March 1834, to try to salvage some sort of political solution from the mess that would keep the Cherokee territory intact. In May 1834, Ridge led his own delegation to Washington, to negotiate separately for a removal treaty, completely destroying any influence either might have had with the federal government. Both leaders recognized that their internal differences threatened their nation as a whole, but even after a series of mediated conferences, were too hardheaded, stubborn, and unyielding in their stances to resolve their differences. Jackson saw this as the perfect opportunity to divide and conquer; he refused to see the Ross delegation, now referred to by its supporters as the "National Party," but made overtures to the minority delegation led by Ridge, referred to as the "Treaty Party." Jackson knew he had identified the weak link in the Cherokee chain of command, and was poised and ready to finally obliterate it. Jackson met again with Ridge, this time with other delegates from the Treaty Party, including Ridge's son John, his nephew Galagina Oowatie, or Elias Boudinot, the editor of the *Cherokee Phoenix* newspaper, and another nephew, Stand Watie, later a Confederate major general. Chief Justice Marshall joined the discussion, urging Ridge to sign a removal treaty as well; although he still believed that their treaty rights should have been enforced, he surely realized that they would not survive the expanding, quickly encroaching tide of white settlers and prospectors taking over Cherokee land.

A third Cherokee political party, formed around John McIntosh and the former principal chief William Hicks, sent yet another delegation to Washington at about the same time, under Ross's brother Andrew, in a last-ditch attempt to negotiate a separate treaty. It, too, was ignored by the Washington power structure, and gave undeniable evidence of the political weakness of the Cherokee nation.

Meanwhile, the state of Georgia also saw no reason to either recognize any of the old Cherokee territorial boundaries or put any sort of restriction on any action being taken against the Cherokee themselves. The mansion and grounds of one of the other Cherokee chiefs, James Vann, the wealthiest man in the nation, were seized by the state and turned over to the militia as a headquarters. Indians were forbidden from participating in any gold-mining activities and stripped of the right to refuse any white settlers moving into their homes and lands; missionaries were banned from the entire territory; and state judges that did try to support Cherokee rights were quickly removed from the bench.

The generally lawless atmosphere that had already developed as a result of the boom-town environment of the gold rush stampede descended into outright terrorism and violence against the Cherokee. The state militia was in the territory, but had woe-fully insufficient manpower to stop the widespread violence, even if they had been ordered to do so, and limited their activities to protecting the white settlers. Influential Cherokee, like Sequoyah, joined the call to remove to the west, especially after New Echota was raided and the newspaper building burned. The lawless atmosphere extended to the differences between the major Chero-kee political factions, and assassinations of those advocating for removal began.

In July 1835 a delegation of Washington officials headed by President Jackson's personal envoy to the Cherokee, John F. Schermerhorn, traveled to Ridge's plantation, near present-day Calhoun, to meet with the Cherokee from both parties. The pro-posed treaty that came out of this meeting was rejected by the Cherokee General Council, but they did appoint a new delegation committee that included both Ross and Ridge, specifically to nego-tiate the best possible removal treaty. Four hundred delegates and other Cherokee gathered at New Echota in December 1835 to negotiate this treaty. Because of an early and heavy winter storm, no delegates from the North Carolina Cherokee bands were able to travel to this meeting; only those from the north Georgia area were in attendance. Ross and other members of the National Party refused to attend as well, despite the General Council's explicit order to do so. Setting aside National Party protests and taking advantage of the inability of absent delegates to vote, Ridge pre-sided over a week of hard negotiations that led to the New Echota Treaty: The United States would pay the Cherokee Nation five million dollars, provide a half-million dollar education grant, and reimburse all Cherokee for land and property they would leave behind. In addition, the Cherokee would be granted territorial rights in perpetuity in the Indian Territory (now Oklahoma) equal to the lands they would give up, and all Cherokee east of the Mis-sissippi River would leave peacefully within two years of ratifica-tion. The treaty originally had a clause allowing that Cherokee wanting to remain could become citizens and be granted a small amount of land, but this was later stricken by Jackson before he forwarded the treaty to the Senate for ratification. The full Cherokee General Council approved the treaty, which passed the Senate, after the typical prolonged violent political infighting typical of the era, by a single-vote margin in May 1836.

Ross and his National Party supporters loudly protested the treaty, asked Congress during their deliberations not to ratify it, and in 1838, sent a petition with sixteen thousand signatures on it to Congress, asking them to void it. Though the General Council had approved the treaty, which was negotiated in good faith on behalf of the Council by Ridge, Ross's position as principal Chief of the Nation, as well as his persuasive call to resist removal at all costs, proved to be a popular stance among the Cherokee. Ross's most effective argument was the long history of broken promises and treaties by the US government, which would doubtlessly continue with this latest treaty. He also pointed out that Ridge had manipulated the vote at New Echota, holding the deliberations during a winter storm, which guaranteed that his most vocal opponents would not be able to attend, and had misrepresented his own authority and position before the US government, when Ross had a much firmer claim to any title of overall chief of the nation. His traditionalist stance and much higher level of general trust from the rest of the Cherokee Nation handily eclipsed Ridge's growing reputation as a usurper and possibly even traitor toward his own people. Within a year of the New Echota negotiations, only about 350 out of the 17,000 members of the Cherokee Nation openly supported Ridge's treaty, and he became a marked man. Ridge quickly departed for the Indian Territory, along with his family and about two thousand other Cherokee.

Ross and his political faction fought tooth and nail against removal, using every political trick and favor he could curry, but it was a hopeless fight against public apathy and Jackson's antipathy. The Cherokee were supposed to be out of their lands by May 1838, but were granted an extension until later that year. Ross tried again during this period to have the New Echota Treaty overturned, and this time enjoyed the support of some whites, particularly the New England transcendentalists like Ralph Waldo Emerson, but once again his efforts failed. The new President, Martin Van Buren, ordered Brigadier General Winfield Scott to take about seven thousand US Army and state militia troops, effectively the entire available combat force of the United States organized into the new "Army of the Cherokee Nation," and escort the Cherokee west across the Mississippi. Much has been written about this removal, the "Trail of Tears," but aside from the issues of winter weather and the difficult trails, Scott to all appearances did what he could do to ease the burdens of the journey; he ordered that no harm be threatened to any Cherokee unless they actively resisted (which some did), that Regular army troops be used whenever possible, to reduce the self-serving intentions of the militia, and that military wagons and horses be used to carry the sick and weak. Chief John Ross was also given permission to mount unaccompanied columns, and organized twelve wagon trains with a thousand Cherokee in each. Scott personally accompanied one of the four military-escorted columns west, but even with his precautions, attacks and rampant theft by white settlers were common, and the death toll from illness and exposure was staggering; out of roughly twelve thousand Cherokee who left in 1838, somewhere between two thousand and four thousand died along the way.

A significant number of Cherokee were able to avoid being removed, and stayed in their lands in the east. About four hundred members of the Qualia tribe under their Chief Yonaguska were already US citizens, and thus were allowed to keep their land. Several hundred other Cherokee in the north Georgia, eastern Tennessee, and western North Carolina mountains escaped the roundups and joined the Qualia; these were later federally recognized as the Eastern Cherokee Nation. Another small band, the Echota Cherokee in Alabama, was also exempted from the roundup and exclusion.

The political infighting did not end when the long-separated groups of Cherokee were reunited in the Indian Territory. One faction had been there since 1828, living in traditional ways and already having had to fight protracted wars with the Plains Indians in the area. Another faction was a similarly resettled, long-separated band of Cherokee from Texas, which the United States considered the same as the others and forced to settle among them. A third faction was the Treaty Party under Ridge that had left by 1837, and then there was the huge glut of the remaining Cherokee who arrived by 1839. There was no happy homecoming among them. A group of Ross's supporters marked Ridge and his supporters for assassination, based on their "giving away" territory in the New Echota Treaty, claiming this was justified under the Cherokee law written by Ridge himself.

On June 22, 1839, a group of about twenty-five warriors from the Ross faction set out to murder a long list of Treaty Party supporters. Major Ridge, who lived near Honey Creek, Missouri, by then, was caught about a mile from the Arkansas-Oklahoma state line, at White Rock Creek near the town of Cane Hill as he was traveling southward and killed with a fusillade of rifle bullets. John Ridge and Elias Boudinot were murdered by this same band of assassins. Stand Watie was also attacked, but managed to ride safely out of the ambush. No other assassinations were carried out by this group, but six years of infighting, sometimes termed the "Cherokee Civil War" resulted, and extended later into the American Civil War. Most Cherokee supported the Confederacy, with a full Indian Brigade led by Watie himself, while Ross led a much smaller group of Union supporters.

In summing up Ridge's life and efforts in the Cherokee nation, it is important to point out that, as "progressive" and as seemingly humane as his actions may have been, he made the vast majority of his political decisions either alone or without significant input from the other major Cherokee leaders, even spurning their counsel when it conflicted with his own ideas. He also took steps, as during the New Echota negotiations, to stack the odds in his own favor by taking advantage of whatever political, meteorological, or other such circumstances presented themselves, and in doing so, consciously condemned the Cherokee to the path which he himself had chosen, one that proved disastrous in the end. He could not help but know that his actions would enrage a great majority of the Cherokee, possibly to the point of endangering his life, but his arrogance and pride would not permit him to back down even in the face of overwhelming evidence that his decisions were faulty. Allegedly, Major Ridge remarked after signing the New Echota Treaty, "I have signed my own death warrant." He in fact did, and despite the fact that he believed he was trying to preserve the Cherokee Nation in doing so, he was widely, roundly, and quite properly condemned for the action and hounded by his enemies until the day of his murder. To this day, his name is synonymous with a curse among many Cherokee descendents, for what he did to his own people.

CHAPTER 5

Harrison W. Riley:
The "Meanest Man in the Mountains"

The Georgia Gold Rush of the early nineteenth century attracted all sorts of people to the fields scattered around Dahlonega and Auraria, but the vast majority can be charitably described as rough-living, hard-working, and harder-playing sorts. One of the most infamous came to the gold fields in the earliest part of the rush, "before a stick of timber had been felled," and was later described as the sort of person who was so utterly corrupt and underhanded, that he was one than "whom the devil is not more artful." Harrison W. Riley was known as a shrewd, cold, and calculating businessman even by his friends and supporters, and by any measure was the most famous person in Georgia to come out of the gold-rush era. He was also a thief, swindler, father of dozens (with possibly even a hundred or more illegitimate children by a dozen or more women, some of whom were his own slaves and not one of whom he ever bothered to marry), an underhanded gambler, brawler, and generally aggressive bully who never stepped away from a fight and started more than one. He may also have been the instigator of mass murder, just so he could steal more money from a dead man's hands.

Gold was the primary reason both early Spanish and English explorers came to the Americas, but relatively minor early finds quickly paved the way to the realization that true wealth lay in other directions: in land, plantations, the abundance of other natural resources, and the exploitable colonies that fed the mercantilist economic system of Europe. Jamestown, the first English colony in North America, almost failed its very first year because so many who came over in the first group were "gentlemen" with no particu-

Photo of Harrison Riley, Lumpkin County
COURTESY OF GEORGIA ARCHIVES, VANISHING GEORGIA COLLECTION, IMAGE LUM163

lar community-building skills, but who had great enthusiasm for gold seeking. Most of them died or returned to England as soon as it became clear that there were no gold deposits along the James River, but, ironically, the first major gold finds in North America were found less than two hundred years later, less than a hundred miles due west from that first settlement. These finds created a bit of interest, but larger finds farther south along the same "belt" in North Carolina received significant publicity. In the 1820s gold was found in more locations and in greater quantities, leading one newspaper editor to remark that reports of these finds "were no longer of interest to his readers." He was wrong, and the stage was set for just one more big find to cause "gold fever" to strike hard and wide.

The Cherokee and earlier Indians in the northern Georgia area could not have helped knowing about the gold deposits, and there is some indication that this gold became part of the near-continent-wide trading network in pre-Columbian times. However, when and where the nineteenth-century "Georgia Gold Rush" began is a matter of no small speculation, and there are few reliable records to compare the claims. The standard tale in Dahlonega for most of the nineteenth and twentieth centuries, which has since been essentially discredited, is that a young man named Benjamin Parks was hunting in the late fall of 1828 at a site in the Cherokee territory near the Chestatee River called Licklog, when he kicked over an unusual rock. He realized it was a sizable nugget of pure gold, and rushed to the nearest town to advertise his discovery, kicking off the gold rush. The problems with this tale include the fact that illegal gold-mining operations by trespassing white settlers had already been going on in the Territory for some years, although exactly when they started and at which first locations is not recorded. It doesn't help Park's case, either, that there is no record of his story until an *Atlanta Constitution* article in 1894, when Parks was well into his nineties. It is clear that gold mining was already underway before this time, but the first newspaper account of the discovery of gold in north Georgia was in the *Georgia Journal* (Milledgeville), August 1, 1829:

A gentleman of the first respectability in Habersham county, writes us thus under date of 22d July: "Two gold mines have just been discovered in this county, and preparations are making to bring these hidden treasures of the earth to use." So it appears that what we long anticipated has come to pass at last, namely, that the gold region of North and South Carolina, would be found to extend into Georgia.

Regardless of who "discovered" the northern Georgia gold fields, news of the truly massive amounts of gold in these fields, which later proved to be part of a more or less continuous belt extending from central Virginia down to northeastern Alabama, spread rapidly in late 1828 and early 1829, kicking off the first "gold rush" in US history. Earlier reports of gold finds had raised both a general awareness and excitement among the public for the chance at "easy wealth," and the finds in the Cherokee Territory, which did not have the complications involved with private property and ownership rights, resulted in thousands being bitten with "gold fever." There are no records of how many miners illegally entered the Territory, but the best guess is roughly ten thousand in 1829 alone. The earliest known record for anything resembling hard numbers is one newspaper article from June 1830, that claimed by that time, over four thousand miners were working one creek alone in Lumpkin County.

The state of Georgia had already been attempting to force the Cherokee off their treaty lands in the north part of the state by the time gold deposits were publicized, with or without help from the federal government, and this gold rush simply gave additional motivation to these clearances. The wild mass of men (and a few women) who rushed into the territory caused then-Governor John Forsyth to order the Georgia Militia up into the gold fields, at first to protect the Cherokee from the excesses of the miners. In short order, though, the militia was ordered to do an about-face and do the very opposite, protecting the miners and their claims against the Cherokee and their treaty properties. The rapid Europeanization and assimilation of the Cherokee into pastoral farming communities made any thought of organized military resistance futile, and their subsequent appeals to the state and federal courts only resulted in their eventual removal from the entire state and neighboring regions. Even before they were removed from their land, in the "Trail of Tears" forced march of the Cherokee to Oklahoma, the state of Georgia simply took over their territory, divided it into individual lots, and held two land lotteries in 1832 to give it all away. With this land organization and the beginning of private ownership of the gold fields came a relative pacifying of the worst excesses of the gold rush environment, with settlements and small towns established, and merchants of all types pouring in to "mine the miners."

The miners who came in the first wave of the rush were by no means the finest examples of genteel society, and one source referred to them collectively as "thieves, gamblers, and murderers—quarrelsome, drunken and malicious—forming altogether a lawless, ungovernable community." In the earliest days, when small groups of tents were the only thing that resembled "civilization" in the territory, sutlers with cartloads of whiskey and gold-panning equipment showed up, adding to the violent atmosphere by hosting gambling contests with plenty of undoubtedly rotgut whiskey, to better separate the miners from their new-found wealth.

One of these sutlers was Harrison W. Riley, born in 1804 in North Carolina. Although he did partner with another prominent man from Dahlonega, J. J. Findley, to operate one profitable gold mine, Riley was much more interested in supplying the means to obtain other miners' gold, legally when convenient, but he was most definitely not beholden to the law. He first shows up in Dahlonega records in 1834, as the head of a household of six. The following year, he purchased one-half of one town lot on the Dahlonega square, and promptly erected a tavern on it. It must have proved profitable, as he shows up in 1838 records as the head of a household of eighteen, including fourteen slaves. In 1840 he and a partner named John M. McAfee purchased several city lots containing roughly the entire southwestern part of the town square at a sheriff's sale, for the then not insignificant sum of $1,739. The following year Riley began construction on that property of the most elaborate and beautiful building in Dahlonega up to that point: the half-block long, two-story Riley (later Eagle) Hotel. A second-story bridge spanned muddy South Chestatee Street to connect with a large tavern, a gambling casino, and a brothel that Riley also owned and operated, each of which proved popular and hugely profitable from the day it opened.

Riley was a brutal and violent man in a brutal and violent time. He was involved in several gunfights on the porch of his hotel and the streets of Dahlonega, and survived at least one assassination attempt following a bitter election contest. He was known to be heavily armed at all times—which to be truthful, was not unusual for that place or time—but was also known to be quick to draw his weapons to intimidate or bully people. Andrew Cain, in his 1932 book *History of Lumpkin County*, gives a colorful and possibly even true account of one time when this did not have the desired effect:

> *An itinerant gambler with a fat roll chanced to sojourn in the village. Riley thought that a stranger with so much money ought not to feel lonely, although in a "strange land." A game was arranged and the stakes piled on the table. In order to give a touch of solemnity to the occasion, Riley drew forth his pocket artillery and placed it on the table with a bang, at the same time saying; "Hark from the tomb, a doleful sound." The visitor promptly drew from his holster a "young cannon" and slammed it down on the table with the refrain: "My ears attend the cry!" The story goes that the gambler went away richer than he came.*

Riley was most decidedly not one who made idle threats or empty boasts of violence, and he had a well-earned reputation for physical violence against anyone who crossed him. Lumpkin

County court records contain a long list of lawsuits against him for what today would be criminal assault and battery. The lack of any serious law enforcement in the gold fields kept him out of jail, but not out of court. One 1838 suit claimed that:

> *Harrison W. with force and arms, to wit with swords, knives, dirks, sticks, rocks, fists, hands, feet and teeth violently and furiously assaulted and beat your petitioner and . . . violently caught hold of your petitioner and threw him on the ground and then and there struck your petitioner a great many violent blows on the head and diverse parts of the body with the rocks, fists, sticks and weapons aforesaid and shook and pulled your petitioner and . . . pulled a great quantity of hair from your petitioner's head by means of which said premise and ill treatment your petitioner was then and there greatly hurt, bruised and wounded and became and was sick, sore, lame and disordered so much that the life of your petitioner was then and there greatly despaired of . . .*

This particular suit was one of the relatively few that Riley lost, costing him $100 in punitive damages and $14.31 in court costs. He did win the majority of suits brought against him, for similar assaults and for alleged land and gold swindles, but the old brick steps of the Lumpkin County Courthouse in Dahlonega bore his boot prints regularly for the rest of his life. Many of the suits were brought simply because he was a notorious figure with deep pockets, but many others were brought because he was indeed a violent and ill-tempered man. Riley was an equal-opportunity offender, though: One 1853 suit for a similar assault was brought against him by a Dahlonega woman.

While Riley is recorded as indisputably being involved in a number of fisticuff altercations and several gun battles in Dahlonega and the vicinity, one historian has uncovered strong evidence to suggest he was also involved in at least one conspiracy to ambush and murder a man in South Carolina. A forty-two-year-old North

Carolina planter and slave trader named William Baxter Jr. had been traveling through northern Georgia in the late summer and early fall of 1838, along with his twelve-year-old son, James Newton Baxter, and his thirteen-year-old niece, Carolina Baxter, en route back from Alabama and Tennessee with a sizable sum of cash—between $2,500 and $8,000—from the earlier sale of slaves and paid-off promissory notes. They were traveling through the northwestern part of Georgia and central Tennessee at the same time the Cherokee Indians were being rounded up into concentration camps, preparing for the "Trail of Tears" westward to Oklahoma. One of the centers of a massive amount of activity related to this roundup was in Calhoun, Tennessee, where Riley was also "transacting mercantile business," including money exchange and slave sales. It is unclear if Baxter had any other fiscal dealing with him, but there is a record that he purchased a slave named Isaac from Riley in Calhoun that September. One source claimed that Riley found out that Baxter had a very large sum of cash on him at the time, possibly from exchanging Alabama currency with him for South and North Carolina currency, which had a much higher value at the time. (In the early nineteenth century, state-issued currency was more highly valued than federal currency, which had suffered from severe devaluation during the Revolution and for decades afterward.)

Following the purchase of the slave Isaac, the Baxter party moved east on the Unicoi Turnpike, which would have brought them into northeastern Georgia southwards to the current vicinity of Helen and Unicoi State Park, northeast of Cleveland. They are known to have passed a prominent overnight stop at Traveler's Rest, Georgia, and crossed Devereaux Jarrett's toll bridge over the Tugaloo River into South Carolina on the late afternoon of September 30. Isaac was seen driving Baxter's carriage, and the party made camp a few miles farther east, next to Chauga Creek in a very remote and isolated spot on the road. Shortly after they crossed, two white men on horseback asked the toll keeper specifically about Baxter and his whereabouts, and then crossed the bridge themselves heading east down the same road. On the morning of October 1, Isaac crossed the toll bridge in the carriage again, this time heading westward alone, while the two unnamed white men followed shortly thereafter, in some bit of a hurry. This aroused some suspicions, and a search party found blood trails along the road the next morning; the bodies of the three Baxters were found shortly thereafter. William Baxter appeared to have been killed in his bed by multiple ax blows to the head, though there was some evidence of a struggle, and James was found dead in his bedroll as well. Carolina appears to have tried to run from the massacre, and her body was found a short distance down the road; she was also slain by ax blows.

News of the vicious murders spread very rapidly throughout the mountains. Isaac returned to Dahlonega about two weeks later, where he was publicly "captured" by Riley and a fellow merchant named David Thompson, along with a few other members of the community. Baxter's father Joseph had traveled to the gold-rush town by that time, along with three surviving members of his family, probably suspecting someone there had something to do with the murders. When Isaac was captured, he returned the carriage, three horses, and about thirteen hundred dollars in cash. For some odd reason, eleven hundred dollars of that money was found in the possession of one of Thompson's slaves, while Isaac himself only had about two hundred dollars in cash on him when he was arrested. The rest of the money William Baxter was known to have been carrying was never recovered.

Isaac was quickly returned to Pickens District, South Carolina, where his trial was swift and the outcome pretty much predetermined. The unusual circumstances of the incident were glossed over, Isaac was sentenced to death with no appeals presented, and brought to the scene of the crime by October 19 for the commission of the sentence, as was habitual in that time. No court records of the trial or sentencing appear to exist today, but one newspaper account claims Isaac was brought to the gallows, and then "chained to an iron bar and burned," a common torture preceding the execution of slaves who killed white people in the early nine-teenth century. On the gallows, Isaac is reported to have confessed to the crime and implicated Riley as the one who ordered him to do it, claiming Riley promised him money and freedom once the deed was done and he returned the rest of Baxter's cash to the notorious businessman in Dahlonega. Riley was already viewed with no little suspicion in other cases of theft and swindling, in at least some of which he was no doubt guilty, and felt enough heat from the doomed slave's confession to pay for notices in several Georgia newspapers denying any involvement and condemning the heinous crime. These notices also had the signatures of eighty-three character references from Lumpkin County, some of whom may not even have had to be paid or threatened in order to give them. It goes without saying that an effective way to carry off a murder conspiracy is to either pay or kill off the other members of the conspiracy; it's even better if the law does it for you, if you are a crass and base sort of person whose conscience would allow it. Riley was most definitely such a person.

Riley did as well in politics as he did in business, getting elected to the state legislature for several terms, and he was one of the delegates to the January 1861 Secession Convention in Milled-geville. He also tried to obtain an officer's commission in the Georgia Militia, first by simply taking over the dormant Dahlonega militia (and asking the Georgia state military command for an appropriate-level commission afterward), and then by assuming the also dormant brigade command of the six mountain county militias, claiming he had "three thousand one hundred and fifteen (3,115) hale, hearty, stout warriors" under his presumed command, and used this assumption to again request a field-grade officer's commission, this time from Georgia Adjutant General Andrew J. Hansell himself (whom he called "my dear friend"). Assuming Hansell even knew who Riley was personally, he probably knew better than to put this untrained, undisciplined hothead in command of fighting men in a real war; the prominent Dahlonega lawyer Weir Boyd was instead given command of what became the

Fifty-Second Georgia Volunteer Infantry Regiment, which served with great distinction in the Western Theater of the war. Nevertheless, Riley assumed the title of "General" for the rest of his life, a stolen valor that was even engraved on his tombstone.

As so often happens when a notorious and feared figure has bought his way into relative respectability, "General" Riley's funeral was a huge affair. He died on Wednesday, November 4, 1874, at his plantation in White County, Georgia, and was buried in Dahlonega's Mount Hope Cemetery on Friday, November 6. According to one newspaper account of the service, "The upmost [sic] respect was shown the deceased. The business houses were closed and the citizens turned out in mass to attend his funeral." Many possibly attended just to make sure the old, violent jerk was really and finally dead. Nevertheless, his notoriety extended to his own grave marker, part of which read, "Let his faults be buried with his bones." At least some of the attention paid to his death and interment had to do with his will; even after losing the modern-day equivalent of $1.5 million during the Civil War, he was still one of the wealthiest men in north Georgia at the time of his death. His will, though, was and still remains a fit testament to the man once referred to as the "meanest man in the mountains." It mentions seven women, none of whom he ever bothered to formally marry, as well as a few children from these women that he did claim as heirs; there were dozens of others alleged to have been his children as well, some of whom tied up this will in court for years. One of the seven women, Eliza (or Elizabeth) Jefferson, was a slave he had purchased in 1819, who had four children when she was purchased, remained with Riley most of the rest of his life, and gave birth to seven more children, one of which, Goliath, is named in the will as Riley's son and heir.

Fittingly, for a man who lived his life in a manner not far distant from that of the Caribbean pirates of lore and legend, Riley was rumored to have left a "buried treasure," allegedly worth many millions of dollars, somewhere in Lumpkin or White Counties. It has never been found.

CHAPTER 6

John P. Gatewood:
Confederate Guerilla Fighter

Just as in the American Revolutionary War, passions for the differing sides ran so high during the Civil War that irregular, guerilla, and partisan fighters from both sides organized to fight in the fringes and shadows of the great armies, carrying the war into nooks and crannies of the backcountry where no regular soldier would ever set foot. Few places turned out more of these fighters, and suffered more extreme carnage from them, than the lower Appalachian Mountains region of eastern Tennessee, western North Carolina, northeastern Alabama, and north Georgia. Very few of these already exceptionally violent and bloodthirsty guerillas were in the same class as John Pemberton Gatewood, a guerilla from central Tennessee operating in the northwestern Georgia mountains, who earned a reputation as "the long-haired, red-headed beast from Georgia." Somewhere between eighteen and twenty-one years old in 1864, he was an imposing figure, two hundred pounds on a tall frame, described as handsome with piercing clear blue eyes, "with the fire of Vulcan in his eye," and long red hair flowing past his shoulders; he was usually wearing a soft felt broad-brimmed hat stuck on the back of his head. A sadistic sociopath, he carved a path of death and destruction all through parts of Georgia, Tennessee, and Alabama, killing dozens if not hundreds of Union soldiers, sympathizers, and others who just got in his way, all because he simply liked killing.

One source claims that Gatewood was born in Sparta, in White County, Tennessee, in the east-central part of the state, while another claims he was from Fentress County farther to the north. Records do show that he enlisted in Captain Willis Scott Bledsoe's cavalry company in August 1861, where he would have had to affirm (or lie) that he was eighteen or older. This company

Grave of one of Gatewood's victims, Captain William Fain, near Ducktown, Tennessee
PHOTO BY JOHN MCKAY

was later reorganized as part of the Fourth Tennessee Cavalry Regiment, and in January 1863, Bledsoe's company and three others were reassigned to the Eighth Tennessee Cavalry. Sometime between then and the big fight at Chickamauga in September, Gatewood deserted and took up the life of a guerilla fighter. The reasons are very obscure—some sources claim Gatewood's sister had been raped by Unionist partisans, and his mother (or father) had been killed by the same group—but it is known that he joined Samuel "Champ" Ferguson's guerilla band in eastern Tennessee sometime in 1863, the best-known and most notorious guerilla outfit of them all. (Possibly in a related move, Bledsoe himself later quit his commission and became another notorious leader of a guerilla band.) Regardless of whether Gatewood was motivated by revenge or something far more sinister, it is undisputed that his focus was not to win a war, but to murder the enemy—as many as he could find.

One of the earliest specific newspaper references to Gatewood came in November 1864, long after he started his own guerilla band, when the Macon *Daily Telegraph* referred to him as "Captain Gatewood" and "Gatewood the Regulator," praising him for presumably protecting civilians from the thousands of dreaded blue-suited Yankees then in north Georgia. Other period newspaper articles suggested that he was operating under the direct supervision of Lieutenant General Joseph Wheeler's cavalry command. Gatewood never held any regular or brevet commission of any rank, and while he did occasionally undertake raids or other missions in coordination with some regular Confederate commands, and rode on occasion with some of Wheeler's far-ranging cavalry patrols, at no time did he consider himself under the discipline and control of any regular military authority. The only authority he did seem to recognize, other than his own instincts, was that of Champ Ferguson, who was quite possibly the only guerilla leader more out of control and bloodthirsty than Gatewood himself. At least one postwar account of Ferguson's activities underscored his very independent ways, referring to him as a "rebel-tinged guerilla."

Gatewood's band of semi-outlaw guerillas was very small for the effect it had; at no time did he directly command more than two to three hundred men, and most of the time his group numbered somewhere between ten and thirty. He was not afraid to take on far more numerous opponents, however; eyewitnesses to raids he conducted on Union formations at Lafayette and Ringgold stated he rode into battle ahead of his men at a full gallop, with reins in his teeth and a Navy model .44 pistol blazing away in each hand, and several more pistols stuck in his belt for backup firepower. He was also notorious for not taking prisoners, or at least for not letting them live much longer after he took them, usually leaving them hanging from the nearest convenient tree, or simply dumping their lifeless bodies in the road. On at least one occasion, after a vicious cavalry battle near Lafayette, where Gatewood was supporting regular Confederate army units, Colonel John R. Hart of the Sixth Georgia Cavalry refused to allow the guerilla leader to take any prisoners away with him afterward, knowing what would undoubtedly happen to them. One of Hart's men mentioned that the Union prisoners knew as well, Gatewood's reputation having preceded him, and that as a result "they stuck to us like brothers," giving the Confederate army no reason to fear escape attempts.

Gatewood operated primarily out of McLemore's Cove, a beautiful and easily defensible valley south of Chattanooga, in northwest Georgia's Walker County. His group frequently clashed with several other groups in this small area: an unnamed pro-Union guerilla outfit headed by Sam Roberts and John Long (who was a native of the valley, one of the rare Unionists there); another independent, small, purely criminal gang headed by Green Cordle, which Gatewood eliminated by assassinating Cordle as he ate supper in a friend's home; and yet another sometime supporter of the Union, a band of cutthroats led by Doc Morse, which was based out of southern Tennessee and spread terror throughout the north Georgia counties. Gatewood sometimes was supported by another independent pro-Confederate guerilla band, the North Georgia Scouts, which was headed by Tom Polk Edmondson and based in nearby Murray County. Adding to the confusion, there are some reports that Gatewood also skirmished with "Captain" Jack Colquitt's group of Confederate deserters (named in at least one report as "Colquitt's Scouts"), who were still presumably pro-Confederate but mostly interested in stealing, robbing, raping, pillaging, and killing in the Floyd County area just south of Gatewood's main base of operations.

Gatewood was not only effective in spreading terror and mayhem in his area of operations, but also had the gift of being able to irritate highly placed opponents. Though the Union command usually considered Gatewood and the other rebel partisans nothing more than sometimes deadly nuisances, Major General William T. Sherman considered him a dangerous threat, especially to his own supply lines in Georgia. "Let all know that such fellows [like Gatewood] will be dealt with summarily," he ordered, meaning they would be immediately hung as spies and saboteurs if caught, without the courtesy of a trial. Sherman ordered a series of large-scale raids to capture the most prominent Confederate guerilla fighters, but all the missions met with very little success, and never came even close to capturing Gatewood himself. The converse was not true, however, and on at least two occasions Gatewood and his men successfully took on superior regular Union forces, killing many and driving the rest from the field.

While Sherman's patrols were searching for Gatewood in his usual haunts in October and November 1864, he was nowhere near the area, having taken his small command north into southern Tennessee on what would become the most notorious raid of his private war, the "Madden Branch Massacre." Taking about fifty men with him, Gatewood did not seem to have any particular objective in mind, other than finding more "Unionists" and Yankee soldiers to kill. Some sources suggest he was out for revenge after yet another Unionist guerilla band leader named William Twiggs conducted several raids in nearby Fannin County; as Gatewood himself had just executed several Confederate soldiers home on leave (accusing them of being deserters), such patriotic motivations seem unlikely.

Moving north into Polk County, Tennessee, along the Federal Road, Gatewood's first victim was a Union-supporting man named Horace Hill, who was sitting on the fence in front of his house watching the approaching column of cavalry. Gatewood greeted him in a friendly manner, dismounted, and walked up to him as if he wanted to strike up a conversation. He then suddenly drew one of his pistols and fired it straight into Hill's ear before he could respond. Moving down the road, his men found three "refugees," two of whom Gatewood shot in the head as soon as they were brought before him. His other men dispatched the third, and then quickly moved farther down the road, stopping at known rebel-sympathizing homes to inquire where the Union men could be found. After killing a half dozen more unarmed men in their homes and fields, Gatewood's band took over the town of Benton, robbing the citizens, looting the stores, and searching through every building for "Unionists." Amazingly, leaving only one man dead there (Thomas Kincer, killed while trying to hide under the floorboards in a friend's house), Gatewood led his men north into McMinn County before sweeping around to the southeast and heading for Ducktown, just north of the Georgia border. Four more men made the fatal error of encountering Gatewood along the way.

Union recruiters were very active in this area of the Tennessee–Georgia border, and one, William Lillard, a Confederate deserter, was particularly active around the Cleveland, Tennessee, vicinity, trying to earn a regular army commission through his efforts.

On November 19, Gatewood's band literally ran into two small groups of new Union recruits heading to rendezvous with Lillard, traveling along the Old Copper Road next to the Ocoee River, right where a small creek called Madden Branch flowed into the river. The Union recruits, several of whom were, in fact, deserters from various Confederate units, attempted to flee at first, but when they saw Gatewood and several of his men wearing federal blue uniform coats (which they had earlier stolen for this exact purpose), the guerilla leader was able to convince the recruits that his group was federal cavalry, and that he meant them no harm. As the Union recruits cautiously came out of the woods and onto the road, his command surrounding them, Gatewood ordered the only armed member of the group, Peter Parris, to give up his pistol, and then had his men line up and search all the rest of them. Gatewood then rode down the line of recruits, shooting each one in the head. Parris ran for the nearby mountains and another man named Wyatt Parton bolted for the river as soon as the shooting began, followed by a hail of bullets from the guerilla fighters. Both were hit multiple times, but both also survived their wounds after months of recovery in nearby friendly homes. The dead bodies of the rest of the recruits were simply left piled in the middle of the road.

Undoubtedly gaining some intelligence as to the whereabouts of Lillard from his recruits before they were killed, Gatewood immediately led his command back north toward Cleveland, catching up with the Union recruiter at his home on November 30. Lillard's brothers and some other men in the home, including Parris's father, returned fire as Gatewood's guerillas rushed it at a full gallop, their own guns blazing. Lillard, who was caught outside unarmed and fled for the nearby woods, was shot as he climbed over a fence. His brothers hid him out in a small cave in the woods, expecting Gatewood to return, and then smuggled him to a hospital in Cleveland, where he eventually recovered. Gatewood instead had turned back for Georgia, along the way capturing five more men en route to enlist in the Union army, some of whom were related to the men he had just murdered at Madden Branch. Amazingly, he simply turned the men loose instead of murdering them as well, telling them that his band had "already killed a lot of men that day." Gatewood returned with his men to McLemore's Cove, leaving the bodies of at least twenty-four murdered men behind.

Gatewood seemed to hold a special place of hatred for Union recruiters in his heart, though otherwise he displayed relatively few pro-Confederate sympathies. In one of the more gruesome encounters with these recruiters, he met Captain William Clayton Fain traveling north from Georgia with a group of new recruits on April 6, 1864, as they were getting off the Edwards Ferry crossing of the Toccoa River from McCaysville. Fain was a well-known lawyer and outspoken Union supporter from Fannin County, Georgia, turned active recruiter for the federal armies. In all likelihood, Gatewood had already heard of Fain and intended to kill him at the first opportunity. Surprised by the guerillas, Fain tried to spur his horse and escape, but was shot off his saddle and killed almost immediately, allegedly by Gatewood himself. (Some sources say another guerilla leader riding with Gatewood that day, Captain Rogers, in fact killed Fain.) The other Union men also tried to escape, but were rounded up, stripped of their arms, robbed, and then murdered. One, Henry Robinson, was tied to a tree while still alive and used as live target practice by the guerillas, expiring after being "shot 15 or 20 times," no doubt to their great amusement.

There were many other guerilla and partisan irregulars like Gatewood operating in Georgia by 1864, on either side, both sides, or neither side of the war. The main avenue of battle in the state ranged down a fairly narrow corridor from Chattanooga to Atlanta in the spring and summer of that year, with some outlying cavalry skirmishes a hundred miles or so to the east, west, and south of the main railroad lines. Outside this corridor, and especially in the mountain counties, the situation was far more anarchic, with local "Home Guards" units frequently behaving more like roving bands of highway robbers, and militias of all sizes and levels of abilities springing up to fill the vacuum of police protection for their communities. One theory that may explain why the situation got so far out of hand is based on the fact that so many prominent and community-stabilizing citizens departed for the Confederate army service early in the war, leaving the relative riff-raff and fringe elements back at home. After the upstanding citizens went to war, these elements had their own private war among themselves, with no one left to restrain them, leaving the meanest, strongest, and fastest on the trigger to survive.

An excellent example of this theory in action is the small gold mining town of Dahlonega, in Lumpkin County on the southern flank of the mountains region. By 1863, this town, which had a population of roughly six thousand, had fully or partially manned and placed into service no fewer than nine companies of infantry and cavalry, with nearly a full sixth of the entire male population going off to war. By 1864, though, the county was wracked with small-unit guerilla actions by impromptu partisan militias, while a formal Union-allied company of deserters from those same nine companies—the 1st Georgia State Troops Volunteers US, aka Brown's First Georgia Cavalry—had formed in the foothills of the north part of the county. At least some of these deserters had left not out of a lessening sense of patriotism to their country, the state of Georgia, but out of the immediate need to directly protect their homes and families from the marauding guerillas. Others left for less important reasons; it is worth noting that the First GSTV earned such a poor reputation that it was never formally accepted into federal service, and was forcibly disbanded as a battalion-sized unit by Union officers on December 15, 1864. Official reports describe the unit as "utterly worthless" and "heterogeneous trash," and damned its actions as actually supporting the health, welfare, and morale of opposing Confederate formations by fleeing the battlefield whenever it was attacked.

It is also worth noting that some of these vicious, inept, former Confederate deserters in the First GSTV later earned a place of

honor in the Marietta National Cemetery, simply by putting on
the blue suit for a brief and dishonorable time; they rest forever
among thousands of men who honorably served the Union armies
and fell in battle.

One of the more effective and dangerous Unionist guerilla
fighters in Lumpkin County was Jefferson Anderson, one of five
sons of a prominent farmer and businessman. The family had
moved into the county before the Cherokee removal, by 1834,
and had significant holdings in land and mining operations in
the Philippi community, just east of Dahlonega. Three of Anderson's brothers fought in different Confederate units, but his other
brother, Thomas, joined a Union regiment for the duration of the
war. Anderson initially enlisted in Captain Thomas Cabiness's
Company H, the "Dahlonega Volunteers," of Colonel James N.
Ramsey's First Georgia Volunteer Infantry Regiment (Confederate), but deserted even before that unit was disbanded after only
a year of service. There are few specifics about what exactly he
did, but there are many reports that he headed a group of "outlaws" hiding out in the mountains and terrorizing the citizenry.
He was arrested in February 1862 by Lumpkin County Sheriff
John Early, on military charges of desertion and civilian charges
of assault, battery, and rape (or attempted rape), but he broke out
of jail before he could be tried, with the help of two of his brothers
and a family friend. He was arrested again six months later, this
time by a company of Confederate artillerymen, and brought back
to Dahlonega before being transferred to an Atlanta jail. A newspaper account of his capture stated that he had been "harboring
runaway negroes, stealing, robbing widows and helpless women
and children whose fathers are in the war, and had become a terror to the whole country."

Anderson later broke out of that jail, along with a group of
accused "bridge burners" and "horse thieves," who were in fact
members of a Union special operations raider company headed by
James J. Andrews. This group had been caught in the early stages
of their mission to disrupt railroads and supply lines between

Atlanta and Chattanooga. After their successful jailbreak, these men, mostly infantrymen from several Ohio regiments traveling in civilian clothes, traveled to Big Shanty (now Kennesaw), just north of Marietta, and stole a train, intending to tear up the Western & Atlantic Railroad line and adjacent telegraph facilities heading north from there. That train's crew, in what later became famous as the "Great Locomotive Chase," successfully pursued them to just north of Ringgold. Anderson is known to have been with the raiders for some time after the jailbreak, but he either did not join them on this operation or successfully escaped at the end. Anderson continued his guerilla activities in the mountains unabated to the end of the war, and then hid out with his Union army veteran brother at his farm near Dalton for a few years. It is thought that he later followed other guerilla fighters to Texas, possibly returning to Lumpkin County in the last few years of his life, a hunted man to the end.

One of the last raids Gatewood led, which particularly infuriated Sherman and helped lead to the demise of the guerilla band, happened on January 4, 1865, at the Lee & Gordon Mill on the south side of the Chickamauga battlefield. A combined force of Confederate raiders under him took on a company of Union regulars guarding a large herd of cattle, killing all forty of the soldiers—many by cutting their throats—and seizing as many as two thousand head of cattle. A squad of no more than ten men from the Forty-Second United States Colored Troops based in Chattanooga was immediately ordered to pursue the raiders, actually catching them en route to Alabama. However, the troops were overwhelmingly outmanned and outgunned by Gatewood's men, and wisely broke off their pursuit. One source relates that Gatewood drove the stolen herd all the way to Corinth, Mississippi, to help feed the starving remnants of the once-proud Confederate Army of Tennessee, broken after their disastrous fight and retreat from Nashville the previous month. Other sources claim he simply distributed the cattle to civilians and scattered, small Confederate units in northern Alabama.

Sherman ordered another series of raids to hunt down the elusive guerilla, and this time met with some limited success. Colonel George A. Gowin of the Sixth Tennessee Mounted Infantry Regiment (US) moved south out of Chattanooga, passing through Ringgold and westward into Summerville, picking up evidence of Gatewood's presence nearby with about seventy-five of his men as he entered the valley of McLemore's Cove. On February 1, 1865, at about 10 p.m., Gowin's cavalry attacked the camp without warning, reporting later that he "made a smash of him [Gatewood], killing a number, capturing several horses, guns, &c. I took no prisoners." Gatewood and some of his men managed to escape the raid, turning and unsuccessfully attacking Gowin the next day, but losing two more guerillas in the process. Gowin did not suffer any losses at all in the raid and later ambush; Gatewood was finally and completely broken.

Very little is known about Gatewood's activities after this raid, nearly at the end of the war, or exactly what he did afterward. He is believed to have survived the vicious end of war and postwar guerilla fighting in north Georgia and Alabama, and gone on to a new life under an assumed name. Like so many other irregular fighters, Gatewood is believed to have "Gone to Texas," possibly also leaving the associated code "GTT" carved on his doorpost, as was a widespread practice. As in the case of many of the fringe characters that manned the guerilla outfits and partisan ranger units, the stories and legends about Gatewood are more prolific than any hard documentation surviving about his life. One source claimed that he married a woman named Sarah C. Cain from Gaylesville, Alabama, which was one of his bases on the westernmost periphery of his guerilla actions during the latter part of the war. This source also claims that Sarah was still alive and attending Confederate reunions as late as 1898, but that Gatewood had died by that time. Another source claims that Gatewood indeed went to Texas, but died in a gunfight in Waco in 1871, while yet another source claims he was killed in a firefight with Union troops on the banks of the Mississippi River. One of the more interesting sources, whose veracity cannot be ascertained, claims that Major John T. Burns of Rome, who became the state of Georgia comptroller general in 1869, was traveling on business in Texas some years after the war, when he happened to run across Gatewood, "and found him engaged in peaceful pursuits."

A problem one often encounters in history, especially military history, is that the truth may never be completely known, as there are few ways of verifying any given source of information about Gatewood. Unconfirmed (and unverifiable) alleged "family" stories handed down about him tell a slightly different story: When Gatewood returned home to Tennessee, he claimed that Yankee "carpetbaggers" had stolen his family's cattle and other valuables near the end of the war, and he subsequently hunted the thieves down and lynched them in his own front yard. He and presumably the rest of his family then left immediately for some unspecified place in Texas. The story continues that two of Pinkerton's detectives were sent out to investigate the deaths of the carpetbaggers, and had put up posters bearing Gatewood's name and likeness. Someone informed on him, and when the detectives later confronted Gatewood, he claimed he was in fact named Jack Smith, and had the identification to prove it in his trunk back in his hotel room. When the detectives accompanied him back to the room, Gatewood opened the trunk, pulled out two fully loaded revolvers, and shot the two Pinkerton men before they could react. The family story concludes that he then left for Dallas, but the trail goes completely cold after that.

The battles in the mountainous regions of Tennessee, Georgia, and North Carolina were almost a separate war within the context of the greater and surrounding Civil War. Along with similar guerilla fighters from Arkansas and Kansas, these men chose one side over the other not out of any overriding sense of patriotism or duty, but primarily because their long-term personal enemies had chosen the other side, or simply because their chosen uniform colors were more convenient for their lethal, blood-drenched purposes. Gatewood, and the vast majority of his fellow irregular and guerilla fighters, should be ultimately viewed not as proper soldiers fighting for a just, if losing cause in a combat environment, but simply as ruffians and outlaws given free reign to commit murderous crimes in the fog and confusion of war.

CHAPTER 7
William T. Sherman:
Pyromaniac across Georgia

On the shortest of all short lists of the criminals, miscreants, and all-around bad guys who've ever set foot in the state of Georgia, one man's name is nearly always at the top. He was an Ohio native; the son of a prominent lawyer and judge; foster child to a senator and brother to other politically powerful men; and an on-again, off-again US Army officer in antebellum days, who nearly single-handedly invented modern battle doctrine and used it to great effect in two wars. This man was also a hotheaded commander who got too many of his own soldiers killed in ill-advised battles, burned down most of Atlanta and a significant portion of Georgia, and allowed the deaths or re-enslavement of hundreds of slaves he had previously liberated, through his neglect and open disdain of their plight.

His friends (somewhat surprisingly, he had quite a number) always called him "Cump," a take on his middle name, Tecumseh, which honored a great Shawnee warrior. However, his last name alone still brings up great passion in this state, 120 years after his death. His reputation in some circles is among the worst that could be imagined, though he was not completely guilty of the main crime with which he is associated, and his main national fame came from what most military historians consider more of a casual march than a martial campaign. Dogged with accusations of insanity through most of the Civil War, and repeatedly relieved of his early commands, William Tecumseh Sherman is now considered in some circles to be both a strategic offensive genius and the poster child of war criminals—sometimes by the same people.

One of eleven children, Sherman was born in Lancaster, Ohio, in 1820, to Mary Hoyt Sherman and Charles Robert Sherman, who was a prominent lawyer in town at the time. The elder

Portrait of Major General William T. Sherman, officer of the Federal Army
COURTESY OF THE LIBRARY OF CONGRESS

Sherman became an Ohio Supreme Court justice in 1823, where he remained until he died, suddenly and unexpectedly, in 1829. His wife, left without any inheritance or funds to keep the family together, was forced to ask other families to adopt some of her children. William was taken in by their friend and neighbor, Thomas Ewing, and his wife, Maria Wills Boyle. Ewing was also a lawyer—a particularly colorful one, to all accounts—and later served as the first secretary of the interior under Presidents Zachary Taylor and Millard Fillmore, as the secretary of the treasury under Presidents William Henry Harrison and John Tyler, and as one of the senators from Ohio. One of Sherman's brothers, Charles Taylor, became a federal judge, while another, Hoyt, became a banker, and yet another, John, became a prominent US senator. Three of his foster brothers became Union army generals in the Civil War: Charles Ewing and Hugh Boyle Ewing, both of whom served under Sherman in the war, and Thomas Ewing Jr., who, ironically, later served as a defense attorney for those accused of conspiring to assassinate Lincoln.

The elder Ewing obtained an appointment to West Point for Sherman, where he did quite well in his studies, though not quite so well in other matters. Due to his sharp tongue and somewhat sloppy manner of dress, he received a number of demerits, which earned him many hours of "walking them off" and caused his class standing to fall. He was commissioned as a US Army second lieutenant in 1840, assigned to the Third US Artillery, and almost immediately saw combat action in Florida during the last two years of the vicious Second Seminole War. His next assignments took him to Fort Morgan in Mobile Bay, Fort Moultrie in Charleston harbor, and to Augusta in northeastern Georgia, where he gained a great topographic picture of the entire northern part of the state while serving in a mapping and engineering position. While there, he went into town several times to see his old West Point roommate, Marcellus A. Stovall, most likely to romance his sister, Cecelia, whom he had met when she visited the military academy. According to one source, Sherman was not the only one smitten with the "noted Georgia belle and beauty," who reportedly "became a favorite among the dancing set at the academy." It is reported that Sherman took every opportunity to use his close friendship with Marcellus to gain any advantage with his sister's heart for some time afterward, but she seemed to not be impressed with the red-headed Yankee. During his presumably last visit to see Miss Cecelia in Augusta, Sherman was pouring out his affections for her in a most un-Sherman-like way, and may have even proposed marriage to her, when she made it abundantly clear that she had not the slightest interest in him, answering, "Your eyes are so cold and cruel. I pity the man who ever becomes your antagonist. Ah, how you would crush an enemy!" Upon taking his leave, he responded prophetically to her, "Even though you were my enemy, my dear, I would love you and protect you."

Cecelia Stovall must have cut quite a figure, as she was wooed by a range of other West Pointers, most notably Joseph Hooker, later a major general in command of the Union's XX Corps under Sherman in Georgia, and Richard Garnett, who in 1845 was a US Army captain and commander of the Augusta Arsenal. Garnett successfully proposed to Cecelia, who seemed to greatly favor the dashing Virginian, but the engagement was broken off when her parents objected. She was to all appearances the true love of Garnett's life, who never married and allegedly carried his devotion to her for the rest of his life. He later became a Confederate brigadier general, commanding a brigade in Lee's Army of Northern Virginia, and died on the third day of the battle of Gettysburg in 1863, leading his men across a mile of open fields into the teeth of Union guns in "Pickett's Charge." Cecelia's parents did later allow her to marry an appropriately wealthy and socially prominent man named Charles Shellman, who in 1851 built a grand mansion for her overlooking the Etowah River near Cartersville, which he named "Shellman Heights."

Sherman then turned to the other "true love of his life," his foster sister, Eleanor "Ellen" Boyle Ewing, who did seem to return his affections. They began a long-distance engagement in the last half of the 1840s, after he accepted a reassignment to California during the Mexican War, where he remained through the start of the gold rush. He saw no combat during that war, and due to that, was doubtlessly limited in his advancement possibilities in the peacetime army. Though he did love the military life, Ellen made it very clear that she did not wish to leave the rest of her family in Lancaster and traipse about the world as an army bride. She also made it clear that Sherman's lack of faith clashed with her devout Roman Catholicism. Despite this, Sherman returned to Ohio, married Ellen in a lavish and well-attended ceremony in May 1850, without converting to Catholicism, and accepted some assignments in Saint Louis and New Orleans. These kept him in the army but still caused frequent absences from Ellen, who let him know of her displeasure in the arrangement. His young marriage threatened, and his military advancement potential hindered because of his lack of combat experience, Sherman reluctantly resigned his commission in 1853. He took a management position in a Saint Louis bank, which caused further strain on his marriage; he ultimately accepted another position in San Francisco. Ellen did travel there with him, but left soon afterward on a several-months-long visit back with her parents in Ohio, leaving two of their children with him. It is very clear that the West Coast job and their frequent separations, primarily caused by Ellen's seeming inability to live without being in the immediate vicinity of her parents, caused great strain on their marriage and Sherman developed blinding headaches and a profound depression. During this time, an apparently unsympathetic Ellen complained in a letter to Sherman's brother John about her husband succumbing to "that melancholy insanity to which your family is subject." In 1856 the bank closed Sherman's branch in San Francisco, which delighted Ellen to no end, as they had no other place to go then but back to the in-laws' house in Ohio. Sherman tried to renew his army commission, but the US Army's antebellum force was small and had no openings.

Sherman went through a series of other banking and business ventures, all of which failed, before several of his old military buddies were able to obtain a new position for him in 1859, as super-intendent of the new Louisiana Seminary of Learning. He was happy with the new position, and the school was soon renamed the Louisiana State Seminary of Learning & Military Academy, but Ellen flatly refused to move south, citing, accurately enough, that there was no adequate (or more accurately, "prominent enough") housing for their family in the small town of Pineville. Hs tenure there, though, was short-lived, ending when Louisiana seceded from the Union in February 1861. Shortly afterward, he traveled to Washington, D.C., to visit his brother John, who was an influ-ential Ohio senator, and was invited to meet newly inaugurated President Lincoln in the White House. The meeting did not go well, Sherman showing his usual impertinence, as he related in either a diary or personal letter (sources vary on this point):

> John then turned to me, and said, "Mr. President, this is my brother, Colonel Sherman, who is just up from Louisiana, he may give you some information you want." "Ah!" said Mr. Lincoln, "how are they getting along down there?" I said, "They think they are getting along swimmingly—they are preparing for war." "Oh, well!" said he, "I guess we'll manage to keep house." I was silenced, said no more to him, and we soon left. I was sadly disappointed, and remember that I broke out on John, d—ning the politicians generally, saying, "You have got things in a hell of a fig, and you may get them out as you best can," adding that the country was sleeping on a volcano that might burst forth at any minute, but that I was going to St. Louis to take care of my family, and would have no more to do with it. John begged me to be more patient, but I said I would not; that I had no time to wait, that I was off for St. Louis; and off I went.

Despite his impertinence, Sherman was asked to reenter the army as a full colonel in May 1861, first serving as an inspec-tor general under the soon-to-retire General of the Army Winfield

Scott, and then taking command of a brigade of infantry in General Daniel Tyler's Division. His performance in the Union defeat at First Bull Run (First Manassas) in July raised his stature in the still-developing army, and he was next sent to Kentucky to serve a staff position, specifically requesting Lincoln himself not to give him another field command. Just before that first great battle Sherman had been horrified at the extreme lack of preparedness of his soldiers and officers—a shortcoming that was very evident in their defeat—and he was quite vocal that he had neither the desire nor the ability to raise a command up to the necessary level of combat effectiveness.

Shortly after Sherman arrived in Kentucky, the Union army there was having a devil of a time subduing the chaotic riot of opposing Union and Confederate militias and regular units. The theater commander, former commander of Fort Sumter, Robert Anderson, cracked under the strain and resigned, and Sherman was given command instead, in direct opposition to his wishes. Sherman did not do well at all, overreacting to the chaotic situation by sending a long series of excited messages back to his command in Washington, demanding to be relieved, and suggesting in the strongest terms that the situation there was simply untenable. He also adopted a deeply pessimistic view of the war in general, which he continued to vocalize even after he was relieved of command and reassigned to a quieter post in Missouri. He was relieved of that new posting shortly after taking it over and sent home to his father-in-law's house in Lancaster for a "brief rest."

Sherman displayed the same lack of diplomacy with the press that he had shown with his comrades in arms, accusing them of being little better than spies, and once remarking that they were "the most contemptible race of men that exist. Cowardly, crying, hanging round, gathering their materials out of the most polluted sources." He was even quoted as saying, "If I had my choice I would kill every reporter in the world but I am sure we would be getting reports from hell before breakfast." During his brief stay back in Lancaster, the national media got their revenge, widely spreading a false rumor that Sherman had "gone off in the head" from the strain of battle; in a December 11, 1861, article, the *Cincinnati Commercial* came right out and stated that he was "insane." Once he was back in command, he had at least one reporter court-martialed as a spy, after the reporter traveled along with his troops, against Sherman's specific and direct order not to. He made life miserable for the rest, personally refusing to speak to any reporter unless directly ordered to by his superiors (who mostly hated the press, as well), and ordered his staff to keep their mouths shut around the "spies" as well. He had no less bitter words for the general public who supported and read those newspapers, either, referring to them as "the non-thinking herd," and, "*Vox populi, vox humbug*" (the voice of the people is the voice of nonsense). This antagonistic relationship with the news media, which was no better and possibly even worse in that day than it is today, plagued Sherman for the rest of his public life.

Sherman returned to service in January 1862, serving in a series of out-of-the-way and relatively unimportant commands, until he again proved his mettle—and showed that he was not, in fact, insane. In early April 1862 he was given a new combat command, this time as a division commander in the Union Army of Tennessee under Major General Ulysses S. Grant at Shiloh. The first day of battle was again a hot mess for the Union army, scattered and battered by a heavy surprise attack from Confederate General Albert Sydney Johnston's Army of Mississippi. Sherman held his ground effectively throughout the morning of the attack, giving way only under great pressure, and had successfully maintained his portion of the battleground when nightfall came. The next day his division was in support of the victorious Union counterattack, and his star began rising again when he was front and center in the May capture of Corinth, Mississippi, which had been the goal of the overall campaign all along.

However, in the fall of 1862, another long campaign against the critical river port of Vicksburg began with a failure of Sherman's attack on the northern fringe of the town, caused primarily by Grant's inability to properly support it. The Northern press immediately renewed their accusations of "insanity" and incompetence against Sherman, who was fortunate to have a commander who shared his view of the media, and who ignored the calls for Sherman's replacement. Sherman's command was taken away by the War Department in Washington, which was more susceptible to pressure from the media, but Grant kept the fiery Ohioan with him in another capacity. The attack on and siege of Vicksburg, the longest in North American history, finally succeeded in July 1863, when Confederate commanding officer John C. Pemberton surrendered, mostly out of fear of a mutiny by his starving men. With the Confederacy split in half, supply lines cut off from Texas and Mexico, and the Mississippi River once again under full Union control, Grant was awarded with a promotion to command the entire Union Army of the West, taking his friend Sherman with him as commanding officer of the Department and Army of the Tennessee. Together, they successfully captured and held the last Confederate strongholds at Chattanooga and Knoxville, Tennessee, making it the first Confederate state to be brought back under Union control.

As a result of this great success, Grant was again promoted in the late fall of 1863, this time to the command of all Union armies, and Sherman was given command of all the western theater armies (specifically, those in Tennessee, Alabama, Mississippi, and Georgia). The two friends developed a grand plan of their own to end the war: Grant would take on General Robert E. Lee's Army of Northern Virginia, with the goal of destroying it and taking the Confederate capital of Richmond, while Sherman would concentrate on taking the crucial city of Atlanta, which would again split the Confederacy and further damage its last few remaining supply and manufacturing channels. A very serious political problem loomed over the already daunting tactical and logistical considerations of these plans: The year 1864 was an election year, and Lincoln was an unpopular Republican president presiding over an even more unpopular war, with a growing peace movement and a downright hostile press. Lincoln was opposed by a popular and dynamic Democrat who—despite proving himself to be pretty much incompetent as a combat commander and having played fast and loose with the truth about his military service—was running as a war hero who promised to "stop the fighting" the moment he became president. In essence, he promised to give the Confederacy the win despite all their losses on the battlefield. By the spring of 1864, Lincoln was convinced that he was going to lose, so he quietly ordered his aides to begin talks with his opponent's aides on how they would go about transferring political power for the first time during a war. The only thing that could change this situation was for Grant and Sherman to do something spectacular, and both knew that fact very well.

Sherman spent the winter months of 1863 to 1864 gathering together a powerful military force in Chattanooga, three grand armies with an eventual aggregate of over 112,000 men, and the supplies and support elements to allow a heavy attack down the one hundred miles of Western and Atlantic Railroad tracks into the heart of Atlanta. Opposing him was Confederate General Joseph Eggleston Johnston, his friend later in life, who commanded a single great army, one of the finest ever assembled in history, the Army of Tennessee, with an eventual total of 65,000 combat-hardened men. Johnston's task was much simpler: It was to keep Sherman from taking the city before the November elections. Sherman and Grant were in the process of developing what would become modern American battle doctrine: using massive amounts of men and material to simply overwhelm the enemy, instead of trying to use maneuver warfare to defeat them through superior strategies and tactics. This was, and is, an effective doctrine, but is costly in terms of both supplies needed and casualties among the soldiers. Johnston, on the other hand, was a natural master of defensive warfare, which is the art of giving just enough resistance and yielding just enough ground to cause the enemy to pay the highest price in men and material for every foot of ground gained, while at the same time keeping his own force as intact and undamaged as possible. Johnston also had his own set of political pressures and problems, primarily the fact that he was actively and publicly disliked by Confederate president Jefferson Davis, who had only given him the command of his army with great reluctance after Lee and others had pressured him to do so. It did not help, either, that one of Johnston's own corps commanders, Lieutenant General John Bell Hood, objected to Johnston's overall strategy and was a close friend of Jefferson Davis.

The Atlanta Campaign opened on May 8, 1864, when Sherman moved his three grand armies south out of their camps near Chattanooga and Ringgold, Georgia, heading toward Dalton. The fighting that began that morning north and west of Dalton, and southwest of the town along Rocky Face Ridge, would continue nearly without a break until September 1. Sherman showed what would become his customary plan of attack at Dalton, hitting the dug-in Confederates with the bulk of his armies, while the rest were sent racing around one flank far to the south, trying to get between Johnston and Atlanta to cut the vital rail link to the city. This was the same deployment Grant had long employed, and Johnston was well versed in how to counter it. Beginning the next morning, he gradually moved the bulk of his own army farther south, along newly constructed roads to well-built trench lines and emplacements ready for him at the next best line of defense, while keeping up a steady resistance to Sherman's attacks along his current line. Johnston employed this "fighting retreat" to Resaca on May 12–13; to Adairsville, Cassville, and Kingston on May 18–19; and to Acworth, Big Shanty, and Allatoona Pass on May 20–21. There, Sherman faced a huge problem: The natural fortress of Kennesaw Mountain would enable Johnston to stop any Union attempts to move down the railroad tracks and roads at its base, and a frontal attack on it was sheer folly to even contemplate.

Recalling the topography of the land north and west of Marietta that he had ridden as a young lieutenant so many years earlier, Sherman realized that he could briefly leave his lines of communication and supply along the railroad, move his armies west toward the small town of Dallas, and then swing back to the east, bypassing Kennesaw Mountain and getting into Marietta south of an unsuspecting Johnston, who would then be forced to either surrender or disperse into the northeastern mountains, thus losing Atlanta to the Union troops. The only real flaw with this plan was that it is nearly impossible to move ninety thousand plus men down dry, dusty, narrow country roads in the heat of late spring without attracting at least some attention. It did, and as Sherman maneuvered his forces to the west, Johnston arrayed his in a seven-mile-long line of defense, northwest from Dallas to a small outpost on a narrow creek called Pickett's Mill. There, the two armies fought three pitched battles over the week of May 25– June 1, all successfully defended by Johnston's men and causing significant Union casualties. Sherman managed to pull another wide flanking maneuver on June 4–5 to bring his forces back to Kennesaw Mountain, resigned to the fact that he would have to crack Johnston's stronghold there.

As the two lines reestablished themselves, small battles erupted at Pine Mountain on June 14 and Gilgal Church on June 15. These were small affairs with one significant exception: At Pine Mountain, Johnston's corps commander and the Episcopalian Bishop of Louisiana, Major General Leonidas K. Polk, was killed by a direct hit from a Union 3-inch rifled cannon. There is an unconfirmed story that the next day, Union scouts found a note pinned to a tree with a ramrod at the bloodstained site, that read, "You damned Yankee sons of bitches have killed our old Gen. Polk. We will fight you forever."

Johnston reestablished a good line of defense around Kennesaw Mountain by June 19, from the crest of Big Kennesaw south approximately five miles to Peter Kolb's Farm along the Powder Springs Road. On June 22 Johnston ordered Hood to send one of his divisions slightly westward, toward the Mt. Zion Church, but when they encountered strong resistance from two Union regiments, Hood rashly ordered his entire corps to attack down the Powder Springs Road, without any reconnaissance and without knowing what Union forces lay in front of him. The attack was a disaster, resulting in Hood's troops becoming bogged down by bad terrain and heavy Union artillery fire, and falling apart before the bulk of both sides' infantry even got within range of each other. Johnston sharply rebuked Hood for his impertinence, to which Hood responded by increasing his correspondence with his friend President Davis, incessantly complaining about Johnston's tactics and insisting the war would be lost if they continued. Sherman had his own subordinate problems: The corps commander facing Hood, Joseph Hooker, who also had been enamored of Sherman's "true love" at West Point, Miss Cecelia, was an excitable sort, and apparently got the idea that his corps was facing Johnston's whole army with no support. He sent a report to Sherman: "We have repulsed two heavy attacks and feel confident, our only apprehension being our extreme right flank. Three entire corps are in front of us." Sherman, and the flanking corps commanders, did not take this missive very well, setting in motion a series of events that would result in Hooker resigning from the army.

Sherman attacked all along the Kennesaw Line on June 27, making small gains in a few isolated spots, but taking incredibly heavy casualties at the point where he had placed his heaviest formations, the Dead Angle at Cheatham's Hill. Despite throwing five full Union brigades at this salient, only held by two Confederate regiments, the line held firm for the next six days of sporadic attacks. This was the last time Sherman tried a frontal assault in the war, a centerpiece tactic in pre-war military thought. The only real success he had at Kennesaw was accomplished by two brigades of Major General John M. Schofield's Army of the Ohio, which managed to slip around the southernmost flank of Hood's position at Kolb's Farm, giving Sherman a route to bypass the mountain and get behind Johnston. To prevent this, Johnston was forced to begin quitting the mountain line on July 1, pulling south to set up another strong line of defense along the Chattahoochee River. Sherman kept the pressure on, though, and before the Confederates could reestablish south of the river, one of Sherman's cavalry regiments forced a crossing around Johnston's right flank, at Sope Creek just south of Roswell. Johnston was forced to hastily retreat south again, this time to a good position at Peachtree Creek, at the site of present-day Piedmont Hospital.

Hood had continued his parade of complaints and laments to his friend Davis, who was increasingly concerned that Johnston was not going to be able to hold Atlanta. The fact that the plan all along was to slowly retreat back into the city, which by that summer was the most heavily fortified city in the world, and hold out until the November elections, seemed to slip the irritable and easily swayed president's mind. Late on the afternoon of July 17, just before Johnston's planned attack on a weak spot in Sherman's line scheduled for the next morning, Davis fired the diminutive general and replaced him with Hood. Sherman could not have been more delighted. In his postwar memoirs he wrote, "I was always anxious with Johnston at my front." He knew Hood was headstrong and "gallant," meaning that he was prone to ordering ill-timed and poorly planned but headline-grabbing movements, and was anxious for him to do so before he could take the still-dangerous Confederate Army of Tennessee inside the defenses of Atlanta. It would be much better to destroy the Confederate forces in the field and then easily take the vital transportation and supply center than to be forced to assault heavily fortified defenses.

Sherman was correct; Hood acted exactly as Sherman had suspected. Hood nearly destroyed his own army over the following six weeks, by attacking larger and better prepared Union formations on three separate occasions. In the end, he ignored the whole point of the Atlanta defensive plan, which was to hold the city at all costs until November, and after a last-ditch effort to keep Sherman from surrounding and cutting off the city at Jonesboro failed on September 1, he ordered the remaining supplies in the city blown up, and the city abandoned by all his military forces. As the last of his Army of Tennessee marched out of the city defenses along the last open road south, his engineers and sappers blew up a large train of munitions and supplies in the southeast part of the city. The thunderous explosion was heard by Sherman fifteen miles away in Jonesboro, and set fires that burned unabated for the next two days, destroying most of that part of the city before they were extinguished. This damage, some of the worst done to the city during the war, was later blamed on Sherman, not Hood.

While Hood moved his battered army to the west and north, on a frankly harebrained scheme to "draw Sherman out" to fight a decisive battle, though Hood had yet to win any battles to date against him, the Union commander set about making the city a large military camp, bringing in trainloads of supplies and preparing to move out again. One of the other problems he faced was the large civilian population still in the city, thirty thousand strong, some of whom were in fact newly unmasked Union supporters. He did not want to "waste" any of his precious supplies on them, so on September 8, Sherman announced one of his most controversial orders of the war: "The city of Atlanta, being exclusively required for wartime purposes, will at once be evacuated by all except the armies of the United States." All civilians would be transported under a flag of truce ten miles south to a settlement called Rough and Ready, now known as Mountain View, and then unceremoniously dumped off without provision for shelter or food. This appalled Hood, and he started a war of words with Sherman, protesting the inhumane actions, writing that "The unprecedented measure you propose transcends, in studied and ingenious cruelty, all acts ever brought to my attention in the dark history of war."

Sherman was not the sort to leave an accusation like that hanging. He hotly replied to Hood that what he had done was based on sound military principal, and that it was not all that unusual in the long history of war:

> In the name of common sense, I ask you not to appeal to a just God in such a sacrilegious manner. You, who in the midst of peace and prosperity have plunged a nation into war, dark and cruel war, who dared and badgered us into battle, insulted our flag, seized our arsenals and forts that

were left in the honorable custody of a peaceful ordnance sergeant, and seized and made prisoners of war the very garrisons sent to protect your people against negroes and Indians. . . . Talk thus to the Marines, but not to me . . . if we must be enemies, let us be men, and fight it out as we propose to do, and not indulge in such hypocritical appeals to God and humanity.

Hood was equally incised, replying, "We will fight you to the death, better die a thousand deaths than submit to live under you."

Sherman finally determined that his best course of action was to streamline his armies down to a more manageable sixty thousand infantry, cavalry, and artillerymen, and then move rapidly southeasterly across the state and seize the vital port city of Savannah. He suspected Hood would maneuver to cut his supply lines back to Atlanta and Chattanooga, but thought he should have sufficient supplies on hand, supplemented by "scavenging" along the way, until he could meet up with Union Navy supply ships on the coast. He also ordered his chief of engineers, Captain Orlando M. Poe, to destroy "anything of military value" in the city once they left, which he planned for November 16. He gave the same order to his field commanders who were chasing after Hood to the north, and within days Rome, Acworth, and Marietta were largely destroyed by flame.

Finally ready to move out, Sherman ordered Poe to start the fires late on the afternoon of November 15. Within a few minutes fires had been set, at first confined to factories and warehouses on the south side of town. A light wind soon built up the fires, spraying sparks and burning cinders in every direction, and spreading very rapidly. Pleased by the sight of the soon out-of-control fires raging through the city, Sherman was moved to remark only that he supposed the flames could be visible from Griffin, about forty-five miles to the south. As a sort of explanation to his staff, who were starting to view the wanton destruction with unease, Sherman remarked,

This city has done more and contributed more to carry on and sustain the war than any other, save perhaps Richmond. We have been fighting Atlanta all the time, in the past; have been capturing guns wagons, etc. etc., marked Atlanta and made here, all the time; and now since they have been doing so much to destroy us and our Government we have to destroy them, at least enough to prevent any more of that.

As the fires built up larger and larger, spreading all across the city into residential areas not earlier specifically targeted, block after block of buildings literally exploded into flame. What initially escaped the fires did not escape Sherman's "bummers," undisciplined wretches from the ranks who ran riot in the burning city, deliberately ignored by their commanding officers, who helped spread the flames by burning homes and businesses to cover up their thefts. In the midst of the chaotic riot, the Thirty-Third Massachusetts Regimental Band stood, calmly and righteously playing, "John Brown's Soul Goes Marching On." Major George Ward Nichols, Sherman's aide-de-camp, remarked without a hint of sarcasm that he had "never heard that noble anthem when it was so grand, so solemn, so inspiring." Other Union soldiers and officers viewed the destruction differently, remarking that the burning and looting of private property was not necessary, and a "disgraceful piece of business." Another summed up the view more widely held by their Confederate opponents, "We hardly deserve success."

As the flames died down overnight, dawn on November 16 revealed that over 4,100 of the 4,500 buildings in town had been leveled by the flames and rioting Union troops, including every single business. Sherman mounted his horse, Sam, and slowly led his men out of the ruined city, bound for Savannah and the Union Navy waiting for him just offshore in the Atlantic Ocean. This march south, the "March to the Sea," was nearly completely unopposed by any Confederate forces, Hood having taken the bulk of his army north in a plan to invade Ohio, and remaining local militias being far too small to take on this great grand army in the field. Despite all this, Sherman showed his usual irritable unease with the situation, ordering his three armies to move together down a path nearly sixty miles wide in places, and to be ready with guns up for any potential trouble. After the war, he wrote about this in his memoirs:

> *Then we turned our horses' heads to the east; Atlanta was soon lost behind the screen of trees, and became a thing of the past. Around it clings many a thought of desperate battle of hope and fear, that now seem like the memory of a dream . . . There was a 'devil-may-care' feeling pervading officers and men, that made me feel the full load of responsibility, for success would be expected as a matter of course, whereas, should we fail, this march would be adjudged the wild adventure of a crazy fool.*

There was a brief fight between a Confederate force that stumbled into one of Sherman's outlying brigades near Griswoldville, but overall, Confederate resistance to this part of the march was nearly nonexistent, and what Confederate forces did show up were grossly outnumbered. The only other resistance of note on the entire march was an attempt to defend the Oconee River bridge east of Griswoldville, where a force of exactly 186 men, the remnants of three separate commands, stood ready to keep Sherman from crossing. Even with nearly one thousand cavalrymen from Wheeler's command backing them up, over twenty thousand Union soldiers moved down that one road toward them. Fortunately, cooler heads prevailed before any fighting could break out, and the tiny force was withdrawn.

Sherman amplified his reputation as a thief and arsonist along this section of the grand march. All along the route, "authorized" foraging parties scoured the countryside, collecting food for both soldiers and animals, and were not above taking whatever else suited them while they were at it, all with Sherman's winking support. A forty-mile-wide path between Milledgeville and Millen was stripped down nearly to the roots, even down to the removal of every fence post. This wanton and truly unnecessary destruction started to disturb many Union officers along the way, although Sherman himself wasn't among them. His attitude was that the Southerners had "forced" him to order such actions by virtue of their secession, and that he only regretted that he "had" to destroy so many useful things that his army simply couldn't carry away with them. The situation deteriorated to the point that even Sherman's blindly admiring personal aide, Major Henry Hitchcock, noted in his memoirs, "I am bound to say I think Sherman lacking in enforcing discipline."

Worse than the wanton and complete destruction along the way was Sherman's attitude toward the slaves he was also setting free, mostly by virtue of killing or scattering their masters and destroying the plantations. The growing numbers of "liberated" slaves following his army quickly became an unendurable burden to Sherman, who claimed he was barely able to feed his own men, and urged the mostly temporarily freed men to stay on their plantations instead. It is worth noting for the accuracy of record that Sherman did have a point, in that his was a combat formation traveling without a supply chain in enemy territory, there was armed opposition in the area, and in the wreckage behind Sherman's passage more damage was done by Confederate deserters, freed slaves playing "catch up" with their former tormentors, and criminals of every stripe. However, he showed his true disdain for the slaves by his approval of an incident at Ebenezer Creek, about twenty miles west of Savannah. His columns were being followed by a group of about 670 newly freed men, women, and children. His rear guard was the XIV Corps, commanded by Brigadier General Jefferson C. Davis (no relation to the Confederate president), a murderer who had made his racist views clear to all, including Sherman. Once his men crossed a pontoon bridge over the swollen, fast-moving creek, he tricked the former slaves into waiting briefly on the other side, and then cut the pontoons free, knowing that a heavy force of Confederate cavalry was pounding down that road toward them, a few minutes away. Davis's men marched out of sight, and when the cavalry arrived, commanded by Brigadier General Joseph Wheeler, the civilians panicked, many trying to swim across the flooded creek, while the cavalrymen shot others as they tried to flee across the open fields, later rounding up and returning to servitude all those who survived. It is unknown how many died in this atrocity, which the callous Sherman clearly permitted to happen.

One more big fight, at Fort McAllister south of Savannah, and a brief siege of the city defenses, was all Sherman needed to finally capture his last objective in Georgia. He did manage to find the time to exchange more "trash-talking" letters, similar to those he had sent Hood, with Savannah's commander, Lieutenant General William J. Hardee. When Hardee seemed ready to mount a sustained defense of the city, Sherman warned him that he had plenty of guns and ammunition, and that he would "make little effort to restrain my army burning to avenge the great national wrong they attach to Savannah and other large cities which have been so prominent in dragging our country into civil war." The implication that Sherman would allow his "bummers" to rape, pillage, and burn their way across his city was very clear, if possibly not completely serious, and Hardee responded in kind. Suggesting that his own troops might be up for a bit of revenge, he replied that he would "deeply regret the adoption of any course by you that may force me to deviate from them in the future."

Despite this bravado, Hardee was already making preparations to abandon the city, which he finished on the night of December 20–21, 1864. The last Confederate units were gone by about 5:30 a.m., and the first Union scouts cautiously entered the abandoned trenchlines a couple of hours later. The capture of Atlanta on September 2 had assured Lincoln's reelection, and the capture of Savannah meant that the war would soon draw to a close. On December 22, Sherman sent a message to Lincoln:

His Excellency President Lincoln,
I beg to present to you, as a Christmas gift, the city of
Savannah, with 150 heavy guns and plenty of ammuni-
tion, and also about 25,000 bales of cotton.
W. T. Sherman
Major General

It is clear that at least part of what Sherman is accused of doing—looting, destroying, and wantonly burning a huge section of Georgia—is accurate and true. He also burned the remaining sections of Atlanta when he left, although it is worth noting that a great deal of the damage to that city was in fact done by Hood's departing men. Sherman has the reputation in some circles of being a great liberator of slaves, and a promoter of equal distribution of property (the "forty acres and a mule" program he promoted was a way to keep the former slaves on the land, so as not to have them wandering the countryside and getting in white people's way), but the incident at Ebenezer Creek showed quite clearly his own character flaws in that regard.

Despite his reputation for being hotheaded, strong willed, and perfectly willing to "show the black flag" and give no quarter to his enemy in battle or afterward, the Yankee general from Ohio was not completely heartless. While campaigning near Cassville and Adairsville, Sherman traveled to the plantation home of Charles Shellman, "Shellman Heights," to pay a visit to his old flame, even though he was then locked in combat with her brother and his old West Point roommate, Marcellus Stovall, and had faced her younger brother George at First Manassas, where George was killed in action. There, the general found that his long-lamented and still-beloved Cecelia had fled with her husband from the approaching Union armies. In a rare show of sentiment, Sherman ordered a picket be set around the property, and that his roaming "bummers" molest none of it. He also left a note for Cecelia with one of the house slaves:

You once said I would crush an enemy, and you pitied my foe. Do you recall my reply? Although many years have passed, my answer is the same now as then, 'I would ever shield and protect you.' That I have done. Forgive me all else. I am only a soldier.
  —W. T. Sherman

Later, in the Georgia Campaign, some of Sherman's staff urged that he march his armies due east from Atlanta to Augusta, to capture and destroy important arms-manufacturing facilities there. Sherman considered that plan, as well as several other possibilities, before deciding on his eventual route to Savannah. Augusta residents were, and still are convinced that he decided against attacking their city because it was the home of his lost love.

Sherman died in 1891. His old antagonist in the Atlanta Campaign, Joseph Johnston, was one of his pallbearers, and died one month later himself of pneumonia he had contracted at the bitterly cold ceremony. His old friend and sometimes opponent on the field of battle, Marcellus Stovall, died in Augusta in 1895. And the "true love" of Sherman's life, Marcellus's sister, who had spurned his proposals, fled from his approaching armies, and apparently never responded to his rather kind-hearted note, died at her home in Cartersville in 1904. Perhaps fittingly, her grand mansion overlooking the Etowah River, which Sherman had ordered protected from the ravages of his men, did not long outlast either of them, burning to the ground on New Year's Eve, 1911.

CHAPTER 8

John Bell Hood:
Hotheaded Southern Commander Who Jeopardized the Confederacy

Sometimes a person causes great harm to himself or others through accident or incompetence, other times through deliberately antagonistic actions, and in other cases through rash and badly-thought-out endeavors. In one specific case, all of these factors combined not only harmed the actor, but also lost the city of Atlanta to an invading army, and in turn doomed the Confederacy itself. Of all the hard luck cases in this state's history, one man rises to the top of the list: John Bell Hood. Son of a wealthy and prominent family, Hood evolved from a mediocre student into a dashing and sometimes dynamic young army officer. Unfortunately, he became best known for engaging in in-fighting and cutthroat politics (at the least appropriate moments), and—most damning of all—being a man his opponents were glad to see come into high command.

Hood was born in 1831 in Owingsville, Kentucky, in the northeastern section of the state, to Theodosia French and John W. Hood, a physician and college professor who owned a number of slaves. His uncle, Congressman Richard French, managed to secure an appointment to West Point for Hood, despite his father's objections; the elder Hood had wanted his son to follow him into the medical field. He graduated low in the rankings of the class of 1853, forty-fourth out of fifty-two in the class, but fared better than the forty-four who dropped out along the way. Hood very nearly did not graduate, having accumulated 196 demerits for various infractions in his senior year. Two hundred demerits would have resulted in his automatic expulsion. Among his friends and class-mates were Philip Henry "Phil" Sheridan (who had been expelled from West Point for a year for excessive demerits), John McAllis-

Lieutenant General John Bell Hood, c. 1864
COURTESY OF THE LIBRARY OF CONGRESS

ter Schofield (who also earned 196 demerits his senior year), and James Birdseye McPherson. One of his primary instructors was Major George Henry "Pap" Thomas; all four of these men would later face Hood in battle. The superintendent of the military academy during the last year of Hood's time there was (brevet) Colonel Robert Edward Lee, who ordered the increase in disciplinary actions that almost resulted in Hood's expulsion. Unimpressed by Hood's academic prowess, his classmates nicknamed him "Old Wooden Head," but friends began calling him "Sam" for some unknown reason; the nickname stuck for the rest of his life.

Hood was commissioned as a second lieutenant of infantry on his graduation, and initially assigned to the Fourth US Infantry in California, but transferred his branch of commission and assignment two years later to the Second US Cavalry in Texas. This new cavalry unit was commanded by one of the great rising stars of the antebellum US Army, Colonel Albert Sydney Johnston, with a host of other future luminaries in the ranks: Lieutenant Colonel Robert E. Lee as the executive officer, along with William Hardee, E. Kirby Smith, and Earl Van Dorn, all of whom later fought for the Confederacy; and John Buford, George Stoneman, and George H. Thomas, all of whom would become significant officers in the Union army. Going into combat almost immediately, Hood suffered the first of his many battlefield injuries on July 20, 1857, when he was shot through the hand by a Comanche arrow at Devil's River, Texas. Hood performed well enough in the ranks that he was offered the post of Chief Instructor of Cavalry at West Point in 1860, despite his poor academic performance there as a cadet, but he declined, desiring to stay with the Second Cavalry.

With the secession of the Southern states beginning in December 1860, the Second Cavalry gradually broke up, each officer choosing which side he would serve. Hood's home state of Kentucky never seceded, so Hood resigned from the US Army, embracing Texas as his new home country, and offered his services to the fledgling Confederate army in the new capital of Montgomery, Alabama. He was almost immediately granted a commission as a

First Lieutenant, first in a training capacity, but later transferred to the first Texas cavalry regiment when it was initially formed. Within a year, he was promoted all the way up to brigadier general and given his own command, the Fourth Texas Infantry Brigade, called Hood's Texas Brigade in the parlance of the day, in Lieutenant General Thomas Jonathan "Stonewall" Jackson's Corps, of General Joseph E. Johnston's superb and capable Army of Northern Virginia. He quickly earned a deserved reputation as an aggressive and highly capable field commander, winning several important victories in the battles of the 1862 Peninsular Campaign, as well as the heartfelt devotion and admiration of his men.

Hood soon became a devoted student of Jackson's battlefield tactics, preferring the offense to the defense, and appreciating the utility and frequent success of quick, stabbing assaults. However, similar to so many other eager students of gifted and inspiring teachers, Hood was quick to utilize the daring and flashy aspects of such tactics, without paying much attention to their careful planning and cultivating patience in waiting for the most appropriate moment to apply them. Hood himself admitted as much, "I was young and buoyant in spirit, my men were mounted and all eager for a chase as well as a fray."

Johnston was seriously wounded at the battle of Seven Pines (also called Fair Oaks), hit in the chest and shoulder with artillery fragments. During his long recuperation, the Army of Northern Virginia was turned over to General Robert E. Lee, a fortuitous event that even Johnston recognized, remarking later that "the shot that struck me down was the best ever fired for the Confederacy." Hood did not appear to have any difficulty in adjusting to working for his old West Point master, even though it was Lee's imposition of sterner discipline measures there that led to his almost being kicked out in his senior year. There does not appear to be any evidence that the two ever discussed the matter, and it would have been contrary to Lee's genteel nature to have brought up the subject.

During Hood's first brigade command, he spent time in Richmond with the movers and shakers of the Confederacy. He was introduced to Confederate President Jefferson Davis, with whom he would later become close friends, as well as some of the other leading generals, politicians, and high-society types. He was not above using his personal magnetism and charm to create alliances that he thought might prove advantageous one day, as observed later by Brigadier General Moxley Sorrel, the chief of staff of Longstreet's Corps:

> *Hood's appearance was very striking; in age only 34, he had a personality that would attract attention anywhere. Very tall and somewhat loose-jointed; a long, oval face shaded by yellowish beard, plentiful hair of same color, and voice of great power and compass. With very winning manners, he is said to have used these advantages actively for his own advancement.*

Some of the more wealthy and powerful people Hood won over included General James Chesnut Jr. and his wife, Mary. The general, a very wealthy and influential planter from Charleston, owned about five square miles of arable land and about five hundred slaves to work it, and was elected a South Carolina senator just before the war. His wife, Mary Boykin Miller Chesnut, was a remarkable woman for her time, well educated and multilingual, the writer of three long but unpublished novels, and the center of attention in both Charleston and Richmond society. She also kept a private diary during the war years, which includes an interesting description of her first impression of Hood in Richmond:

> *The famous colonel of the Fourth Texas, by name John Bell Hood, is here—him we call Sam, because his classmates at West Point did so—for what cause is not known. John Darby asked if he might bring his hero to us; bragged of him extensively; said he had won his three stars, etc., under Stonewall's eye, and that he was promoted by Stonewall's request. When Hood came with his sad Quixote face, the face of an old Crusader, who believed in his cause, his cross,*

and his crown, we were not prepared for such a man as a beau-ideal of the wild Texans. He is tall, thin, and shy; has blue eyes and light hair; a tawny beard, and a vast amount of it, covering the lower part of his face, the whole appearance that of awkward strength. Some one said that his great reserve of manner he carried only into the society of ladies. Major Venable added that he had often heard of the light of battle shining in a man's eyes. He had seen it once—when he carried to Hood orders from Lee, and found in the hottest of the fight that the man was transfigured. The fierce light of Hood's eyes I can never forget.

Hood led a decisive charge at the battle of Gaines Mill during the Peninsular Campaign, the only field grade officer in the unit to escape death or serious injury in the attack, and as a reward was promoted to command of a full division in Major General James "Pete" Longstreet's Corps. There, he performed with great gallantry during the Northern Virginia Campaign, and was in the vanguard of Longstreet's massive smashing attack at Second Manassas (Second Bull Run), which shattered, scattered, and almost completely smothered Major General John Pope's Army of Virginia, which was never reconstituted after that debacle. Hood's division was in turn almost completely wiped out that September in the West Woods at the battle of Sharpsburg (Antietam), while successfully defending the threatened flank of Lieutenant General Thomas J. "Stonewall" Jackson's Corps. His leadership in that defense suitably impressed Lee, who again promoted him, this time to Major General in charge of a reconstituted division. His division missed most of the actions at Fredericksburg and Chancellorsville, but was front and center in Longstreet's Corps at Gettysburg.

Longstreet arrived at Gettysburg too late to take part in the first day's action, but Lee directed his "old war horse" to mount what he thought would be a decisive assault on the Union's left flank on July 2, at a low-ranging hill covered with huge boulders called the Devil's Den, just north of two small outcroppings called

Big and Little Round Top. Longstreet saw an opportunity to roll up the Union line by maneuvering farther to the south and coming up on the other side of this low range of hills, but Lee refused him permission, ordering him to directly assault the Union positions there. Hood was ordered to lead this assault, and in turn hotly protested his order with Longstreet, who simply replied that it was Lee's order, that was the end of it, and get to it. Hood led his division up toward the Devil's Den, but before he could move to contact, an air burst from a Union artillery piece nearly severed his left arm. Doctors were able to save it, but it remained hanging useless in a sling the rest of his life. His second in command, Brigadier General Evander Law, attempted to carry out the assault as ordered, but the disruption of command at a critical time, combined with the difficult terrain and the well-emplaced Union defenders, resulted in a failure to take and hold the objective, with heavy losses in the ranks.

After a brief recovery period in Richmond, Hood traveled with Longstreet west to reinforce General Braxton Bragg's Army of the Tennessee, about to engage Major General William Starke Rosecrans's Army of the Cumberland at Chickamauga, in far northwestern Georgia. In a nearly unbelievable stroke of luck, Longstreet's Corps attacked shortly after arriving on the center of the battlefield, at the exact place and time a Union division had been mistakenly moved out of the way, leaving a nearly vacant hole in their line. Longstreet was able to exploit the breech most successfully and carry the day, but Hood suffered another serious wound, this time resulting in the amputation of nearly all of his right leg. He was once again sent back to recover in Richmond, this time spending a significant amount of time with his new friend, Jefferson Davis.

Hood recuperated from his injuries over the winter of 1863–64 in Richmond, spending many hours with Jefferson Davis and hotly pursuing the flighty but prominent socialite, Sally Buchanan Preston. This spirited campaign for "Buck's" hand would prove fruitless (but did demonstrate what a gallant figure Hood was to the Richmond social circles), but his friendship with Davis proved the opposite. As soon as Hood was able to return to service, Davis appointed him to the command of a full corps in the Army of Tennessee, which had just been reassigned to Davis's least favorite general and antagonist, Joseph Johnston. This was somewhat controversial, both because of Hood's age (he was one of the youngest lieutenant generals at age thirty-three), and because of his extensive injuries and amputations, which made mounting his horse a team effort: He had to be lashed to the saddle and followed by an aide carrying his crutches and spare artificial legs. A large Union army was building up under Major General William Tecumseh Sherman in Chattanooga, with Atlanta being their obvious target. The Army of Tennessee's critical task was to keep that city in Confederate hands, at least until the November 1864 elections would hopefully provide a more amicable Union president for the Confederacy to exploit politically.

Johnston had a host of problems other than the enmity of his president: His total strength in the field was only a little over half that fielded by Sherman (65,000 to 112,000 at the peak of both armies); he had far more limited supplies and the logistical trains to provide them compared to the Northern armies; and he could not afford to lose this campaign and have any hope for a final Confederate victory, while Sherman had a bit more leeway in this regard. However, Johnston did have some serious advantages: His Army of Tennessee by the spring of 1864 was one of the finest and most capable armies ever fielded, with some of the best combat commanders of that day leading in the ranks; he had a relatively small area to maneuver in, but this simply shortened his lines of communications, making defensive stands easier; and his engineers and those under Lemuel Pratt Grant created a series of outstanding fixed defenses, making Atlanta the most heavily fortified city in the world at that time.

Johnston was a cautious and conservative commander, which worked well for the size and composition of his army and the task that they faced. His overall strategy was originally planned to keep Sherman away from Atlanta as long as practicable, and then withdraw inside its formidable defenses and wait through a siege by the Northern armies until after the November elections. Lincoln was running for reelection, the first such vote during wartime in American political history, and his opponent, Major General George McClellan, was running on a peace platform, promising to end the war as soon as possible and give the South its independence and freedom. Sherman, on the other hand, felt the pressure to make something happen before the November election. Namely, either he or Grant would have to do something spectacular that would reenergize the voters into a Lincoln victory, or all they had fought for, for three long years, would be lost. His overall strategy for the grand army he had assembled was simple but brutal: to frontally assault and chew up Johnston's army, or at least push it out of the way, and grab the prize of Atlanta as soon as possible, at least several weeks before the election.

The Atlanta Campaign kicked off when Sherman moved his forces south in early May, striking Johnston's defenses around Dalton and Rocky Face Ridge. His frustrations with Johnston's capable defenses showed early, as he was normally loathe to engage in flanking maneuvers, but sent one of his corps far to the west around Johnston, heading for Resaca. He would return to this flanking tactic several times, as Johnston's defenses proved too formidable for a direct assault to carry, gradually pushing Johnston's army farther and farther south, ending up south of the Chattahoochee River and just outside the gates of Atlanta by mid-July. Two of Johnston's corps commanders, Hood and Lieutenant General William J. Hardee, did not approve of this "death by entrenching" style of warfare, and let their objections be known to Johnston, who politely deflected their criticisms. His other two major commanders, Lieutenant General Leonidas K. Polk and Major General Joseph Wheeler, tacitly agreed with the overall strategy. Ironically, an impatient Hood had himself blown a carefully planned and staged ambush of one of Sherman's columns at Cassville, when he suddenly and without orders or prior notice to Johnston, pulled his corps out of the line of battle and retreated farther south before contact was made, when a small Union unit appeared unexpectedly on his right rear flank. Hood's action at Cassville was unfortunately all too typical of the impetuous and hotheaded commander, who admitted in his memoirs that he was sometimes too hasty in his orders and movements, without giving sufficient thought as to the general strategic situation. It is possible that his poor decisions here, and continuing later in the Atlanta Campaign, were provoked by the pain from and medications for his extensive and crippling injuries, but they were more likely a result of his impertinent personality, mixed with a growing sense of irritation over Johnston's purely defensive strategies.

Hood and Hardee are both alleged to have sent a series of clandestine letters to Davis, increasingly complaining about the strategy Johnston had chosen, and predicting that Atlanta, and ultimately the Confederacy, would fall unless he was replaced. Hardee was an old political enemy of Davis, and his letters doubtlessly were ignored, but Hood's communiqués had the desired effect, as Davis dispatched his close friend, Mexican War comrade and then-military advisor General Braxton Bragg, on an inspection tour of Johnston's army in July. He reported back that Johnston should be replaced, hinting that he would like his old job back, but recommending Hardee for the command.

It should be noted that Bragg, no friend of Johnston, had formerly commanded the Army of Tennessee, was roundly hated by the men in the ranks, as well as a plurality of his officers, and proved only middling competent in command, winning several important victories but failing to adequately follow up on any of them. Longstreet once said of his command stint under Bragg, "Nothing but the hand of God can save us or help us as long as we have our present commander." Bragg's own cavalry commander, Lieutenant General Nathan Bedford Forrest, fought bitterly with him on several issues, and when he had finally had enough of the prickly general, personally threatened him in a letter, writing, "You have played the part of a damned scoundrel. If you ever again try to interfere with me or cross my path it will be at the peril of your life."

Davis was most reluctant to even consider Hardee for the command, but then asked his most able field commander, Robert E. Lee, for his opinion of Hood in that place of command. Lee responded in his usual very cautious and polite manner, actually suggesting Hardee for the position and damning Hood with faint praise, but phrasing it in such a way that Davis could, and did, read what he wanted into it:

> *. . . Hood is a good fighter, very industrious on the battle-field, careless off, and I have had no opportunity of judging his action, when the whole responsibility rested upon him. I have a very high opinion of his gallantry, earnestness and zeal. Gen. Hardee has more experience in managing an army. May God give you wisdom to decide in this momentous matter.*

By July 17 Johnston's army was arrayed north of Atlanta along a low series of hills overlooking Peachtree Creek. Sherman had moved his three grand armies south, but had been experiencing some difficulty in keeping the four columns of troops in contact with each other in the rough and overgrown terrain. Johnston had spotted a gap in Sherman's line and had issued orders in preparation for an assault into the weak point the next morning when a telegram arrived from Confederate Adjutant General Samuel Cooper, advising him that he had been relieved of his post, effective immediately. Hood was promoted to (brevet) full General and placed in command of the Army of Tennessee within the hour. Mary Chesnut neatly summed up the stark differences between the two generals, both of whom she knew so well:

> *Joe Johnston is a fine military critic, a capital writer, an accomplished soldier, as brave as Cæsar in his own person, but cautious to a fault in manipulating an army. Hood has*

all the dash and fire of a reckless young soldier, and his Texans would follow him to the death. Too much caution might be followed easily by too much headlong rush. That is where the swing-back of the pendulum might ruin us.

The disruption in change of command and some staff delayed any combat actions, while Sherman closed the dangerous gaps in his own deployments and established a strong line of entrenchments and redoubts on the north side of the Peachtree Creek valley. Mary Chesnut's analysis proved prophetic: Hood soon moved his army out of their own defensive works, assaulting the Union lines at Peachtree Creek on July 20. He lost about five thousand men to no gain there, and was forced to retreat south into the city on July 21. He kept his army moving through town into the late afternoon and night, panicking the residents who thought the army was abandoning them. He redeployed his troops on the morning of July 22 across from the Union works on the east, ordering a general attack in the afternoon. Losing another 8,500 men to no other gain again, he moved back inside the defenses of Atlanta until July 28, when he once again tried a frontal attack on Union defensive works, this time at Ezra Church. They did manage to temporarily halt further Union maneuvering in that part of the area, but at the cost of yet another three thousand men. Several smaller battles and skirmishes, including a swirling and extended one at Utoy Creek on August 4–7, gradually closed off every avenue of approach to the city, cutting off Hood inside the defenses. Although this was part of the original plan—to simply hold the city behind its formidable defenses when no additional offensive actions were possible (defenses that Sherman had no hope of carrying in a pitched fight)—the irrational, hotheaded Hood preferred risking the lives of his men and the people of Atlanta in a show of military might rather than relying on the safety of the city's defenses while patiently waiting to realize a major political gain for the Confederacy.

By the end of August, Sherman's forces had cut all rail access into the city save one, the Macon & Western Railroad from Macon, and had begun to heavily bombard the city, causing relatively few casualties, but badly rattling everyone's nerves, civilians and soldiers alike. When that last rail line was threatened in the Jonesboro area, Hood could no longer restrain his aggressive nature, and ordered Hardee to take what was left of his corps and defend it. A last assault on the Union lines at Jonesboro proved no more fruitful than the other Confederate attempts to break Sherman's emplacements. Hardee was left cut off and unable to get back inside the city defenses, losing another three thousand men and causing a crisis for Hood. With Hardee's corps out of the Atlanta defenses, his remaining men were insufficient to adequately man the extensive set of works surrounding the city, which would allow Sherman to successfully assault through them in a carefully coordinated, multipronged attack. All hope for keeping the Gate City out of Union hands gone, Hood ordered his remaining supplies destroyed, so they would not fall into the hands of the already well-supplied Union force's hands, and ordered the remaining formations of his once-proud Army of Tennessee to march south to Lovejoy on the night of September 1–2. As they left down the one remaining open road, Confederate engineers and sappers blew up Hood's ammunition and logistics trains, destroying several blocks around the rail station from the blasts, and starting a fire that burned down a significant part of the south side of the city. This destruction, recreated in the "Atlanta burning" scene in *Gone With the Wind*, would later be blamed on Sherman. Union troops entered the city the next morning, met by Atlanta Mayor James M. Calhoun, who formally surrendered the city.

With nearly 35,000 of his original 65,000-man force, dead, wounded, missing, or captured in the hundred-mile campaign from Dalton to Atlanta, Hood redeployed his remaining force near Lovejoy, expecting Sherman to continue chasing after him. Sherman, though, was busy consolidating his defenses and forces in Atlanta, and bringing in additional supplies for his next move, which he was still pondering. Davis begged Hood to do everything practicable to get the city back, but this was too tall a task for even Hood to reasonably pull off. Instead, he proposed to the Confederate president a new plan, to take his now roughly thirty thousand-man force north and west around Atlanta, which presumably would "force" Sherman to come out of the grand defense works of the city and attack Hood at a ground of his own choosing. The fact that neither Hood nor Johnston had successfully won a single major offensive action against Sherman, even when their army was at its peak and still intact, did not phase the ever-optimistic general. Amazingly, Davis signed off on the unlikely plan, and Hood headed north on September 18.

Having predicted that Hood would do something like this, Sherman had already sent Major General George Henry Thomas with a full corps back north to Nashville, to guard the critical supply base established there, and had ordered reinforcements placed along the critical Western & Atlantic Railroad line running north to Nashville from Atlanta. Hood struck first on October 4 at Big Shanty (now Kennesaw) and Acworth, easily capturing small garrisons in both towns, and then assaulted a stronger Union emplacement at Allatoona Pass a few miles north on October 5. Hood assumed the pass was only lightly held, but Sherman had seen the danger and already ordered a full division under Brigadier General John M. Corse to man two small forts atop the pass. A full day of pitched battle there failed to dislodge the Union forces, resulting in the identical number of 706 casualties for each side, and Hood abandoning the attempt to carry the Union works at sunset. Hood moved out north and west around Rome through Cedartown, Cave Springs, and Coosaville, while Sherman sent a force of forty thousand men (fifty-five thousand in some accounts) after him, vindicating in Hood's mind his unlikely and audacious plan. Wheeler's cavalry joined the campaign at this point, screening his movement from Sherman's force. Strong attacks at Resaca on October 12 and 13 were failures, but elements of Hood's army were able to capture the railroad north of Resaca the next day. In one of the only real successes in north Georgia, a two-thousand-man Union garrison at Dalton was forced to surrender, but with the large Union blocking force hot on his heels, Hood was unable to hold the city, and again struck off for the north and west.

All this time, Davis sent message after message to his friend Hood, begging him "not to abandon Georgia to Sherman but defeat him in detail before marching into Tennessee." Hood replied back that it was his intent to "draw out Sherman where he can be dealt with north of Atlanta," and that he had a new plan to "force" Sherman to chase after him. He now planned to move westward across northern Alabama, bypassing significant Union formations there, and strike north through Spring Hill and Franklin, assault and take the major Union base at Nashville, and then march farther north to the Cumberland River, where he could possibly take the war into Kentucky or Ohio. In his postwar memoirs, Hood clung to this unrealistic stance and his former hopes of defeating both Sherman and Thomas's powerful force in Tennessee:

> *I conceived the plan of marching into Tennessee . . . to move upon Thomas and Schofield and capture their army before it could reach Nashville and afterward march northeast, past the Cumberland River in that position I could threaten Cincinnati from Kentucky and Tennessee . . . if blessed with a victory [over Sherman coming north after him], to send reinforcements to Lee, in Virginia, or to march through gaps in the Cumberland Mountains and attack Grant in the rear.*

Reluctantly, once again, Davis approved of Hood's plan. Sherman's boss, though, Lieutenant General Ulysses S. Grant, had more confidence in Hood than his own men had by that point, and was worried that Hood might slip away from the force Sherman had chasing after him, possibly even threatening the Union supply chain in Tennessee. Sherman was confident that the badly reduced if still potent Army of Tennessee posed little threat to his plans, writing back to Grant that, "No single force can catch Hood, and I am convinced that the best results will follow from our defeating Jeff Davis's cherished plan of making me leave Georgia by maneuvering." As Hood continued his movement north, to Sherman's utter delight, the Union general recalled his blocking force chasing after the Confederates, and told an aide that he was quite approving of Hood's schemes, "If he will go to the Ohio River, I will give him rations." Stripping down his own force in preparation for a rapid march across Georgia to Savannah, Sherman sent Major General John M. Schofield's entire Army of the Ohio north to Nashville, to reinforce Thomas's strong command already there.

Hood left Georgia on October 17, taking the last major military force in the state that opposed Sherman with him. He spent a month preparing for his new, ill-conceived Tennessee Campaign, finally heading north again on November 19. He managed to eke out a slender victory at Columbia, Tennessee, on November 24–29, but suffered a loss at a relatively small fight at Spring Hill on November 29–30, which should have been an easily won victory and hard blow to Schofield's army, if it had not been for serious errors made by Major General Benjamin F. "Frank" Cheatham and Lieutenant General Alexander P. Stewart. Hood was enraged by his subordinates' failure; one staff officer mentioned that the next morning Hood was "wrathy as a rattlesnake," while his corps commanders were equally as upset and fought with each other over the debacle. Hood had already let it be known that he considered the long, defensive Atlanta campaign ruinous to the fighting spirit of an army, and had clashed with his other generals over his overall strategy of daring (and to others, reckless) offensive actions in the face of overwhelming opposition.

Hood moved up to Franklin on November 30, hot on the heels of Schofield's Army of the Ohio, which was trying to avoid contact with the Confederates until they got to Nashville. A difficult river crossing slowed the federal advance, and Hood decided late in the afternoon to take advantage of this, despite having only three hours of sunlight left (night actions were very rare during this war), and only two of his three corps immediately available. There are some historians who claim Hood, Cheatham, and Stewart engaged in a hot debate about the wisdom of this action, but the evidence for this is inconclusive. Hood ordered an all-out charge against the Union defenses, across over a mile of fairly open ground, at 4 p.m. Hammering attacks on the federal entrenchments over the next three hours caused about 2,500 total Union casualties, but failed to dislodge them from their works. Before dawn the next morning, Schofield abandoned the works and his wounded, and moved the rest of his army into the defenses of Nashville. Hood, on the other hand, suffered massive losses to no gain, including fourteen generals (six killed in action, seven seriously wounded, and one captured), fifty-five regimental commanders, and nearly 6,200 casualties in the ranks. His most serious loss was that of Major General Patrick Ronayne Cleburne, who had been commanding a division in Cheatham's Corps and was one of the most dynamic and capable combat commanders in the entire Confederate army. He was last seen alive advancing on foot into the Federal works, after his horse was shot out from underneath him, sword in hand, leading his men into the fray. Corporal Sam Watkins of the Maury Grays, 1/27th Tennessee Infantry, usually verbose and frequently humorous in his accounts of the actions he witnessed, was stunned nearly to silence by what he witnessed at Franklin:

> *Kind reader, right here my pen, and courage, and ability fail me. I shrink from butchery. Would to God I could tear the page from these memoirs and from my own memory. It is the blackest page in the history of the war of the Lost Cause. It was the bloodiest battle of modern times in any war. It was the finishing stroke to the independence of the Southern Confederacy. I was there. I saw it. My flesh trembles, and creeps, and crawls when I think of it today. My heart almost ceases to beat at the horrid recollection. Would to God that I had never witnessed such a scene!*

After suffering this galling loss, Hood had two simple choices: He could withdraw, reform and reconstitute his army and either modify, abandon, or retry his original plan, or he could keep his face toward the enemy and carry on. Doubtlessly in his overconfident, intrepid mind, there was no choice. He marched what was left of his army north to Nashville, detaching his cavalry command under Lieutenant General Nathan Bedford Forrest to separately attack federal forces at Murfreesboro, further reducing the force he had available to attack Thomas. Nashville ended up being one of the most lopsided Union victories of the war, with Hood unable to mount any sort of offensive movements from his initial positions outside the town, against the strong, seven-mile-wide federal line of entrenchments and redoubts, reinforced by US Navy gunboats in the Cumberland River on each end of that line.

Thomas allowed Hood's army to "cool off" for two weeks in the freezing cold and rain, and then mounted a massive frontal assault on Hood's works on December 15–16. Many of the hardened veterans of the once mighty Army of Tennessee had had enough by then, over 4,500 dropping their rifles in surrender or simply deserting the ranks, leaving a wildly outnumbered but hard core remaining to strongly resist the Union assault. Hood finally capitulated to the overwhelming Union pressure about 4 p.m., retreating under constant attacks by federal cavalry all the way back south to Corinth, Mississippi.

Hood insisted then and later that his losses were "very small" in this last campaign, but only about ten thousand to fifteen thousand (some sources claim as many as twenty thousand, but this is unlikely) of the sixty thousand plus men he inherited with his promotion at Peachtree Creek remained with him by the time the army arrived in Corinth. He quietly asked to be relieved of command on Friday, January 13, 1865.

Hood was and still is a very polarizing figure, but one of the better-known and most widespread charges against him seems to be entirely spurious: that he was either an alcoholic or a habitual abuser of painkilling drugs, especially during and after the Atlanta Campaign. Lately, this debate has actually been heating up, especially between the John Bell Hood Historical Society (JBHHS), an admittedly hagiographic group that seeks to honor the true heroism and courage the general displayed on the fields of battle, and historian Wiley Sword, who in two books, *The Confederacy's Last Hurrah: Spring Hill, Franklin, and Nashville* (1993) and *Courage Under Fire: Profiles in Bravery from the Battlefields of the Civil War* (2007), takes the complete opposite view of Hood's actions and character, harshly condemning the general for his behaviors and actions specifically in these last campaigns of the western theater. Both sides have carefully chosen the evidence they use to promote their point of view, while accusing the other side of lies, distortions, libelous posts and articles, and slanderous public comments, to the point where Sword complained in 2009 that he had become the subject of a "hate mail" campaign from supporters of the JBHHS over his books and other writings about Hood.

Throwing some more gasoline on this fiery debate over Hood's alleged chemical romances, historian Steve Davis, in his book *Atlanta Will Fall* (2001) and other writings, has pointed out that not a single known period source about Hood mentions these assumptions, several contain passages that would seemingly refute such behaviors, and in fact there are several references to his marked and very highly public abstinence after being baptized as a born-again Christian in February 1864. This, however, brings up a more troubling possibility: It has been long assumed by many military historians and students of the military sciences that Hood was impaired, either by drink or drugs, when he made the long series of ill-considered decisions during the latter part of the Atlanta Campaign and throughout the Tennessee Campaign, both of which brought great disaster to his own army and country. If this is not the case, and Hood was not impaired by such intoxicants, then the only conclusion that can be reached is that he fell far short in an attempt to exceed his level of personal skills and abilities, when he took command of the Army of Tennessee, if not long before then, as a corps commander. Regardless of the cause of Hood's ill-advised actions, the falsely inflated ego of the clean and sober general who refuses to recognize his limitations can be as damaging as the clouded mind of the drug-addled casualty commanding the ranks.

CHAPTER 9

Henry Wirz:
Commander of the
Andersonville POW Camp

One of the most notorious figures from Georgia's history was not in fact from Georgia; he wasn't even from the South or a citizen of the United States. He was Swiss, a somewhat shadowy figure who was accused of one of the most heinous war crimes ever in military history, short of what occurred in Nazi Germany or Imperial Japan. Yet later he was hailed in some circles as a martyr and viewed as a scapegoat for crimes in fact committed by the opposing side. Eventually, a large obelisk was erected in his honor, near the site of his alleged crimes, and it stands today as the only monument to a convicted war criminal in the United States. In any book about criminals and miscreants, this character would seem to be a shoe-in for inclusion, but as so very often happens in an investigation of a highly charged historical event, the facts about his life and actions do not completely fit the popular narrative, in either direction.

Heinrich Hartmann "Henry" Wirz was born November 25, 1823, in Zürich, Switzerland. His father was a businessman and his mother a housewife, and although both tried to steer Wirz into a business career, he reportedly desired from his youth to be a doctor. He was described as a "stooped, frail fellow," with hazel eyes, dark black hair, and a full beard. He reportedly married in 1845, had two children, and attended the University of Zürich, but there is no record of his obtaining a degree there. He was imprisoned for a short time in the late 1840s, possibly for debt, but no record as to the charges could be located. One source claims Wirz served in a military unit during this period, although there is no mention of which one (or even which country's military); there is an outside chance that his imprisonment was related to this service. Wirz divorced his wife and abandoned his children after his release, and emigrated to the United States in 1849, presumably to avoid the Swiss Civil War (the Sonderbund War) or the fallout from the various other revolutions that broke out in Europe the year before, though one account holds that he was expelled from the country following his prison sentence. He arrived in New York City, where he appears to have failed in setting up a medical practice or apprenticeship, and moved on to New Orleans a year later. In 1854 he relocated to Hopkinsville, Kentucky, shortly afterward moving to Louisville, where he finally established a medical practice. That same year he met and married a widow named Elizabeth Wolfe in Cadiz, Kentucky, who already had two teenage daughters. They had another daughter together in 1855, and the following year moved to Milliken's Bend, Louisiana, where Wirz found work as a plantation doctor.

Louisiana seceded from the Union on January 26, 1861, the sixth state to do so and join the fledgling Confederate States of America. Four months later Wirz enlisted as a private in the Madison Infantry of the Louisiana State Troops, which in short order became Company A of the Fourth Battalion Infantry, Louisiana Volunteers, moving out to Virginia by early July. Wirz does not appear in a postwar muster list of all the known Louisianans who served in the war, but an August 26, 1861, order from the Confederate Secretary of War office in Richmond makes it clear that he was present and serving in the state volunteers' ranks at that time: "Private Henry Wirz, of the Madison Infantry Louisiana Volunteers will report for duty to General J. H. Winder in this city." He served under Winder as a clerk and prison camp administrator, while the rest of the Fourth Battalion were assigned as bodyguards for Confederate President Jefferson Davis and as guards in the prisoner of war (POW) camps in Richmond and at Tuscaloosa, Alabama. It is not known when he was transferred, but by December Wirz was a sergeant and Assistant Commander of the military prison at Tuscaloosa. After this, his war record becomes less cer-

Monument to Wirz in the middle of old town Andersonville
PHOTO BY JOHN MCKAY

tain and subject to some seriously conflicting reports. According to most sources, probably based on his own later claims, Wirz fought with the Fourth Battalion at the battle of Seven Pines in Virginia, on May 31, 1862, where he reportedly was severely wounded. However, this is contradicted by evidence showing he remained at Tuscaloosa until early June 1862, when he was recalled to Richmond, promoted to captain by Winder, and placed in charge of all the prison camps in the city.

The standard for POWs at that time was to hold them for a relatively brief time, a few weeks up to three or four months, and then they would either be exchanged one for one with prisoners of the other side, or they would be given a parole, signing an oath promising to go home and not fight any more, a very old military practice held over from the European armies. As a result, there were no long-range plans made for housing large numbers of prisoners on either side, and even temporarily housing the numbers of prisoners captured put a huge strain on both side's resources from the very beginning of the war. The war started relatively suddenly and lasted longer than the "one big battle" both sides had expected, so literally no plans were ready by the time the first batches of battlefield prisoners were taken. Both sides initially tried to house POWs in regular jails, alongside regular criminals and other riff-raff, but quickly ran out of space in those facilities. The North began using coastal fortifications and the South old factory and warehouse buildings, but neither could humanely or adequately hold prisoners. This system suffered from the lack of any centralized command or control over the camps, until both sides separately established such in 1863. Union Colonel William H. Hoffman (who had been a POW himself at the beginning of the war) was assigned that year to set up a vast bureaucratic network of regulations, inspections, and standards for his camps. The South followed suit, also in that same year, by assigning Confederate Brigadier General John H. Winder as the Provost Marshal, in overall charge of all the burgeoning numbers of POW camps springing up across the South.

This system became even more strained in 1863, when local Union commanders stopped routine prisoner exchanges and releases, and became far worse in August 1864, when Lieutenant General Ulysses S. Grant, overall commander of the Union armies, signed an order completely ending the practices of exchange and parole. This was done specifically to cause further economic harm to the South, which was forced to house, feed, clothe, and give at least rudimentary medical care to ever-increasing numbers of federal prisoners, with ever-decreasing amounts and sources of supplies. From a military standpoint, this was a sound decision, as it helped cripple the Southern economy without unduly impacting the Northern one at the same time (the North was far better able to take care of Confederate prisoners, though records are clear that they often chose not to). The fact that most Union prisoners did honor their paroles and go back home, while most Southerners honored them just long enough to join the nearest Confederate fighting unit, played no small part in this decision. Some Confederate prisoners were captured three or four times over in battle, going right back into the fray as soon as they were paroled. Northern newspapers did take great note at the time that this sound military policy was implemented on the backs of Union prisoners of war, but as usual in such matters, forgot about their previously printed outrages over this policy, which had resulted in the deaths of thousands of Union soldiers, and replaced them instead with their printed jubilation and hagiographies of their own leaders at the end of the war. However, the newspapers did soon find another target on which to focus their fire, bile, and headline-grabbing semi-truths.

Wirz's duties included escorting groups of prisoners from holding camps all over the Confederacy to either Richmond or Vicksburg, Mississippi, for exchange. On one of these journeys, in December 1862, he was involved in a stagecoach accident and severely injured. From then until March 1863, he was placed on medical leave at his home in Louisiana. A telling insight into his less than honorable personality is the fact that he later claimed to have suffered these injuries in battle. Once Wirz returned to duty, he was promptly sent off to Europe on what appears to be completely undocumented and somewhat mysterious errands, probably involving delivering messages or other documents to Confederate agents across the Atlantic. Shortly after he returned the following year, aboard a blockade runner into the Wilmington, North Carolina, harbor, he was reassigned to command of a new prisoner-of-war camp still under construction in southwest Georgia.

In the summer of 1863, urgent searches were made by Confederate officials to find appropriate places to house the growing number of Union prisoners. One of these officials, Captain William Sidney Winder (General Winder's son), reported back that he had found an ideal spot, on the Georgia Southwestern Railroad line just north of Americus, Georgia, at an outpost simply called Station No. 8. He reported that the site featured good land and fair weather, provided "plentiful food" and sufficient water for the number of prisoners expected, and that it was far from any expected avenues of invasion or areas of battle, with abundant transportation lines available to bring in needed supplies and to transport the prisoners. The plans were approved by Provost Marshal Winder in Richmond, and Colonel Alexander W. Persons was named as the first commander of the planned outpost. Construction of the facility, called Camp Sumter, was delayed several weeks due to a lack of sufficient labor in the area, as well as the objections of the inhabitants of a nearby village called Anderson. By the time work started in early January 1864, funding shortages and rapidly increasing numbers of Union prisoners caused the original plans of wooden barracks buildings to be scrapped and replaced with just a strong outer wall fence, without any interior buildings to house the POWs. Under pressure to have the facility ready at the earliest opportunity, the contracted slave workmen ignored the original mostly forested site plan, and simply stripped the entire area of all but two trees, using the tall pines to build a fifteen-foot-high double wall of roughly shaved logs butted closely together, originally enclosing a space of about sixteen-and-a-half acres. Guard towers, known as "pigeon roosts," were built against the outside of the interior wall spaced every thirty feet, to house the regiment of infantry assigned to watch over the six thousand prisoners expected.

A small fort on the southwest corner and six other earthwork emplacements guarded against any Union cavalry attempt to free the prisoners, and inward-facing cannon redoubts guarded against prisoner uprisings. A smaller enclosure called Castle Reed located half a mile west housed the only officer prisoners sent to this area, until all were transferred to Macon's Camp Oglethorpe in May 1864. Afterward, only enlisted prisoners were sent to Camp Sumter. The first Union prisoners arrived in what they quickly dubbed "Andersonville" on February 25, 1864, using their own shelter halves, blankets, ponchos, and scrap wood left lying around to build crude huts to escape the freezing weather. Just two days later, Private J. H. "Adam" Swarner, of Company H, Second Regiment, New York Cavalry, became the first prisoner to die, expiring from the pneumonia he had contracted before his arrival at the camp. Within a week, the first escape attempts were mounted. Although they proved unsuccessful, they led Persons to order the establishment of the later-notorious "dead-line": a light rail mounted about a foot off the ground, ten feet inside the stock-ade wall. Any prisoner who stepped over this line would be imme-diately shot dead by the guards, no questions asked. The dead-line was not unique or original to Camp Sumter, but by that time was a common feature in POW camps in both the North and South.

By late May 1864, the camp held over 23,000 prisoners, and the stockade walls were moved outward to contain a twenty-six acre plot, still insufficient for this number of occupants. Many of the prisoners arriving later had been held in other POW camps, and were already weak, sick, and malnourished when they arrived in the overcrowded facility. The prisoners' sickly conditions, com-bined with the rapidly warming, late spring weather, set the stage for a real disaster to break out. On June 17 General Winder was reassigned to command of the rapidly growing overall set of facil-ities in the area, bringing with him Wirz as commander of the stockade itself. By August, over 33,000 prisoners were being held at the camp, making the twenty-six acres the fifth largest city in the Confederacy. The Atlanta Campaign was drawing to a close farther to the north of the state by that time, with Union Major General William T. Sherman's cavalry ranging over a fair part of the state, disrupting sources of transport and supply, and tearing up many of the railroad tracks that helped feed those prisoners.

Conditions inside Camp Sumter rapidly deteriorated as the heat of summer wore on. Many new prisoners vomited uncontrol-lably on entering the gates, the overpowering stench of open sew-ers, dead bodies, and rotting flesh hanging like a cloud over the open field. The new ones would stand for hours at first, trying not to touch or sit on anything, given that almost every inch of ground was covered with thick layers of greasy slime, contaminated dirt, mold, dead lice, and other vermin. The prisoners themselves were nearly universally filthy, lice- and flea-infested and covered with open sores and rashes. Bathing was almost nonexistent for most prisoners, unable to work themselves through the crowds to the single water source, which itself was already becoming heavily contaminated. Many soon became despondent, not caring what happened to themselves or others, and quit bothering to use the slit latrines to relieve themselves, or even covering up the mess afterward. Diarrhea, dysentery, and typhoid fever ran rampant, killing many more prisoners than starvation or failed escape attempts. Neither Winder nor Wirz did anything of significance to relieve this situation on their arrival.

One Union prisoner, Private Samuel Elliot of Company A, Seventh Pennsylvania Reserves, kept a diary while he was confined at Camp Sumter. His first entry well expressed the dread he felt as soon as he arrived in the camp:

> *Sunday, May 22: The camp contains about fifteen thousand Union men, most of whom have been prisoners from eight to ten months, and were once strong, able bodied men, but are now nothing more than walking skeletons, covered with filth and vermin, and can hardly be recognized as white men. The horrible sights are almost enough to make us give up in despair—the ground is covered with filth, and, vermin can be seen crawling in the sand. In the centre of the camp is a stream of dirty water so warm and greasy we can scarcely drink it. The sights I saw on this, my first day . . . so filled me with horror that I can give but a poor idea of this prison den.*

Food supplies began dropping, as rail lines and available stocked warehouses were destroyed or captured by Union forces. Rations dwindled down to near nothing, with many prisoners subsiding on rats (until they ran out), the occasional bird that fell into their hands, or rough cornmeal that was the only regularly distributed food by mid-September, delivered four days a week on good weeks. Water, too, became a serious issue. The "sufficient water supplies," were only really sufficient for the originally planned six thousand, consisting of a single, moderately-sized stream running through the middle of the camp. It provided the only drinking, cleaning, and bathing water, which became contaminated after the poorly situated prison kitchen started dumping their refuse in it upstream from the prisoners. It became further contaminated when the infrequent but heavy summer showers washed all the prisoner's soiled waste down into it. In August, a dry spell almost completely dried up this single source of water for the camp, until, during a violent thunderstorm, a lightning bolt struck the ground inside the stockade, missing the prisoners but opening up an old spring that had been covered up by accident during construction of the camp. The prisoners, who believed God had provided them with this additional water source in their direst hour of need, named it Providence Spring.

Through all of this, Wirz frequently displayed a disturbing lack of personal command leadership. Although the guard force was nominally under his command (and directly under their own regiment commander's), Wirz had little interaction with them, and failed to restrain some of the "games" they played. The more sadistic game involved guards dropping bits of their own bread ration into the crowds of prisoners just to watch the ensuing riot. The sociopathic guards would even drop bits of food inside the dead-line, daring prisoners to cross to grab them, and then shooting anyone who did. During the few times Wirz actually responded to problems inside his command, his directions were erratic and often ill-advised. For example, when he was notified that there was some evidence the prisoners were starting to construct escape tunnels (most of the "tunnels" were either deep holes dug to escape the brutal heat of the summer day or attempts to dig wells for more water), Wirz ordered that no prisoner dig any hole, or build or inhabit any sort of overhead shelter. This insane command was soon overturned by Winder during one of the few times he seemed to have paid much attention at all to what was going on inside the stockade. There were also reports that Wirz habitually walked around the stockade wearing his large LeMat revolver, allegedly frequently with it in his hand, and some allegations that he personally shot several prisoners (although this last point is the object of seriously heated debate). Camp Sumter's best known inmate,

Union Private John Ransom (author of *Andersonville Diary*), certainly was no great fan of Wirz:

May 10.—Capt. Wirtz [sic] very domineering and abusive. Is afraid to come into camp anymore. There are a thousand men in here who would willingly die if they could kill him first. Certainly the worst man I ever saw.

Whether Wirz actively abused and threatened the prisoners under his charge or not is highly debated today, but it is very clear that he at least passively allowed an incredible amount of suffering to go on, even considering the difficulties he was having in obtaining supplies. After the second camp expansion, there never was any further attempt made to expand it again in order to more properly contain the exploding numbers of incoming prisoners, which led directly to the rampant spread of camp diseases. The number of prisoners dying from starvation, diarrhea, dysentery, cholera, and other diseases started to skyrocket by the end of the summer of 1864, with already over 4,500 dying inside the stockade in just the six-month period between February and August. The peak population of the camp was reached in late August, with over 32,000 Union prisoners held in a spot that would have been overcrowded with a third of that number. Deaths were so common that some prisoners managed to escape by pretending they were dead, so that they would be carried outside the walls to the rude "death house." By the end of the war, over 45,000 prisoners had been held inside the stockade of Camp Sumter, exactly 12,919 died there, and another 329 successfully escaped. Another large field close by the northern stockade wall became the prison's cemetery, the dead buried shoulder to shoulder about three feet deep. These were not true mass graves, because each deceased soldier was buried individually with some level of dignity, instead of being dumped into a jumble at the bottom of a pit, but the long rows of tombstones that have barely a gap between them is a startling and sobering sight.

Largely through the work of a single prisoner, Union Private Dorence Atwater of the Second New York Cavalry, one of the original prisoners, only 460 of the graves are marked as "Unknown Dead." Atwater had been assigned by Wirz with the responsibility to record the names of all who died at the camp, and fearing the loss or destruction of this record in the Confederate archives (a justified fear, as most of the camp records were either lost or deliberately destroyed in the postwar turmoil), Atwater painstakingly hand-wrote another, which he kept in hopes of notifying the families of the deceased once he was released. Private Elliot wrote about what he saw while taking one of his deceased friends to the "dead house":

Thursday 25 (August 1864). Charles Jarimer, a recruit of our Company, and a bunk-mate of mine, died to-day, after a long and painful illness; helped to carry his body to the "dead house" —a house built in the rear of the hospital, outside the stockade. There were about twenty-five other bodies, most of which had been stripped of all their clothing, and were so black and swollen they could not be recognized. While I was there I saw them piling the bodies one on top of the other, into the wagon, to be hauled to their graves or ditches. I passed through the hospital on my way back, and the sights I saw there were enough to make one sick: the tents were filled with what could once have been called men, but were now nothing but mere skeletons. The short time I was there I saw several die. A man is never admitted to the hospital until there is no hope of his recovery, and when once there it is seldom, if ever, he returns.

On top of all the death, suffering and deprivation, the prisoners were attacked inside the camp by some of their own. A group of thugs known as the "Mosby Raiders" beat, robbed, terrorized, and even murdered their fellow prisoners quite openly for many months. Led by a particularly unpleasant character, Union Private William "Mosby" Collins of Company D, Eighty-Eighth Pennsylvania Infantry, they were finally brought down by another group of prisoners. With Wirz's permission and cooperation, twenty-four of the Raiders were subjected to a trial by the prisoners themselves, and six were convicted and immediately hung. All the others spared in the trial were later severely beaten by large groups of their former victims, three more dying in the process. The six hung and three who died from the retribution are buried in a special part of the cemetery separated from the rest, by request of the other prisoners.

To his credit, although Wirz did not display any capacity for personal command, he did seem to eventually recognize how desperate the situation in his camp had become, and tried to alleviate it through several sincere, if ineffective means. He sent letters to Confederate high command officials in Richmond, over the head of his boss, General Winder (who seemed to have mentally "checked out" by this time), begging for increased rations and medical supplies. Confederate Surgeon General Dr. James Jones traveled to Camp Sumter in the later summer, and reported back to Richmond of the serious issues he found. There being a dearth of needed supplies, and few ways to send what little there was, his report had no more impact on the situation than Wirz's own pleading letters. Wirz also released on his own parole a group of several hundred prisoners, with passes to get by any Confederate checkpoints, to go to a major Union base at Jacksonville. Remarkably, the Union commander at Jacksonville refused to accept their parole or allow them in his base, but forced them to return to Camp Sumter, in accordance with Grant's orders.

After the peak of prisoner numbers was reached in early September, a series of Union victories caused the camp's population to quickly dwindle. Atlanta fell to Sherman on September 2, and it was assumed that he would either mount a full-on campaign to relieve the camp or at least send a strong cavalry unit to forcibly take it. In fact, Sherman did order one of his cavalry commanders, Major General George Stoneman, to take his corps to relieve "Andersonville," which was already notorious among Northern troops, thanks to reports from the few successful escapees. Stoneman was not exactly a great cavalry leader in the mold of Nathan Bedford Forrest or J. E. B. Stuart; he was captured along with most of his officers and a significant number of enlisted men near Macon, and became an occupant of Camp Oglethorpe himself. Ironically, he was paroled out just three months later, at the personal request of Sherman, returning to service during the fall Georgia Campaign down to Savannah.

The healthiest of the thousands of unfortunate prisoners for whom Sherman did not request a parole were moved to the much larger Camp Lawton near Millen, Georgia, that had been specifically constructed in September 1864 to finally help relieve the overcrowding at Camp Sumter. It had to be abandoned on November 25, with Sherman's forces close approaching, and the prisoners temporarily moved to other camps near Blackshear and Thomasville, before being returned to Camp Sumter. Other prisoners were moved to Florence and Columbia, South Carolina. About eight thousand of the sickest prisoners were left at Camp Sumter, the majority dying there. By early December, only 1,359 were still alive, soon joined by prisoners transferred back from Blackshear and Thomasville, and all were finally released in May 1865 to a special Union train sent to take them home. Some of the released former Camp Sumter prisoners were on the SS *Sultana* on the Mississippi River on April 21, 1865, when its boiler exploded, killing about 1,800 of the 2,500 people on board.

Conditions at the other camps proved even worse than what Andersonville POWs had experienced. Private Elliot was sent to South Carolina, where he wrote:

Monday 31 (September 1864). While at Andersonville I did not suppose the rebels had a worse prison in the South, but I have now found out that they have. This den is ten times worse than that at Andersonville. Our rations are smaller and of poorer quality, wood more scarce, lice plentier, shelters worn out, and cold weather coming on. I have stood my prison life wonderfully, but now I am commencing to feel it more sensibly, and am getting too weak to move about. To add to my misery I have the scurvy in the gums.

Wirz was not even able for one reason or another to take proper care of his own men. The conditions at Camp Sumter proved to be no less hazardous for the guards than the prisoners. Over the few months the camp was active, it had a guard force of roughly 1,000 men; 226 of them died there, 117 buried in a small, separate Confederate cemetery outside the walls of the National Historic Site property there today. This 23 percent death rate is not much lower than the 29 percent death rate among their Union prisoners.

Although he was replaced by Colonel George C. Gibbs as stockade commander in October, Wirz remained at Anderson until his arrest on May 7, 1865, by Union Captain H. E. Noyes, of Union Brigadier General James H. Wilson's staff. Wilson had just completed a long raid through Alabama and Georgia, culminating three days later in capturing Confederate President Jefferson Davis eighty miles to the southeast, near Irwinville, Georgia. Though Wirz was not in command of the camp at the end, he had been subordinate to the actual commander for his entire assignment (General Winder) and thus had a price on his head. With the war coming to a close, the public—fueled by the usual screaming headlines, half-truths, and mostly fictional stories spun by the press about the camp, as well as the assassination of Abraham Lincoln—was demanding nothing short of a blood sacrifice. And since Winder had died three months before, Wirz was just about the perfect lamb to be slaughtered to satisfy that lust, regardless of his relative guilt or innocence.

Wirz was brought to Washington, D.C., and placed on trial before a military tribunal beginning on August 23, 1865, on one charge of conspiring to assassinate Lincoln (which should underscore what a mockery this trial was from the very beginning), and thirteen specific charges of murder or deadly assault on prisoners, in violation of the US Articles of War. Although there were plenty of named sources for stories about the camp in the press (and several magazine articles and books had been published by this time about the horrid conditions of the prison camp), and despite the possession by the military tribunal of a copy of Atwater's list of the dead (ordered compiled by Wirz himself), the thirteen allegedly murdered prisoners were each listed as an anonymous "United States soldier whose name is not known." Wirz had five lawyers assigned to help his defense at first, and they did put up a spirited defense in pretrial motions. Their most effective arguments were shot down quickly by the tribunal; the surrender of Lee and Johnston had provided a blanket pardon for all Confederate soldiers, but the tribunal quickly ruled the pardon did not extend to "war criminals." His lawyers argued that, as Wirz was now a civilian who had never served in the US military, a military tribunal was not the proper forum in which to conduct his trial. In response, the tribunal ruled that the humbled and utterly defeated former Confederate states remained "a rebellious, armed camp," and that combat might break out again *at any second*, making their military tribunal the necessary and proper venue in which to try the former Confederate officer. The defense's last motion argued that the charges were unconstitutionally vague and unspecific, violating several Sixth Amendment provisions; the tribunal dismissed the motion without comment. With that, three of his lawyers quit the case, stating it was clear that it was a sham court assembled just to put a fig leaf of legality over what was sure to be the murder of the accused.

One hundred sixty witnesses were called by the prosecution; 145 of them were former prisoners. All testified movingly of their intense suffering inside the camp, but most could only relate rumors about any specific charges against Wirz, ten giving "friend of a friend" hearsay testimony, and only two claiming to be eyewitnesses to the crimes with which Wirz was charged. One of these two supposed eyewitnesses testified that out of over thirty thousand men in the small camp that day (and contrary to what John Ransom had written about Wirz some weeks earlier), he alone witnessed Wirz come into the camp alone, pistol in hand, pick out a random prisoner, and shoot him to death. The problem was that the date he testified in open court that this happened did not match the date printed in the indictment for this specific crime; this small problem was corrected by illegally "fixing" the date later in the document.

The other eyewitness was the star of the trial, one former Private Felix de la Baume, a flamboyant and well-groomed man who testified that he personally saw Wirz shoot several prisoners, each one exactly on the day the indictments said these crimes occurred. He seemed to have a phenomenal, near photographic memory, especially considering the hellish conditions he would have been suffering through as a prisoner in the camp; he was able to provide exact dates and times, as well as exceptionally detailed and lurid accounts of multiple outrages Wirz allegedly committed all over the crowded camp. The newspapers ate it all up, providing the public with daily new lists of horrors and debauchery committed by the Swiss former commandant, though at least one observer at the trial smelled something fishy about his testimony, "His omnipresence while at Andersonville seemed something bordering on the supernatural. Nothing escaped him. Witness de la Baume held the surging crowd like an inspiration." Baume was later lauded by the tribunal itself for his brave and "zealous testimony," which he used as leverage to get appointed to a government job.

There was really only one problem with Baume's testimony about Wirz, which was the primary evidence used to convict him: It was all a lie. "Private Felix de la Baume" was in fact ex-Private Felix Oeser, a deserter from the Seventh New York Volunteer Infantry Regiment, who had never spent a day in Georgia, much less at Camp Sumter. The regiment itself had been disbanded more than a year before Camp Sumter was built, even if he had served honorably in its ranks. Once exposed, shortly after the trial and before Wirz was executed, "Baume" admitted his lies and false testimony against the accused. Once again, though pressured to set aside the sentence and re-try Wirz, the military tribunal simply ignored his confession and let the sentence stand. Although the trial was a farce, with the witnesses relating hearsay or in fact perjuring themselves, the outcome fit the desired narrative.

Wirz's defense team was prevented from calling any effective eyewitnesses who would testify to the efforts he made to relieve the suffering at the camp. The tribunal issued a special rule for the trial that all defense witnesses had to first be interviewed and approved by the prosecution. The court ruled as irrelevant testimony about Wirz releasing several hundred prisoners to Jacksonville, as well as documents showing he had released and sent to Washington four other prisoners, to plead there for the reinstitution of parole and exchange. Other documents showing his frequent desperate requests for food and medicine from the Confederate high command were also dismissed as irrelevant. The sixty-eight witnesses who were allowed to testify in his defense consistently claimed that, although he was a personally unpleasant, frequently irritable man, he did try with all his might to bring relief to the suffering prisoners. Most of this testimony, as well, was ruled as irrelevant to the charges against him.

Both sides rested their cases in late October, and the defense made a routine request for a brief recess in order to prepare their closing arguments. This, too, was denied, and both of Wirz's remaining lawyers quit in disgust, telling what few reporters were willing to listen to them that the trial was clearly "a fraud and shamble." On October 25, Colonel N. P. Chipman, the lead prosecutor, gave both the prosecution and defense closing arguments to the tribunal. The following day, Wirz was declared guilty on all counts (including the conspiracy to assassinate Lincoln, making him the only person to be convicted of such), and sentenced to death. Two weeks later, on November 10, inside Old Capital Prison in Washington, in sight of the Capitol's dome, Wirz was brought out before a chanting, screaming mob, repeatedly calling out "Andersonville! Andersonville!" and mounted the gallows.

Wirz was bound by the hands and feet, the hangman placed the noose loosely around his neck, and Major Russell, in charge of the execution, spent about fifteen minutes reading the specific charges to him, which could not be heard by the witnesses due to all the noise and chants from the assembled soldiers. Wirz smiled tightly and shook his head a few times, as if denying the charges, but said nothing until asked for his last words, "I am innocent—I will have to die, and will die like a man, and my hopes are in the future."

The trap was pulled at 10:30, Wirz fell to the end of the rope, but the civilian executioner had botched the knot, and his neck did not break. Instead, he slowly strangled to death, twisting slowly in the light wind as the crowd jeered, mocked, and hurled abuses on his soon lifeless body.

In an ironic twist to his end, Wirz was indeed a most unpleasant, nasty, lying, and pretty much criminally incompetent officer, placed in a position far above what his talents and abilities could handle, most likely as a result of his "boot-licking" of Winder for such a high command. However, the "crimes" for which he was actually executed could have been more properly laid at the feet of his own prosecutors, the Union army high command, which destroyed the lives of its own men by allowing them to be held in foreign prisons as a military tactic. Still, Wirz was certainly not one to admire or hold up as an example of Southern honor and chivalry. He was by any view a rogue and scoundrel who cast a blind eye on human suffering and caused the deaths of thousands through both his actions and inactions.

CHAPTER 10

Charles B. Blacker:
Deputy US Marshal in the Georgia Moonshine War, 1876–77

With the passage of time, some of the less enlightened stereo-types about the people who live in the north Georgia mountains have faded, the area turning largely into a recreation and vacation region, with some of the more southerly communities now serving as "bedroom" suburbs for Atlanta. Less than thirty years ago, though, it was common to see allegedly humorous caricatures of these folks printed on various tourism and souvenir items, portraying them as raggedly clothed lazy idlers, usually with a gallon jug of "hootch" either in their hands or sitting nearby. These "hillbillies" have been lampooned in popular media for nearly two centuries as an odd mix of ignorant, illiterate, socially backward racists, and dangerous, cunning, thieving, in-bred sociopaths.

Between *The Beverley Hillbillies* and *Deliverance*, there is a sliver of truth mixed in with all the ignorant attitudes about them, but the larger reality is that, as a class of people, they represent the independent, self-sufficient frontier spirit that settled and grew this country. In the process, they also helped establish the government, and then proceeded to attract that very institution's animosity and wrath. The breaking point between the people and the government in this region came from the oldest conflict in this country's history: the imposition of taxes without that people's consent and the government's aggressive use of sovereign powers to collect them. One of the agents of this excessive use of power was Deputy US Marshal Charles B. Blacker, who with his fellow adherents and the backing of the US Army in the north Georgia mountains, managed to turn the simple collection of excise taxes into a full-blown war.

The north Georgia mountains are more appropriately viewed as a part of Appalachia than the rest of the state, a region that stretches from northern Virginia and Maryland southwest across North Carolina, Tennessee, north Georgia, and parts of northwestern South Carolina and northeastern Alabama. Even today, this has some of the poorest areas per capita in the nation, though the rise of tourism and the construction of large highways in the area have greatly diminished the inequity. While most European settlers preferred the relatively flat lands south of the Chattahoochee River, and consigned the Cherokee and Creek Indians to the "useless" mountain regions, a few hardy souls preferred the isolated and rugged terrain. Preceded by Methodist and Moravian missionaries and a handful of government agents, the earliest settlers came mostly from Ireland and Scotland, with a significant number of Protestants from the Ulster region, known as the Scots-Irish. In their old countries, brewing and distilling beers and whiskeys was a time-honored profession, a way for farmers to effectively use their leftover crops, and the only way that the most remote settlements could trade in distant markets.

The primary cash crop in the mountain regions was corn, which in Ireland or Scotland was a term for pretty much any grain product, but in the United States almost universally indicates maize, or sweet corn. This crop has a short shelf life, and in the regions where it would take several weeks to carry wagonloads of it to the markets, all or most of the product could be lost through spoilage before it could be sold. However, setting up a simple, inexpensive distillery system could convert the grains into a product that not only had a long shelf life, but was also actually worth more per unit than the fresh grain. When these groups immigrated to the United States, they brought this ancient tradition with them, quickly establishing a new tradition of farm distillation that included such luminaries as George Washington in its practice. The practice was so socially accepted and widespread that by 1800, "columns of steel blue smoke poured from hundreds of stills over the six-hundred-mile backcountry along the Appalachian mountain chain." Some of these areas produced staggering quantities of whiskey—in 1840, Surry County, North Carolina, alone produced thirty-nine gallons per capita, selling for around fifty cents per gallon (a little over ten dollars in modern dollars), bringing in roughly twice the amount that the bushels of corn used to make it could bring in the market. Small-time distilling in the colonial period served both the farmers and drinkers in the community, and even provided a stable currency in the newly independent United States; a gallon of "Monongahely rye" brought as much as a dollar per gallon in the larger northeastern cities, and proved to be a more stable and acceptable means of exchange than the government's own "Continental" dollars.

The original politician who would "never waste a good crisis," Alexander Hamilton, by 1791 the first Secretary of the Treasury in the Washington administration, proposed correcting this politically unacceptable situation by leveling an excise tax against all distilled spirits made in the United States. This was the first proposed tax for anything produced domestically. Hamilton's overt purpose was to raise money to settle the massive national debt stemming from the Revolutionary War, but he also had the fiscal and political support of social reformers to whom he wanted to grant this political favor. Any taxes were politically unfavorable, but Hamilton argued that whiskey and other distilled spirits were "luxuries," and that by passing a "sin tax" on them, imbibers would have the government-provided opportunity to reevaluate their sinful ways as they paid the higher prices. The temperance movement was small and in its barest infancy at the time, but several prominent members had Hamilton's ear, and the opportunity for raising money for the government while imposing such noble and uplifting sentiments on the citizenry he oversaw proved irresistible. Washington approved the tax, which went into effect in March 1791, with an organization of "revenue agents" to collect the tax set up in November of that year.

The reaction to the tax was swift and almost entirely negative on the state level, from the farmers all the way up to the state houses. The tax would eat up the profits that farmers made in producing liquor, and it would fall hardest on the poorest and most isolated people in the nation, the western settlers, who had very little cash to begin with and used whiskey for barter and trade, not for cash sales. Within a year, violent protest against this law, centered in the Pennsylvania backcountry but spread across the whole of Appalachia, resulted in numerous attacks on revenue agents and very little tax money collected. Characteristically, Hamilton called for federal troops to be sent in to forcibly collect the tax revenue, violently if necessary. The revolt grew much worse in 1794, when US District Attorney for Philadelphia William Rawle issued more than sixty subpoenas for western farmers, requiring them to make the long, expensive trip to appear in the Philadelphia federal court, right in the middle of the growing season, and sent US Marshals out to serve them.

On July 16 and 17, 1794, a large armed group of backcountry Pennsylvania militia exchanged gunfire with one of the federal marshals and a handful of US Army troops accompanying them, in what was later called the "Battle of Bower Hill." Several militiamen and at least one soldier were killed in the exchange. This was followed two weeks later by a massive rally, when over seven thousand mostly poor famers gathered at Braddock's Field, about eight miles east of Pittsburgh, threatening to march on Philadelphia and forcibly take over the government there in order to end the excise tax. President Washington responded by calling up militias to put down the insurrection; he was shocked when most failed to rally to the federal cause, "liberty poles" (patriotic displays first used by the Patriots during the Revolutionary War) started reappearing, this time against the US government, and a draft to raise enough of a force resulted in a massive show of resistance to any support of a federal armed operation. Washington was forced to personally intervene to raise enough troops, the only time in US history that a sitting president has taken to the field as commander in chief of the military, and was helped by other popular Revolutionary War figures such as General Henry "Light Horse

Harry" Lee. With Washington finally raising sufficient troops and leading the federal force westward into the backcountry area in October, the incipient rebellion collapsed. Few if any of the tax protestors were willing to oppose the man whom so many deeply admired and had followed in the previous war. The crisis was over, for the time being, but clear warning signs that such divisions between the wealthy Easterners and the poor backcountry farmers could easily break out in civil war remained. The tax itself was dropped when Thomas Jefferson ascended to the presidency in 1800.

Except for a three-year period following the War of 1812, the federal excise tax remained suspended for the next sixty-two years. Distillation of spirits remained a small-operator business, but the practice was exceptionally widespread; in 1819, more than two million gallons of whiskey were shipped to New Orleans, over eight hundred thousand gallons coming from Tennessee alone. This golden age of small-producer distilling came to a screeching halt during yet another war, when President Abraham Lincoln signed into law the Revenue Act of 1862, establishing both the first progressive income tax in US history and the office of Commissioner of Internal Revenue to collect it. It was intended to be a self-limiting tax to pay for the war effort, to expire after just four (later ten) years, and be limited to personal income over five hundred dollars, but as with so many other government programs, it proved longer lived and quickly grew far wider in scope. The same act permitted Congress to reimpose an excise tax on "luxury" goods, primarily on alcohol and tobacco, which they did that same year and refined in 1868, requiring the use of tax stamps on these products. This is the same system we still have today, and a throwback to the Stamp Act of 1765, a British Parliament revenue action that led to violent resistance during the Colonial period and the earliest beginnings of the Revolutionary War.

Once the Civil War ended, this federal excise tax on whiskey was imposed on the newly readmitted Southern states. With occupying Federal troops ranging all through the South, happily enforcing whatever degradations Washington chose to impose, some whiskey producers attempted to go along with the tax and revenue system, while others, primarily in the easier-to-monitor southern flatlands, chose to quit producing it altogether. Others, primarily the poorest mountain residents who depended on the untaxed whiskey for a significant portion of their income, went underground with their stills, sometimes literally. Even the legal, licensed, and inspected producers were soon selling batches off the books and "under the table," as the profits were so high. So much of this illicit distilling went on at night that it soon acquired the nickname "moonshining," with the resulting "illegal" corn whiskey simply called "moonshine." This product gained a deservedly bad reputation much later, but at the time did not indicate a poorly produced or dangerous, highly alcoholic beverage, but simply any whiskey that was sold without the government's stamp of approval.

Through most of the "Reconstruction" period, there were too few revenue agents in the field, and most of their attention was paid to large-scale illicit whiskey producers in the Midwest. A series of scandals involving every level of supervision of revenue collecting in the IRS resulted in a massive overhaul of the system in 1875; afterward, most individual revenue agents came from the ranks of federal marshals and former military officers, like newly installed Marshal Charles Blacker. All worked almost completely autonomously, and had the power to summon help from the US Army whenever they saw fit. Commanding General of the Army of the United States William Tecumseh Sherman worried about this last provision, concerned that his troops would get pulled into violent revenue collection attempts, and that any of his soldiers who shot civilians in the process might be brought up on state charges of murder or manslaughter. He was right to worry—a war was about to start in the lower Appalachian Mountains that would place his troops at front and center.

Many of the initial problems with revenue agents in the north Georgia mountains stemmed from two facts: During the war most had been open and active Unionists or Union army soldiers not

Captain Charles Blacker, approximately 1865
THE BLACKER EPIC BY LOYN BLACKER

from those communities, and all were paid a fee instead of a regular salary, strictly based on the number of illegal stills they destroyed and "moonshiners" they arrested, a practice that actually encouraged perjury and corruption in the ranks of the "revenuers." To further complicate matters, the agents had the full backing of the federal government, and they were going into a hostile area to end the only real source of income for the poorest of all residents. Those residents were not only highly unlikely to give up without a struggle, but would also likely use any amount of force necessary to fight what many residents considered a hostile foreign government. Simply put, the inevitable conflict was a recipe for disaster. The temptation for agents to make false arrests to pad their fee intake was obvious, as was the motivation to divide the communities by encouraging and rewarding informants. Many local and national government officials voiced warnings about how this system could be abused too easily, especially given the kickback and bribery scandals that had already occurred, but the government had to have its money.

A further complication to this already volatile situation was an ongoing federal crackdown on the Ku Klux Klan (KKK) and other such groups across the South. The original KKK grew out of a "joke" society formed in Pulaski, Tennessee, by a group of bored ex-Confederate officers a few months after the end of the war. The ominous-sounding name (which was a then-humorous variant on the Celtic and Latin terms for "circle of friends and family") was quickly adopted by night-riding terrorists not thought to have had any connection to the original group, and who were targeting newly freed blacks and their Northern-sympathizing neighbors. Without any sort of effective national or even state organization, the Klan quickly grew into a loose, violent, anti-Reconstruction and anti-Republican association of small groups across the Deep South. In many areas across the rural landscape of the ruined South, the Klan proved to be the only local defense against vengeance groups formed by freed ex-slaves, and against land- and property-stealing carpetbaggers officially protected by federal troops. In this capacity, the Klan gained a widespread admiration and respect from the Southern civilians, while it gained an equal notoriety among Northern politicians and soldiers. Congress passed the Force Acts in 1870 and 1871—overtly to protect the voting rights of blacks in the South—which outlawed the Klan and specifically authorized the use of military forces to destroy Klan factions. The military crackdown on the Klan did eventually bring its end in the late 1870s, but resulted in a wave of violence across the South, and the rise of several other Klan-allied groups, such as the White League and Knights of the White Camelia in Louisiana, and the Red Shirts in Mississippi and the Carolinas. As part of their resistance against the federal government, the Klan in northern Georgia pledged their support of the moonshiners to protect their operations and families from the revenuers and soldiers. Blacker and his fellow federal marshals and revenue agents would use this pledge as further ammunition to justify their own underhanded tactics.

Though the anti-moonshining revenue collection efforts ranged all through the Appalachian Mountains region, the most violent and long-lasting efforts centered in a few north Georgia counties. Between 1875 and 1881, during the height of what became known as the "North Georgia Moonshine War," more than twice as many revenue agents were killed or wounded than in the next most violent region. Federal revenue agents uncovered and destroyed at least five thousand stills and made over eight thousand arrests, but suffered twenty-nine killed and sixty-three seriously injured among their ranks. At least as many moonshiners suffered the same ends, though records for their suffering simply do not exist in most cases.

Violence against informants, known as "Judases," was even more extreme. If an informant's name leaked out to the community, that person could most likely expect a visit from the local Klan, and to at least have his fields and barns burned. Informants would never again be trusted within the small, tightly knit communities, and most chose to leave shortly afterward. Those who stayed, defiant against the neighbors whom they were betraying, were often ambushed or attacked by night riders. This situation went on for many years after the Moonshine War presumably ended; in Pickens County, Georgia, an anti-informant group called the "Honest Man's Friend & Protector," or simply the HMF&P, was formed in the late 1880s to spy on suspected "reporters" in their area and take action against the property of those they determined were informing the federal authorities about moonshining activities. Seven members of the group were eventually arrested and sentenced to long prison terms for their activities.

There were "informants" on the other side, as well: The tight-knit mountain communities deployed their own warning systems when revenue agents came into the area, despite the lack of phones, electric devices of any sort, or even decent roads. The first farmer or hunter to spot the agents would send runners, usually teenage or younger, up into the "hollers" where the stills were located, while the women would stop their housework and get out their "blowing horns," modified cow horns similar to Jewish shofars. One agent working the east Tennessee mountains in the 1880s, Joseph Spurrier, related how effective this system was:

> The moonshiners found out I was in the mountains before I fully knew the fact myself. And the way they spread that information would do credit to a long distance telephone. The first man that heard of me blew a horn. I think he had a certain number of toots for my name. The horn could be heard three miles, and everybody within hearing took up the alarm till the echoes were awakened by the sound of the horns. In an hour after the first blast people one hundred miles away knew that Spurrier was on a raid. I didn't get a dog's chance to seize a distillery.

One of the revenuers centrally involved in some of the more violent incidents in north Georgia was US Marshal Charles B. Blacker. He was born on August 3, 1834, in Clutton, Sommerset,

England, and immigrated to Saint Clair in Schuylkill County, Pennsylvania in 1854 (some of his genealogical records state 1848) with his wife, Mary Moore Parfait Blacker. He volunteered for federal service at the very beginning of the Civil War, enlisting on April 30, 1861, and serving as the First Sergeant of Company B, Fourteenth Pennsylvania Infantry. The Fourteenth saw little action during its ninety-day service (a common length of enlistment at the very beginning of what everyone thought would be a one-battle war), mustering out on August 1. Later that month he joined the newly formed Seventh Pennsylvania Cavalry as a corporal, eventually rising to the rank of sergeant. By May of 1865, after serving with distinction in several battles, Blacker was promoted and detached to another special duty, as the first (and only) captain of Company B, 137th United States Colored Infantry, formed of ex-slaves with professional, white army officers.

Blacker's command soon moved to Macon, Georgia, and mustered into federal service on June 1. They were assigned to the Department of Georgia, but few records exist that might explain what exactly their duties were. Some companies of the 137th were sent to Andersonville prison camp in south Georgia to help out in cleanup and burial details, but it is not known if Company B was a part of this. The entire regiment was mustered out in Macon on January 15, 1866. Blacker remained in Georgia, assigned to various duties with the military Reconstruction command there, before resigning his commission and accepting a post with the US Marshals Service sometime in the early 1870s.

These Georgia-based marshals were primarily working with (and sometimes as) revenue agents of the Internal Revenue Bureau (later Service), enforcing alcohol stamp tax laws, investigating revenue evasion efforts, and raiding known moonshining locations. Blacker first shows up in IRS records as being fired on by moonshiners in the Fightingtown (also called Boardtown) area of Fannin County in 1872, while accompanying a group of US Army cavalry conducting a raid in the area. He quickly developed a reputation among the mountaineers for using force—preferably military force—to shut down illicit distilling operations, and arresting the operators, frequently traveling with Lietenant Augustine McIntyre and the men of his Company E, Second US Infantry.

One such raid on January 14, 1876, underscored the violence that Blacker both met and dispatched. He had gained some information that an elderly man named John Emory was running a still in the Santa Luca area of Gilmer County, and when he found four men sitting in the dark woods, waiting for sunrise near Emory's house, he had them arrested without charge or warrant. When Emory heard the commotion and came outside, he was killed by a single shot to the head by Private William O'Grady, one of Lieutenant McIntyre's men. For some reason, O'Grady and two other soldiers attempted to hide Emory's body by burying it under a pile of leaves at a nearby creek, while Blacker and McIntyre were occupied with their prisoners. Emory's wife discovered his corpse the next day, and the county district attorney immediately filed warrants for the arrests of the three soldiers. They were arrested in Atlanta, but almost immediately transferred to the federal court's custody in a personal writ from President Ulysses S. Grant. An all-black jury found them innocent at their subsequent trial in the US District Court, which reconfirmed to the mountaineers that they should neither expect nor give justice in the fight for their own homes, lives, and property. Instead of adopting a less confrontational and more conciliatory approach in the wake of this grave injustice, Blacker and his fellow revenue agents used the opportunity to call for more federal troops, stating, accurately, that Emory's death would cause an increase in organized resistance to their actions.

The increasingly violent situation came to a head in February 1877, when Lieutenant McIntyre led a detachment of federal troops from McPherson Barracks in Atlanta, to join Blacker and other revenue agents in Ellijay for a series of raids into the mountains. Blacker, along with another revenue agent, W. L. Goodwin, and Lieutenant McIntyre with a small detachment of his company, left Ellijay on the afternoon of February 9, heading to the home of a suspected moonshiner, Ayers Jones, in the Frog Mountain region of the county. Arriving at what they thought was Jones's stillhouse at 2:45 a.m., Blacker and several of his men burst inside, only to find it was Jones's cabin, with his wife and children huddled around a small fire trying to keep from freezing to death. Mrs. Jones later testified that Blacker was violently profane, repeatedly demanding to know where her husband was and where his stillhouse was located. She said that Blacker became enraged when she did not answer his questions and asked him to leave, profanely shouting that he would stay as long as he pleased. He, McIntyre, and three other men remained in the cabin while the rest of the small command went out into the darkness to try to locate Jones's still.

About fifteen minutes later, Blacker reported that they heard movement outside and opened the door to admit what they thought was the rest of their patrol. Instead, they were confronted by a large, enraged mountain man with a dark beard, shouting at Blacker, "You're in the wrong place tonight!" A vicious, close-quarters battle erupted between the small group of revenuers inside the cabin and an unknown number of mountaineers outside, who made at least four attempts to shoot their way into the cabin itself. Two of Blacker's men escaped through a rear door as soon as the shooting began, and as the remaining three attempted to return as much fire as they were receiving, McIntyre was hit. He reportedly cried out, "Blacker, I'm shot through the heart," and turned to run out the back door himself. Blacker attempted to help him, but with an increasing volume of fire now coming through the open front door and McIntyre quickly slipping away, was forced to leave the dying officer in order to save himself. He later reported that as he and the remaining soldier with him fled down the dark mountainside, they heard a voice back in the cabin shouting, "Oh, yes, we've got one of the damned son of a bitches!"

Blacker made contact with five other members of his command, and at dawn, returned to the cabin, finding McIntyre's lifeless body on the floor. Mrs. Jones and her children were still huddled in the bed, and she later testified that Blacker cursed her for the violence, demanding to know where her husband was, and when she pleaded ignorance of his whereabouts, swore that he would return in three weeks to burn down every cabin in the area. As his men prepared to remove McIntyre's body, they were once again confronted with a large group of armed, angry mountaineers. They were able to escape for a second time without any further deaths or injuries. Later that same afternoon, a full company of infantry under Lieutenant James Ulio finally recovered McIntyre's body, removing it on horseback while under fire down the mountain ravine, killing at least three more mountaineers and suffering at least one casualty. Ulio reported later that the mountaineers had laughed and hooted at them as they moved in to collect McIntyre's remains, shouting, "Here is the damned son of a bitch—take him away from here—he is dead where you all ought to be, you dam [sic] sons of bitches you." He also reported that McIntyre's body "had a hobnailed boot print on his forehead," and was missing his watch and other jewelry, as well as the twenty dollars he was known to have with him.

On February 23, a large force of revenue agents backed by numerous army troops swept the entire Frog Mountain area, arresting about eighty people, mostly without cause or warrants, and took them all to Atlanta for arraignment and trial. Over four hundred more arrests were made in that area over the subsequent weeks, again, mostly without warrants or for any specific crimes. On March 12, sixty-nine of the original arrestees plead guilty to whatever charges had been drummed up against them, and all were immediately released on suspended sentences. Another 247 had their charges dropped that same week, while all the rest either plead guilty and were released on suspended sentences, or simply had their charges dropped in the subsequent weeks. The worst part was that no return transportation was provided for them; all were forced to walk the 130-mile route back home in freezing weather.

Four men were arrested later in Nashville for the death of Lieutenant McIntyre, but all were released when it was revealed that the only evidence against them was that they used to live in the Frog Mountain area. Ayers Jones himself, who the army maintained was the one charging the doorway to his cabin that night, was finally arrested in 1879, not for the murder but on federal charges of violating the Ku Klux Klan Acts of 1870–71, allegedly conspiring with his brother Tom to prevent Blacker from serving his warrants on them that fatal night. Both were tried in federal court and found not guilty. Ayers, an illiterate but wealthy landowner, was murdered by his son, John, on September 11, 1893.

Georgia Governor Alfred Colquitt sent one of his secretaries, Colonel Samuel Williams, into the district to investigate the violent actions, and reported back that the mountaineers thought they were being attacked by corrupt revenuers, not army troops, and responded to the middle of the night raid by trying to protect their homes and families. He found that the mountaineers were quite open about the events, even admitting that Ayers Jones had been warned the patrol was after him, and that he had later bragged that he carried the pistol that had killed McIntyre. Williams's report, however, was also a blistering condemnation of the revenue collection practices, and specifically the frequent use of violent means by Blacker and his fellow agents. He listed several hundred cases of certifiably false arrests they had made for moonshining and tax avoidance, along with reams of reports of blackmail threats and demands for kickbacks and bribes by the federal agents. He further found that the "ambush" as reported at the Jones's cabin was not supported by the ground evidence: The cabin was so poorly maintained and so open to the elements that if the murder of Blacker's party was the desired result, two men with pistols would have easily swept the cabin by firing through the gaping openings between the logs from outside. He also put down that he believed the "unknown size party" attacking Blacker was probably only five or six men, not the thirty or more that had been suggested.

During this investigation, Blacker moved on to Dawson County, along with his military escort, and continued the warrantless raids on suspected moonshiners' homes. He was wounded while trying to arrest a Cumming tavern owner, Harrison Barker, and pursued him all the way to Kentucky before cornering him. The revenuers' actions were already producing unexpected results in both Atlanta and Washington: Several US marshals accused of criminal improprieties in the report were fired, most fleeing the country to avoid prosecution, and President Grant signed clemency orders for all violators of the revenue laws as one of his last acts in office. Acting partially in response to Governor Colquitt's outraged protests based on Colonel Williams's report, Congress passed the Posse Comitatus Act in 1879, subsequently signed by President Rutherford B. Hayes, that forbid the use of military force to enforce civilian laws. With that, the Moonshine War came to a sudden and abrupt end.

Barker was indicted for moonshining; he pleaded guilty and was given a suspended sentence. He was also indicted but never tried for shooting Blacker—by that time the entire federal revenue collection system in the north Georgia mountains had been thoroughly discredited. Blacker recovered from his wounds and managed to avoid the fallout from Williams's report and the new mood of Congress. He was never officially reprimanded or indicted for his own part in the Moonshine War, but quietly resigned from the US Marshal's service and returned to Pennsylvania. He and his wife Mary had one daughter, Lillian, who later moved to Berkeley, California. Charles Blacker died in September 1919.

CHAPTER 11

Tom Woolfolk:
Mass Murderer of His Own Family

The worst mass murder in Georgia history took place at a farmhouse near Macon, somewhere between 2 and 4 a.m. on Saturday, August 6, 1887. Nine people, ranging in age from eighty-four years down to eighteen months old, were all axed to death in their sleep or near their beds with a short-handled ax that belonged to the sole survivor of the family and was left at the scene. That sole survivor, who ran to the neighbors the next morning to report the crime, was blood-splattered, haggard, and had been widely regarded in the community as nearly insane and unstable. He was quickly arrested as the only possible suspect, the third child and first son of his now-dead war hero father, the stepson of his now-lifeless and unbeloved stepmother, and the stepbrother to six brutally murdered children from his father's second marriage, all hacked to death in the night. Though the crime has faded from the public memory, replaced by other and even more brutal "crimes of the century," and even his family's name and story has been largely forgotten, Tom Woolfolk has officially remained as the most notorious mass murderer in all of Georgia history.

Very little is known about Tom's early life other than the barest of chronological facts. He was born on the eve of the Civil War, on June 18, 1860, to Richard F. and Susan M. Woolfolk, their third child and only son, at their plantation home near Macon. Susan died soon afterward, and his father nearly immediately enlisted in Company A, the "Bibb Hussars," Eighth Battalion Georgia Cavalry (State Guards), riding off to defend his state and country. The infant Tom was sent to live with his mother's sister, Fannie Moore Crane, the wife of a prominent builder in Athens. He remained in the care of his aunt even after his father returned from the war, resettled at a new plantation in the remote Hazzard District of Bibb County, twelve miles east of Macon, and remarried. Finally, in 1867, Tom was sent to live with his father and his new family at "The Homeplace"; the family soon grew to include six more step-siblings in its thousand acres of rolling countryside. His two older sisters, married by that time, remained in the Athens area with their own families.

It seems a bit odd that the elder Woolfolk would not imme-diately seek to be reunited with his only son, and his war record has its own set of mysteries. While still with Company A of the Eighth Cavalry, Woolfolk had been granted a commission and promoted to First Lieutenant, but that unit saw no combat action and was only used to guard railroads around the northern part of the state for the latter half of 1863 before being disbanded. His name does not appear in any other of the admittedly incomplete records of Confederate units, although there are listings of other Woolfolks in other Georgia regiments, and misspelled and miss-ing names in military records during the Civil War are far from uncommon. He was referred to as "Captain" Woolfolk postwar, which may have indicated a later promotion, or may have sim-ply been part of the very common habit of referring to honored veterans by that or higher-ranked titles as a means of respect. There are hints and clues that his service time was difficult and harrowing, though; in a photograph taken shortly after the war, before Tom came back to live with him, a stern-faced Richard Woolfolk glares at the camera, with narrowed eyes deeply set in a face that reflects a lengthy period of hardship, possibly from battle, possibly from the economic turmoil that haunted the South for so long during and after the war. Whatever the cause, it is clear that the senior Woolfolk brought these painful experi-ences and his post-traumatic stress back to his family, possibly contributing to their horrifying end.

Tom's new stepmother was Mattie E. Howard, a well-educated graduate of the Forsyth Female Collegiate Institute (later Tift College) in nearby Monroe County. According to his two natural sisters, Tom was the first of them to accept Mattie into the family, and to all appearances, their first months were happy ones together. Mattie gave birth to her first child, Richard Jr., that same year. Three years later, she gave birth to their first daughter, Pearl, with another boy and three more girls born over the following sixteen years. These new siblings created increasing strife between Tom and Mattie, especially after she began pressing Captain Woolfolk to change his will with each new member of the family, to ensure that each would inherit a share of the prosperous plantation business. There are no surviving letters or diaries to describe exactly what went on within the walls of the Woolfolk home, but nearly every subsequent retelling of the murders mentions without citation or documentation to back it up that Tom was "agitated" and a "problem child" who was presumably consumed with the notion of one day inheriting his father's estate.

There is, again, little documentation, but Tom apparently went into a number of business endeavors after reaching his late teens, all of which seemed to have failed quickly. He also did not succeed as a plantation manager, grocery store owner, and streetcar driver, finally being reduced to working his own father's plantation for wages by the summer of 1887. Shortly before that, though, he had married a woman named Georgia Bird, the daughter of a wealthy Jones County farmer, in a bizarre ceremony aboard a moving train. Though he had told her about a massive plantation that he owned outside of Macon, the only home he could take her to afterward was that of his father's, that modest structure already crowded with eight other family members. Their marriage lasted only three weeks before she quit and returned to her father's home near Holton. Tom later told friends that he "had been a fool" to marry her, and made at least one unsettling comment about her, that he might have "to frail her out" (an archaic Southernism, meaning that he might have to beat her until she was crippled for life). Allegedly, she later said that Tom was too much to live with, but "not crazy. It is simple meanness. He is the meanest man I ever saw, and there is nothing too mean for him to do." From some other remarks Tom later made, it was clear that he was deeply depressed about his situation, and was reportedly acting increasingly paranoid and agitated as the summer of 1887 wore on, even going about his rounds openly armed. Surviving family members later reported that Tom was exceptionally violent and agitated in the weeks leading up to the murders, stalking the streets talking angrily to himself, openly carrying a large revolver, and (some sources claimed) even making pointed threats about his stepsiblings and how they might "take away" his rightful inheritance. By this time, that inheritance likely seemed the only insurance he still had for his future.

Tom was not the only agitated person in the area; troublesome vagrants were passing through the area, begging food from the Woolfolks and other families, adding to the deep sense of paranoia and fear that still gripped this postwar region. Though the initial postwar guerrilla activity and former slave retaliations had calmed down to almost nothing by the late 1880s, most of the men of the area still openly worried about the "coloreds" and the potential harm they could pose to their rebuilding communities. Antivagrancy laws were on the books and enforced, but it was still far from unusual to see solitary roaming men, or even small groups of the dispossessed, wandering through, usually stopping only at the former slave quarters of poor sharecroppers to ask for food and shelter. Most of these wanderers would accept a bit of work on one of the many plantations for a time, either at the behest of the local sheriff or from the need to be making a little bit of "folding money" before taking to the road again. Captain Woolfolk was known to have hired some of these vagrants, and Tom is known to have had conflicts with some of them, the less tactful of the former slaves undoubtedly finding some humor in the fact that "massah's" son was toiling in the fields alongside them.

Early on the morning of Saturday, August 6, 1887, some of the sharecroppers working the Woolfolk plantation were awakened by the sounds of terrified screams and cries for help coming from the darkened plantation house. Well accustomed to "staying out of white folk's business," none of the black sharecroppers made any move to investigate what was going on. Shortly before 4 a.m., a half-dressed and manic Tom Woolfolk came running to one of them, the home of Greene Lockett, begging for help, screaming at the terrified sharecropper that someone had gotten into his house, and "they're killin' Pa!" Lockett decided that going up to the house with Tom, with a possible murderer (or more) still on the scene, was not the best course of action, and instead sent his young son running to other neighbors to get more help. Tom returned to the house with another sharecropper, Anderson Smith, whom he later claimed ran off while he went in to see if anyone was still alive. Other sharecroppers drifted to the Lockett cabin, alerted by the noise and agitation, as Tom later returned there, squatting nearby under a tree, saying nothing to the gathering crowd. Just before dawn, William H. Smith, Woolfolk's sawmill foreman, rode up and escorted Tom and Lockett back to the plantation house. They heard a noise inside the house shortly after arriving, and Tom went in alone to investigate, while Smith met another neighbor, George Yates, who was just riding up. Tom emerged a few minutes later, splattered with blood, saying that he had re-checked all the bodies, and everyone was indeed dead.

No one else entered the house until one of Captain Woolfolk's close friends arrived a bit later, Samuel Chambliss, who owned a smaller plantation in nearby Lorane, bringing with him his family and several armed men. Though Chambliss was also a Civil War veteran, he was shocked and horrified at what they found inside the darkened house. Richard Jr. and his five-year-old brother Charlie lay next to each other, just inside the entrance to their parent's bedroom, Richard displaying multiple deep cuts all across his arms and face from a fight he put up to save his life; deep ax blows to his head and Charlie's proved to be the killing injuries. The remains of Captain Woolfolk and Mattie lay entangled on the bed, where they had obviously been attacked while asleep; brain matter and blood splattered all over the walls, while the bed itself was soaked with their combined blood. Their eighteen month old, also named Mattie, lay tangled up in the bloody sheets between them, a single ax wound splitting her head in half. Seventeen-year-old Pearl was laid across the foot of their bed, with multiple blunt force and deep ax wounds all across her lifeless body, the slashing wounds to her hands mute evidence to the struggle she put up against her attacker. A blood-stained, short-handled axe, with matted brain matter and hair covering the shaft, leaned against a wall near the bed. Several reports later claimed that Pearl had also been raped before being axed to death.

Moving across the hall to the "girl's room," Chambliss discovered the body of Temperance West, the eighty-four-year-old aunt of Mattie Woolfolk, lying as if still just asleep, though with a deep ax wound in her skull. Seven-year-old Rosebud lay dead next to her on the floor, while ten-year-old Annie was found with multiple ax blows across her arms, back and head, one arm still hooked over the nearby windowsill, over which she had apparently tried to escape during the frenzied killings. In each room Chambliss found a single set of bloody footprints, which Tom admitted were his. Until Chambliss told him to put on some more clothes, Tom had been dressed only in a nightshirt, underwear, and blood-soaked socks. He changed into a set of his brother's clothes before exiting the house, but did not explain why he did not put on his own clothes.

A large crowd had quickly gathered soon after sunup around the house, and most in the crowd immediately and vocally blamed Tom for the massacre. The arrival of Bibb County Sheriff George Westcott with a party of deputies a bit later in the morning dampened the growing spirit to lynch Tom on the spot, but did not entirely erase it. A coroner's jury was convened from men of the crowd on scene, while witnesses were examined and Sheriff Westcott's deputies carefully watched the crowd for any signs of trouble. Just a year earlier, a man accused of raping a child had been removed from his own jail in Macon and lynched, and Westcott was not about to have a repeat of that sort of vigilante justice.

Throughout the inquest and growing unrest in the crowd, Tom remained strangely calm and detached, further agitating the onlookers. He could not explain how he had managed to escape successfully, while everyone else in the house was brutally murdered, nor could he explain what had happened to his clothes. He also could not explain why his were the only bloody prints in the house, why he had a bloody handprint on his thigh that he could not have made, and why he had stopped to wash his feet in his bedroom before going to the neighbor's house a second time, leaving a large wet spot in front of his fireplace. When Tom refused a drink from the well, Sheriff Westcott sent one of the field hands from the crowd down in it. He brought back a tightly bound set of clothes and a hat, said to be Tom's, with large bloody stains on the front and sleeves of the shirt. One of the sharecropper's wives, Sarah Hardin, the Woolfolk's laundress, later testified that a bloodstained undershirt found in the same bundle was his. She told one of Westcott's deputies that the shirt also found in the well shirt belonged to Richard Jr., and the hat found with it to Silas Woolfolk, one of the sharecropper field hands. A pair of bloodstained socks allegedly belonging to Tom was found in the same well on a later search, though how he would come to be wearing two different sets of socks at the same murder scene was never explained.

Tom was taken first to the jail in Macon, and then moved to the more secure facility in Atlanta to avoid any repeat of lynch-mob justice. From the very first day, responding to the overwhelming amount of physical and eyewitness evidence against him, the *Atlanta Constitution* newspaper whipped up a storm of frenzy about the murders, clearly and repeatedly tying only Tom to them, and coining the name "Bloody Tom" for him in their front-page articles, all in the best traditions of nineteenth-century yellow journalism. Other newspapers around the country picked up on the sensational crime, making it front page news in the *New York Times* and *Cincinnati Enquirer*. A Macon photographer managed to sneak into the crime scene even before the coroner's jury began their inquest, taking pictures of the mangled bodies and bloodied floors and walls, and selling them to all the local newspapers, who dutifully printed them for the enlightenment of the public.

Tom was tried five times for the crimes, each time with a courthouse filled with enraged onlookers who harbored not a single doubt that he was the murderer. The first trial lasted ten days, interrupted by repeated outbursts from the onlookers to "hang him!" Judge George W. Gustin ordered each one of the vocal members of the audience ejected from the courtroom, but did not clear the court or order a mistrial afterward. The jury took twenty minutes to convict Tom on all counts. Judge Gustin heard motions for a retrial and overruled them. Tom's lawyers succeeded in getting a new trial ordered from the Georgia Supreme Court, but in the same Macon venue, under the same Judge Gustin. The circus atmosphere surrounding the courthouse was even worse the second time around, and when a juryman in the second trial was overheard telling a friend that he would force a mistrial rather than allowing any possibility that Tom would be found innocent, even the hardheaded Judge Gustin was forced to declare a mistrial.

The venue was changed to neighboring Houston County, where a third mistrial was declared, an acceptable jury unable to be impaneled. The fourth trial ended in yet another mistrial when outbursts from the courtroom spectators interrupted jury selection there. The fifth and last trial finally seated a jury on June 8, 1889. By this time, Tom had apparently given up any pretense of participating in his own defense, and spent most of the proceedings sitting at the defense table, reading John Tyler Headley's *Napoleon and His Marshals*. Sixteen days later, the jury was charged, spent forty-five minutes in the jury room debating, and returned another guilty verdict. Tom was sentenced to death by hanging. Higher courts denied all further appeals. Shortly after the verdict and sentencing, Georgia Woolfolk formally divorced Tom and returned to her maiden name.

On October 29, 1890, escorted by the heavily armed local militia, the Perry Rifles under Captain W. C. Davis, Sheriff Melton L. Cooper and a deputy drove Tom in a carriage to the gallows about a mile west of the courthouse in Perry, followed by at least ten thousand spectators. Expecting to hear Tom finally confess to his crimes atop the gallows, they instead heard him once again proclaim his innocence. He calmly shook the sheriff's hand before he bound Tom's arms and legs, lowered the hood over his head and adjusted the knot around his neck. When Cooper pulled the trap, Tom dropped, but the knot had slipped, slowly strangulating him instead of breaking his neck, which would have resulted in a near instantaneous death. It took Tom twenty long minutes to die, dangling in agony at the end of the rope in front of the multitude that wanted him to suffer even more than that dreadful end.

Tom claimed to the very end of his life that an unknown assailant had committed the unspeakable crime, and additionally claimed that he had actually brushed past this unknown person as he reentered the house. It is heartbreaking and chilling to consider that he just might have been telling the truth, despite all evidence to the contrary. Two other cases lend evidence that either one of two groups of strangers committed the horrendous crime. The first, which admittedly has the slimmest credibility, stems from an 1893 letter written to the editor of the *Pittsburgh Dispatch* newspaper, claiming that the writer had met a "tramp" wandering the nearby countryside, who not only claimed to have committed the 1892 Borden family ax murders in Massachusetts, but confessed to murdering an entire "farm family" near Macon, Georgia, a few years earlier. The tramp allegedly stated that while his group was traveling near Macon, they got into a bit of trouble with an unnamed farmer, later invading his home and killing everyone they found, so they would not be arrested for the scrap they had with him. He also allegedly stated that one person, whom he thought was the famer's son, managed to escape their murderous rage by jumping out of a window and running away. This letter was later reprinted in the *Macon Telegraph* newspaper, with a commentary on the amazing similarities between the Borden and Woolfolk murders; both involved unbeloved stepmothers; financial difficulties, personality issues, and adamant claims of innocence among the suspects; and both occurred in early August, five years apart.

The second case has somewhat more credibility. Ten years after the Woolfolk murders, another family was murdered in an almost identical fashion in Sumpter County, South Carolina. This time, a neighbor witnessed the brutal death of one of them, a farm worker who ran to the scene of the mass murder of the Benjamin Wilson family, meeting his end with them as well. Three white family members and two black workers were axed to death there without a trace of mercy, just as the Woolfolks had been. The identified assailant was a black man named Simon Cooper, who had been terrorizing the area for days before those murders, along with three other members of his gang. One of the gang, Isaac Boyles, turned himself in to the sheriff a few days later, telling him that Cooper had not only raped Wilson's wife during the crime spree, as Pearl had allegedly also been raped, but also boasted of killing the Woolfolks in Macon ten years earlier. Another gang member confessed the location of Cooper's hideout, and after a lengthy standoff and gun battle, Cooper was taken alive by a sheriff's posse.

Described as six-foot-six, hulking, and notoriously violent but "pleasant-looking," Simon Cooper was the grandson of John Ashemore, a notorious white antebellum criminal in South Carolina. Cooper bragged to the posse members of his multiple murders over the years, and threatened to do the same to each of them and their families, calling some out by name. When he started to relate details of his outrages to Mrs. Wilson before killing her, one of the enraged posse members shot him in the head. Still alive, he was dragged away with a logging chain around his neck into an adjacent swamp by some of the posse, while others restrained the deputy sheriff accompanying them. The next morning, his battered and deeply tortured body was found on the side of a nearby road. The sheriff searched his hideout, finding letters, legal documents, and other evidence that Cooper had been a surprisingly learned and literate man, though consumed with a passionate hatred for all whites.

When Cooper's papers and other effects were sent to a friend back in Georgia, a diary was found detailing his extensive crimes in the two states over a ten-year period. Cooper bragged in the diary about committing several previously unsolved murders and other crimes. He also included a section detailing his employment at the Woolfolk plantation, his run-ins with Tom Woolfolk, and a detailed account of the murders that closely matched several of the details of what Tom had claimed happened, and which matched some of the evidence found at the scene. The diary entry about the Woolfolks ended with what possibly amounted to a confession, and an exoneration of Tom Woolfolk: "Tom Woolfolk was mighty slick, but I fixed him. I would have killed him with the rest of the damn family, but he was not at home."

The story Cooper wrote has some "ring of truth" about it, but it remains the solitary claim of a notorious criminal, who could well have simply overheard enough details about the Woolfolk murders to create a false claim of responsibility. To what end this would serve might only exist in the unrecorded thoughts of Cooper himself, but might have been done simply to add to his "street cred" as a violent and dangerous outlaw. Other than this diary, there is not a shred of physical evidence that places Cooper at the Woolfolk home at any point, nor that links him to the murders themselves.

Tom Woolfolk is a divisive figure today, the work of several local historians and family members devoted to proving his innocence lending more support to his claims than was seriously considered at the time. His grave in a borrowed plot in the back section of a large cemetery in Hawkinsville, Georgia, was later vandalized,

Tom Woolfolk's vandalized tombstone in Orange Hill Cemetery, Hawkinsville
PHOTO BY JOHN MCKAY

the tombstone broken into several pieces where his family name was carved upon it. This is something that is simply not done in the South, a long tradition of respecting the dead, good and bad as they may have been in life broken along with his grave marker, mute evidence of the deep and abiding hostility that still remains for Georgia's official worst mass murderer.

CHAPTER 12

Thomas Watson:
Populist Politician, KKK Supporter

Georgia has a long tradition of peculiar men in its political institutions, ranging from the foaming-at-the-mouth racist segregationists, through the axe-handle-wielding, backward-bicycle-riding restaurateur turned governor, to the submarine commander turned segregationist George Wallace protégée turned liberal president, to dozens of sober, serious, and conservative statesmen and nearly everything in between. One of the oddest, though, remains a sometimes Populist, sometimes Democrat, and sometimes Socialist lawyer and publisher, an early champion of agrarian reform and the poverty-stricken common working men of his age, both black and white, who also became a major force behind the resurrection of the Ku Klux Klan in the early twentieth century. Thomas E. Watson eventually became a powerful force behind all Georgia politics of his age, even making it difficult at one point to gain any office without his support. However, his primary legacy in the state's criminal history is his vicious and long-lasting published attacks against a Jewish business owner that led directly to the businessman's lynching. While many Georgia politicians have figurative blood on their hands from their stances and proclamations over the past two hundred years, Tom Watson stands alone as the only one who bears literal as well as innocent blood on his.

Edward Thomas Watson (later changed to Thomas Edward, for unknown reasons) was born at his parents' plantation on September 5, 1856, near Thomson, the county seat of what was then Columbia County, Georgia, the second child and first son of John Smith and Ann Eliza Maddox Watson, themselves the descendents of Quaker immigrants to early colonial Georgia. After his father left for combat duty, Thomas Edward spent the intervening Civil War years on the plantation of his grandfather, Squire Thomas

Miles "Long-Tom" Watson, which was not some grand *Gone With the Wind*-style Greek Revival mansion, but "just a plain house" as he later described it, three miles outside of Thomson. The war years were difficult for his family; besides the shortages of food and other supplies, his beloved grandfather and the rock-steady foundation of the family, Squire Watson, died of a stroke during the war, his father was wounded twice in battle (but survived, albeit driven by combat-induced demons the rest of his life), and two of his uncles returned home as invalids, having acquired terminal wounds and illnesses during the four-year-long struggle. The collapse of the Southern economy during the war left the Watsons destitute afterward; they lost their plantation as well as a series of smaller purchased farms, eventually ending up in Augusta, where they ran a boarding house and saloon. This situation was helped along in no small way by the elder Watson's post-traumatic stress from the war, resulting in severe alcohol abuse and gambling addictions, but Watson later claimed that the poverty and destitution he witnessed in the urban streets of Augusta shaped his political leanings and destiny, and forever put him opposed to capitalist policies.

Watson was also profoundly influenced by both the "Southern cavalier" attitude of his father, uncle, and neighbors fighting for the Confederacy, and by the harsh conditions of the postwar Reconstruction occupation government. His father remained prominent in ex-Confederate circles, where the young Watson gained the chance to meet and get to know some of the luminaries of that lost cause; in a late-life newspaper interview, he related, "It was in this way that I came to know of such Southern leaders as Howell Cobb, Ranee Wright, John B. Gordon, Robert Toombs and Benjamin H. Hill." It was in these circles that the notorious Ku Klux Klan was viewed as a heroic band of resistance fighters, out to protect the flower of Southern life and guard against the feared (for good reason) backlash from newly freed ex-slaves. C. Vann Woodward related one event in June 1869 at which young Watson was present, which nearly broke out into renewed civil warfare:

Thomas Edward Watson, Thomson, 1904

The squad of Blue Coats stationed at Thomson was received with bitter protests and demonstrations. A mass meeting of citizens was called a few miles out of the town at Union Church. A Methodist preacher was in the midst of a fiery speech when a squad of horsemen in uniform trotted by. Striking a defiant pose, the orator shouted, "We can't even hold a quiet, peaceable meeting without being spied upon and disturbed by these military masters!" His face flushed with excitement, young Tom stood below the platform with his father. "I remember even now," he said when an old man, "the flame of wrath that leapt into the eyes of that preacher, when he saw the Blue Coat cavalry. . . . I actually believe that if the squad of cavalry had not taken another road on their return to Thomson a great tragedy would have resulted."

. . . Politics, as Tom Watson first knew the art, was an heroic business of mysterious, white-robed horsemen galloping at midnight, and majestic orators, whose long hair waved in the breezes as the periods rolled. Politics was also a potent magic whereby a distraught and oppressed people might conjure up forgotten, as well as imaginary, grandeurs, unite with intense purpose, and cast off their oppressors.

The general economic blight of the postwar South also affected Watson's education; he attended a small primary school in nearby Thomson, but later was able to stay at Mercer University for only two years. His parents had lost their last real estate holdings while he was studying at Mercer, but despite his limited education and lack of resources, he passed the Georgia bar examination in 1875. Two years later, he began a private law practice in Thomson, quickly settling into prominence as one of the most dynamic and effective trial lawyers in the state. He also settled into married life about the same time, wedding Georgia Dunham of Augusta, the adopted daughter of an ex-Confederate surgeon who claimed that he had found her as a young, parentless child wandering the streets of Savannah during the war. Their marriage was apparently a very happy one, for although "in many ways [she was] the very antithesis of her husband's, for that she was serene, patient, and reserved," they had three children and worked together in harmony and dynamically in their joint business ventures. Watson, quite contrary to his public nature, was still writing sentimental love poems to her many years into their relationship.

While Watson quickly grew his law practice, becoming well-known across the state and quite wealthy from the spoils of court life within just a few years, he was just as quickly drawn to the life of politics. He first ran for office as a Democrat to represent McDuffie County in the state legislature in 1882, successfully employing a campaign platform as the defender of the "old ways." Despite this platform, he later embraced the plight of the black voting population of the state, working to fund public education for both races, and loudly proclaiming himself as the great white hope of poor farmers and sharecroppers in the state legislature. Ever the aggressive and energetic social and political climber, he left the state legislature even before his two-year term was up, heading to bigger and better things on the national stage.

Although initially Watson ran for office as a Democrat—the only way any politician could be elected to office in Georgia up until the 1980s—he was in fact a Populist politician from the very beginning of his political life. As such, Watson was the epitome of what would become political "progressives," and very much a polar opposite to the pro-capitalist and New South promoter Henry W. Grady, the influential and prominent editor of the *Atlanta Constitution* in the late nineteenth century. Very simply put, progressivism as a political movement emphasizes the equivalency of outcome of economic and social changes across the greater society, while conservative or capitalist movements emphasize the availability of opportunities and freedom of the market from government manipulation as that which will bring the greatest rewards to those who are the most industrious.

Both of these movements in their most overt and honest forms are seeking the advancement of both civilizations and individuals to the maximum potential possible. In the outlying trenches of the less altruistic, though, unrestrained and unrestricted capitalism produced the excesses of the "robber baron" class, which used its vast wealth and political influence to manipulate government agencies to its gain, and through its single-minded efforts to maximize its gains, exploited without equivalent reward the efforts of its own workers. Similarly, the less-enlightened progressives created widespread havoc, invariably turning to the darker sides of human nature when their desire for equal outcome for all based on theories of finite and equal distribution of wealth and power turned out to be nothing more than a pipe dream, resulting in violent reactions ranging from the various National Socialist totalitarian movements of the early to mid-twentieth century, down to the anarchic street circuses of the assorted "Occupy" movements of late 2011. Watson's own Populists in essence were liberal social reformists seeking to attract the lower-middle-class and poverty-stricken city dwellers, as well as the poor rural tenant farmers and sharecroppers, both black and white. However, despite his initial foray into politics under the auspices of lifting up society's poor and downtrodden, Watson eventually used both his political office and his nationally distributed magazine to do everything in his power to prevent blacks, Jews, and Catholics from being politically or socially accepted into the white majority Protestant society as equals.

It was on the Progressive platform that Watson first ran for the US Congress, winning a seat representing the Georgia Tenth District in 1890. Echoing, but never fully endorsing the then-powerful Farmer's Alliance movement during his run, Watson campaigned on promises to redistribute land the state had granted to large corporations, to end the national banking system (a throwback to Andrew Jackson's wars with the First and Second Bank of the United States), to end the practice of printing paper money and return to specie with the unlimited issue of silver coinage, and to end or drastically reduce all taxes for low-income and poor citizens. Although Watson had deep pro-Confederate roots, like many of that same era and political caste, he fought for the unity of the races in their agrarian-based political groups and in voting rights. Soon after entering Congress, Watson broke with the Democrats and openly supported the newly formed People's Party, or Populists, the political branch of the Farmer's Alliance. As a result, he was nominated for speaker of house by the Populists, but after refusing to endorse Georgia Democrat Charles F. Crisp for office in 1891, he was defeated at the end of his first term by another Democrat. He tried again for Congress in the next session, but lost that 1894 election as well, both defeats his supporters claimed were the results of deep electoral fraud by the Democratic Party. Although deeply angered by the party's actions against him, Watson was convinced to support, albeit very reluctantly, the Democratic nomination of William Jennings Bryan in 1896, with the promise that he would be Bryan's vice presidential nominee, and that his own Populists would merge with the larger party. The result was a disaster on many levels; after gaining Watson's support, Bryan picked Arthur Sewell as his running mate, the Populist Party soon disappeared from the scene, "Gold" Democrats split from the main party and named their own slate of candidates, and the Republican nominee, William McKinley, won in the end. Deeply embittered by yet another crass deception by the Democrats, yet still deeply opposed to the pro-business Republicans, Watson dropped out of politics altogether, returning to his law practice in Thomson.

Watson did return to politics after the turn of the century, running as the Populist candidate for president in 1904 and 1908. He also grew his reputation as a "king maker," obliging any Georgia political candidate who desired success to first gain his endorsement. But something had happened to him in the meantime. While back in Thomson, Watson turned to writing to fill up the void his law practice could not cover, producing several biographies of noted historical personages, a history of France, and even a novel, but his most striking outlet came in the form of a weekly newspaper he founded and largely wrote, the *Weekly Jeffersonian,* that proved quite popular across the South. A subsequent national commercial publication, *Watson's Jeffersonian Magazine*, proved popular across the country and featured lengthy diatribes written by Watson outlining his deeply felt and growing antibusiness and pro-socialist philosophies. They also reflected his surprising move to apparently deeply held antiblack and anti-Semitic positions, openly opposing the rise of black leaders like W. E. B. Du Bois and Booker T. Washington, despite their own polar opposite views on racial integration and social equality, eventually calling for the complete and utter disenfranchisement of all black voters. He also launched strong attacks against the Roman Catholic Church, blaming its missionary efforts and political influence as being too "openly pro-capitalist." Ironically, the Roman Catholic Church responded to his attacks by launching a successful boycott against those businesses who advertised in Watson's newspaper and magazine, nearly bringing both publications into bankruptcy.

While Watson had openly disparaged the Socialists and heatedly claimed his own Populists shared none of their views, he began just as openly supporting their party and causes after the outbreak of World War I in 1914, leading to more backlashes against his publishing businesses, the refusal of the US Postal Service to distribute them (which led to the end of his publishing empire), and even an obscenity trial based on certain obscure Latin phrases he had published in his diatribes against the Catholics, from which he was quickly acquitted. His deepest notoriety, though, stemmed from a lengthy series of front-page articles he wrote in his newspaper and magazine, condemning in harsh and nearly obscene ways one specific and obscure manager of a pencil factory in downtown Atlanta, Leo Frank. Frank had been accused of a heinous and violent crime, but his greatest offense in Watson's mind was the fact that Frank was Jewish.

Early on the morning of April 27, 1913, the night watchman at Frank's National Pencil Factory frantically called the police, stating that he had just found the dead body of a young girl in the basement there, fourteen-year-old factory employee Mary Phagan. What the policemen discovered when they arrived shortly afterward horrified them. The body was so covered with grime and soot from the floor of the basement that it was at first unclear what race she was. Her dress had been pulled up and some of her underwear torn off, a strip of which was wrapped around her neck, under a long length of three-quarter-inch cord, which had been used to strangle her. Her face was battered and bruised, her cheeks were slashed by a knife or some other sharp object, dried blood was coming out of both her mouth and ears, and some of her fingers had pulled out of joint, apparently in a struggle with her attacker. An autopsy would later reveal that her skull had been broken in multiple places, she had suffered bite marks on her shoulders, and displayed "strange violence" to her sexual organs, though the report did not explicitly conclude that she had been raped. There were many bloody fingerprints, stained doors, and a blood-stained metal bar found at the scene, none of which were subjected to any sort of testing. Two mysterious, barely literate notes were also found at the scene, bearing inscriptions that seemed to point to the night watchman himself, Newt Lee, as the guilty party.

The police investigation was lengthy and comprehensive for the day, and all the evidence pointed at either Lee or the facility janitor, Jim Conley, as the guilty party. Some detectives were initially suspicious of Frank, who was "dazed and confused" when they got him out of bed about 4 a.m., but there was no physical evidence at all that pointed to him as the culprit. At first, it appeared that the two black workers would stand trial for the crime, but two media-driven events soon changed the entire focus of the investigation: The length of the investigation soon brought angry editorials demanding a termination of the "endless" detective work and a speedy trial, and the media disclosed that Frank was Jewish, which at the time was unpopular and subject to journalistic suspicion on its own.

The more mainstream and somewhat more legitimate *Atlanta Constitution* broke the story that same morning, with a special edition hitting the streets literally minutes after Phagan's mother was given the grim news. This touched off a wild free-for-all competition for headlines with the William Randolph Hearst-owned yellow journal tabloid *Atlanta Georgian*, which put out no fewer than forty special editions that first day. Frank soon became a target of both papers, which carried increasingly anti-Semitic editorials against the "Yankee Jew" as the police investigation dragged on through the month of May. The *Atlanta Georgian* eventually muted its tone, responding to an outraged backlash from the Jewish community in town, but also paid for an attorney to represent Conley. The *Constitution*, though, continued with attacks against Frank, mixed with loud complaints about how long the investigation was taking.

With great media pressure hastening their examination of the evidence, a grand jury returned a murder indictment against Frank on May 24, and his widely covered "trial of the century" began on July 28. Conley became the state's leading witness, creating a story on the stand of how Frank had allegedly come to him for help in hiding the body of a girl he had accidently killed, and then dictated these mysterious notes for him to write. He embellished the story further on the witness stand during direct examination, adding that Frank frequently had sexual relations with women in his factory office, while Conley served as a lookout for him. Defense witnesses showed the great holes in Conley's claims, and the lack of any physical evidence tying Frank to the crime should have ended the case against him before it started, but the newspaper-driven public outrage was too much for the jury to ignore. Frank was found guilty on August 25, and given a sentence of death. His initial appeals failed, though Supreme Court Justice Oliver Wendell Holmes led an effort to bring his case before the nation's highest court. This appeal, too, failed by 7-2, with Holmes writing in his dissent, "Mob law does not become due process of law by securing the assent of a terrorized jury."

Watson had covered the trial at a much less inflamed level than the two leading local papers, but when Frank's appeals began to show some fruit, his outrage at Frank's religion overcame his moderate approach. Every legal appeal was met by howls of printed derision in the *Weekly Jeffersonian*, with Watson's own front-page editorials leading the parade of abuse. Watson referred to Frank as "a Jew Pervert," and in one of his other publications, *Watson's Magazine,* wrote a series of long diatribes about several issues in the Frank case, culminating in a forty-six-page rant about the trial and evidence, along with an "examination of the Jewish race" in the September 1915 edition. In the midst of all this bloodlust sound and fury, Frank's lawyer made a final appeal for a commutation of his sentence to life in prison to Georgia Governor John M. Slaton. Slaton held a new hearing, carefully reviewed the evidence, and finally convinced that Frank had in the least not received a fair trial, commuted his sentence to life the day before his scheduled execution date. Slaton himself left office six days later, and though he had been a widely admired and respected governor, was forced to leave the state in the ensuing public outcry over his decision, led once again by Watson's own editorials in the pages of the widely read and admired *Weekly Jeffersonian.*

Watson did not back down after Slaton's pardon, redoubling his printed rage against Frank and then openly calling for vigilantism. In September 1915 Watson had called for "another Ku Klux Klan . . . to restore HOME RULE" in his *Jeffersonian* magazine. Inspired by the popular Populist kingmaker's rants, a group of prominent politicians, professionals, and lawmen in short order formed an open lynching society, the "Knights of Mary Phagan," advertising in all the Atlanta newspapers for handymen with the necessary skills to join them in "serving justice" to Frank. One of the ringleaders of the Knights was none other than two-term former Georgia Governor Joseph M. Brown. On the afternoon of August 16, the group of twenty-eight men traveled to Milledgeville, took control of the state prison without meeting much, if any, resistance from the warden, seized Frank, and drove throughout the night back to Marietta. At 7 a.m., the mob threw a rope over a branch of a large oak tree, placed a noose around Frank's neck, turned him to face the direction of Phagan's house, and hanged him. Although they apparently had served their purpose, the Knights of Mary Phagan did not simply disband after lynching Frank. Instead, they found another purpose under another name for the same sort of underground terrorism that Watson had called for, as the resurrected Ku Klux Klan. Thanks to the same glowing approval for their motivations and efforts finding its way once again into Watson's newspaper—and the sympathy of a South largely transformed by Watson's own hateful diatribes—this version of the Klan proved harder to eliminate, still proving violently effective more than fifty years later, and not essentially dying out until nearly the turn of the twenty-first century.

With the notoriety that Franks's lynching and the heavy-handed federal prosecution of him had brought, Watson was convinced to return to politics one last time, successfully running for one of the US Senate seats from Georgia in 1920. He suddenly died on September 26, 1922, while serving his second year in the Senate. His replacement, named by Georgia Governor Thomas E. Hardwick, was his old friend Rebecca Latimer Felton. She was the first woman to serve in the Senate, the oldest freshman senator, at age eighty-six, and had the shortest tenure in office in Senate history, serving just one day as the end result of a political move by Hardwick. She was also the last former slave owner in the Senate, and, in an absolute mirroring of Watson's worst efforts in his later political years, a rabid and quite outspoken racist, who once called for the lynching of a thousand black men a week if that was what would be necessary to "protect woman's dearest possession." Further continuing Watson's work in ending black suffrage, she also claimed that granting voting rights to black men led directly to the rapes of white women. Felton died eight years later, in 1930.

Watson's later political and editorial legacy has been nearly fully repudiated in the intervening years, but his early reputation as a Populist and friend to the poor and oppressed has not. He is honored by a twelve-foot-high statue just outside the state capitol in Atlanta, bearing the inscription, "A champion of right who never faltered in the cause."

CHAPTER 13

George R. Harsh:
Thrill Killer Turned
"Great Escape" War Hero

At first glance, George Rutherford Harsh Jr. would seem to be a prime candidate for the title of "jerk" in Georgia history, and many of the elements of his life underscore that assumption. An archetypical "rich kid," with too much money and too few morals, it looked like he had screwed up his life beyond repair at the tender age of nineteen. Partially redeeming himself by saving someone's life years later while in prison, he was granted a pardon and returned to the streets, resigned to live a life on or outside the margins of polite society, forever branded as a convict. Harsh's story, though, only really began at this point.

"Junie" Harsh, originally from Milwaukee, was the son of the elder George Rutherford Harsh, a wealthy businessman who had founded a once well-regarded business, the Harsh-Chapline Shoe Company in that city. George Sr. died of a brain aneurysm in 1921 and left the younger George one hundred thousand dollars (some sources claim it was five hundred thousand dollars), a quite substantial fortune at the time. He left Milwaukee shortly afterward, and by the fall of 1928 was a student at Atlanta's Oglethorpe University, when he and four other similarly privileged and bored students decided to form a robbing crew, just for the "thrill" of committing such crimes. As Harsh himself described it, the group met one evening in the spring of 1929 over a gallon jug of corn liquor in an illegal speakeasy just south of Atlanta, and one of the young men convinced the others that all they needed to pull off any manner of crimes "was organization, careful planning, and intelligence," which he further proposed that they all shared in abundance, being the elitists that they were. This same young member of the group, about whom Harsh later said, "had the mysterious quality called leadership," owned and fetched from his car a Colt Model 1911 .45 caliber pistol to illustrate how they would pull these crimes off. Each member of the gang would later draw straws to see which one would wield it in the ensuing robbery.

The "Polite Bandits," as some in the ever-excitable press of the day soon dubbed them, cut quite a swath through Atlanta businesses over the ensuing weeks, following the same pattern each time. Two members of the gang would crash into the business, one armed with the single .45 pistol they possessed, terrifying the employees in what would later be called a "takeover" style robbery, while the other three watched from a nearby car, ready to intercept and shake off any police pursuit that might happen upon the scene. In at least one case, a member of the gang posed as the clerk they had just robbed and tied up in the back of the store, to gain more cash from unsuspecting customers. Newspaper reports of the crimes, which netted them anywhere from less than five dollars to several hundred dollars, emphasized how calm and casual the robbers appeared to be, and highlighted the fact that they frequently left a small amount of their takings with the clerk, presumably for streetcar fare back home. Other reports mentioned how well dressed and prosperous the robbers appeared, which undoubtedly helped in accessing the stores they intended to rob.

Harsh later said, "There were several gun battles, the .45 had now drawn its first blood, and a man had been killed." The dead man was Willard A. Smith, killed by one of the gang members during a robbery of Smith's Drug Store on September 26, but a careful search of crime reports in the late spring, summer, and early fall of 1929 do not show any other such "gun battles" or incidents that can definitely be attributed to Harsh's gang, and no other member of their group was ever charged with any crime.

On the evening of Sunday, October 6, 1929, Harsh drew the short straw to carry the .45, and with fellow bandit Richard Gray Gallogly, entered the A&P grocery store at 1004 Hemphill Avenue.

Harsh later claimed that as soon as he entered and announced, "This is a holdup, don't move!" manager I. V. Ellis pulled out a .38 caliber revolver, wildly firing as he swung it around to point at Harsh, allegedly killing store clerk E. H. Meeks in the process. Harsh returned fire, wounding Ellis, but was wounded in the groin by one of Ellis's own shots in the exchange. With Gallogly's help, Harsh was able to get back to their getaway car, and made it safely to Gallogly's apartment on Sixteenth Street. With the rest of Gallogly's family off on a trip, Harsh was able to rest there and recover from his relatively minor wound, returning to his classes at Oglethorpe University within a few days.

This A&P robbery attempt was assigned to Atlanta detective John Lowe, who initially suspected a notorious Alabama criminal, Roy Dickerson, who as chance would have it, had escaped from prison a few days before the crime. Lowe soon eliminated Dickerson from his list of suspects after considering the Alabama criminal's history of relative nonviolence and the conflicting great violence of the A&P crime scene, but was left with no solid leads as a result. Nearly four weeks later, a solid lead finally came in. Gallogly's maid, who had found the suit Harsh had worn the night of the A&P robbery rolled up in the bottom of a closet, had sent the bloodstained clothes to the cleaners, who in turn alerted the police when they found a bullet hole in the pants. (Harsh's and Lowe's recall of the sequence and details of this event differ significantly.) Through a previous cleaner's laundry mark, Lowe was able to trace the suit back to Harsh and quickly issue a warrant for his and Gallogly's arrest. Harsh was picked up on Saturday, October 26, while walking along Peachtree Street at North Avenue, by Atlanta motorcycle patrolman William Mashburn, who was asked by Lowe to serve the warrant because he knew Harsh by sight, apparently having had some previous (though unrecorded) encounters with the troubled young man.

While the real story about what happened in the subsequent interrogation would be difficult to firmly establish, Harsh claimed that he maintained his innocence for some hours, until Gallogly's family surrendered him to the police, high-priced attorneys in tow. Gallogly was the son of the very wealthy and prominent editor of the *Atlanta Journal* newspaper, James Richard Gray Jr., and the grandson of its founders and majority owners James Richard Gray Sr. and May Inman Gray (a fact that apparently didn't seem worthy of mention in most news reports), as well as being the stepson of prominent Atlanta physician Worth Edwin Yankey Sr. In contrast to Harsh's account of the interrogation, Lowe told a reporter a few days later that "We had not been together five minutes before Harsh started to confess. . . . We got from him every criminal move he has made since the first of this month, when he started his life of lawlessness." Harsh's own family provided him with even higher-priced legal help, hiring former US Congressman William Schley Howard (whose grandson Pierre was the Lieutenant Governor of Georgia throughout the 1990s) and a full team of other prominent attorneys. Despite the "full" confessions of both young men, no other members of their former gang were ever identified or prosecuted, and neither was charged with any of their earlier robberies.

Harsh was charged with the murders of both Smith and Meek, and his lawyers entered a plea of not guilty by reason of insanity. Much psychiatric absurdity resulted from this, with no fewer than twelve psychiatrists being brought in to examine Harsh, one later theorizing to a newspaper reporter that the two outlaws had a "master and slave complex," with Harsh doing all the planning and "leading" in their crimes, fueled by the quantities of illicit liquor both were testified to have been imbibing, and that both wealthy young men exhibited what he would term "snob psychology." This same reporter dug up a couple of Harsh's fellow Oglethorpe students, one of whom he dutifully reported claimed that both defendants were "attractive" to her, to whatever end that was supposed to lead the reader. This defense only served to further inflame the press, which produced an absolute carnival atmosphere in its "trial of the century" sensationalism. Meanwhile, reporters managed to completely ignore the close ties this same media had with the other murder defendant, which likely would have had a dire effect on the court proceedings. Despite Harsh's high-powered army of attorneys and psychiatric entourage, the jury came back with a guilty verdict within fifteen minutes of starting their deliberations, and Judge E. D. Thomas imposed a sentence of death.

In the other gang member's subsequent trial, Harsh refused to testify against Gallogly, which ultimately spared his own life. The prosecution had a very weak case with only casual circumstantial evidence against him, and when his lawyers offered to plead guilty in exchange for a life sentence, so long as Harsh's sentence was also commuted to life, the prosecution agreed. Faced with effective legal defenses backed with nearly limitless monetary resources, and potentially years of appeals that might have worked to free the men at some point, Judge Thomas reluctantly agreed to the deal, but added that Harsh would spend his sentence as a chain gang prisoner in one of Georgia's notorious work camps, a de facto death sentence.

Harsh began his work camp sentence at one of the worst work camps in the state. Instead of wooden barracks, the camp still featured iron cages mounted on wagons that the men slept in at night, a relic from the old convict lease system that had finally died an overdue death a few years previously. Records are spotty, to say the least, but it appears that Harsh stayed in this southern Georgia camp for at least two years, before another member of the chain gang he was on overpowered their "boss," killing him with his own pistol, stealing clothes from the other two guards, and escaping in the county work truck with another prisoner. In his autobiography, *Lonesome Road*, written in 1971, Harsh claimed the pair were killed two weeks later at a roadblock in Louisiana, but the fallout from the investigation ended up closing the camp and transferring him to a less brutal camp in Fulton County. While there, he eventually worked up to a trustee position and a job in the prison hospital at the Bellwood prison camp, where he became a trusted assistant to the camp physician.

One surprising fact about being made a trustee that Harsh mentioned in his autobiography was that he at last had his iron chains and shackles cut off. Under the chain gang system in Georgia and other Southern states, prisoners assigned to the work camps would have these shackles permanently riveted on as soon as they arrived in camp; they were usually removed only upon release or death. Harsh mentioned how difficult it was to change clothing with these on, especially if the clothes became soiled through sickness in the week they wore each set, and how "old timers" on the gang learned to walk in a particular "pigeon-toed" way, so they would not trip over their own chains. Obviously having picked up at least some literary references in his abbreviated college career (and in poring over the pile of books that amounted to a library in his work camp days), he mentioned in his autobiography that, "Lord Byron tells us that The Prisoner of Chillon lost his chains 'with a sigh.' . . . I lost my chains with a glad cry—not vocally but in my soul."

Harsh spent the last five years of his prison life working as a physician's assistant at the Bellwood hospital, primarily working on the massive national syphilis education and eradication program going on in the late 1930s. Gaining the trust of the director of the prison syphilis program, Dr. Paul McDonald, Harsh gradually took over more direct care of the inmates at Bellwood, to the point that Dr. McDonald was soon informally training him in advanced (for the time) medical and surgical techniques. Harsh again showed his classical education in recollecting these days: "All during this time I remembered a Molière play I had read in French class in boarding school: Le Médecin Malgré Lui. I'm afraid that's what I was becoming . . . a doctor in spite of myself."

The single event that finally gained Harsh his freedom occurred when a black chain-gang prisoner developed acute appendicitis in the middle of one of Atlanta's famed severe ice storms. Harsh stated in his book that this occurred in October 1940, but there is no record of such a storm that month; however, there was such a severe storm in January of that year. The roads were impassible and the phone lines down, forcing Harsh to operate on the sixty-one-year-old prisoner with the help of only another trustee. When Dr. McDonald was at last able to travel through the debris-choked streets to the hospital, he found a recovering patient and a still nervous Harsh. Congratulating him for a job well done, especially under the circumstances, he did have just one minor critique: "But George . . . that incision, good God. . . . You weren't doing a Caesarean on an elephant, you know." McDonald was indeed impressed with Harsh's devotion to his duty and his attentiveness to his patients, and set about trying to reward him for his diligence. McDonald wrote a long letter detailing both this incident and his personal observation of Harsh to outgoing Georgia Governor Eurith Dickenson (E. D.) Rivers, and then personally visited him (along with Harsh's lawyer and two personal friends) to present the letter and ask the governor for a pardon. In the meantime, Harsh was released from prison on parole, to await the governor's decision.

As one of his last acts in office, Governor Rivers formally and fully pardoned both Harsh and Gallogly, who was still in prison facing a longer term after a failed escape attempt. At a January 13, 1941, public ceremony announcing the pardons, Governor Rivers took the occasion to note protests from both murder victims' families as well as the state's solicitor general (forerunner of the attorney general's office), while explicitly blasting the *Atlanta Journal* for running multiple editorials calling for Harsh's continued imprisonment but continuing to carefully leave Gallogly's name out of print. Rivers stated that both men were equally guilty, but both had earned a pardon through their lives and efforts while in custody.

Harsh stayed in Atlanta for only six weeks, roaming the streets "like a fleshed out ghost" in his own words. With little prospect for gainful employment, even with the great pre-war defense boom starting to fire up, he left for brighter prospects in Canada. World War II had been underway for over a year and a half, with Canada as part of the British Commonwealth supplying men in huge numbers. American drifters like Harsh were readily accepted into military service there, and their official if inaccurate denial of any criminal past was usually accepted with a wink and nod, especially given the fact that the Axis powers were still winning the war at that point. Harsh joined the Royal Canadian Air Force, even after having to get over yet another obstacle: the fact that at age twenty-eight he was too old for combat service. The veteran pilot Group Captain commanding the intake station personally intervened, not only accepting Harsh into the air service, but also giving him the chance to become a pilot, perhaps even offering Harsh the much-sought-after Spitfire fighter pilot assignment. (Harsh hinted at this possibility in his memoirs, but never made it explicitly clear if he was offered such a position.) Instead, Harsh volunteered for the most dangerous job available, as a turret gunner on the bombers. In his autobiography, he gives a rambling, somewhat incoherent explanation for this duty request, apparently made on the spur of the moment, but it seems clear that he had no real desire to outlive the war, and wanted what action and glory he could find in it. After mentioning that he had to forfeit his US citizenship, and swear allegiance to His Britannic Majesty, Harsh mentioned, "At the time I realized that someday this would present a problem for me, but I would worry about that when the time came. And besides, if I didn't come back from the war . . . well, it was just not worth worrying about at the time."

He was sent in short order to the Royal Canadian Air Force (RCAF) air gunnery school in Ontario, and soon after graduating, was selected for commissioning as an officer. After shipping over to England, and bouncing around a couple of other bomber squadrons, he was finally assigned sometime after February 1942 as the squadron gunnery officer of B Flight, 102 Squadron, No. 4 Group (Bomber Command) based at Royal Air Force (RAF) Driffield, Yorkshire, flying in Handley Page Halifax Mk.II's. His normal flying station was in the four-engine bomber's rear power turret, manning four .303 Browning machine guns. He flew on a number of missions over the following eight months, but had little to say later on the details of these. He did, however, emphasize the sheer terror involved in flying night bombing missions over the heart of the Third Reich.

The night of his last mission, October 5–6, 1942, Harsh was not assigned to fly, but was standing at the end of the active runway with the squadron operations officer, doing last minute checks of the departing bombers. As Halifax number W7824 taxied up for takeoff, though, pilot W/O F. A. Schaw waved at Harsh, indicating that the rear turret gunner was having some sort of issue with his equipment. The gunner, a new replacement on his first mission (as were the rest of the crew), had managed to damage the turret's gunsight beyond any hope of quick repair. Realizing that the crew would stand no chance without an effective rear gunner to foil attacks of the far-too-effective German night fighters, Harsh quickly took the man's place, hoping his experience would allow him to effectively utilize his guns without benefit of a proper sight.

Taking off at 6:41 p.m., the lone bomber never managed to regroup with the rest of the already-departed 102 Squadron and other Halifax squadrons en route to bomb the German town of Aachen (Harsh wrote in his book that the target was Dusseldorf). Harsh stated that they flew alone without encountering any serious antiaircraft fire or night fighters, until he spotted the signature twin spire of the Cologne Cathedral below, forty-six miles east of their intended target. Before they could turn away, the highly effective, radar controlled Cologne antiaircraft batteries shot his bomber out of the sky. Harsh was blown out of the crashing bomber, as were most other members of the crew. Schaw, like Harsh a "foreigner" in the RAF, in his case a member of the Royal New Zealand Air Force, was killed in the crash. Harsh and the other six crew members were captured as soon as they landed by parachute. Harsh had been injured quite badly by shrapnel from all the antiaircraft fire, as well as from a particularly bad landing he made, and was first taken to the Cologne city hospital, where he recovered over the next two weeks.

Barely able to walk, he was transferred to the Luftwaffe interrogation center at Dulag Luft in Wetzlar near Frankfort, a standard treatment for any downed airman, even if the chances were slim that they had any information that the Germans could find useful. After some perfunctory questioning, and some deliberate attempts to humiliate if not exactly torture Harsh, he was transferred to another camp, Stalig Luft III, near the town of Sagan, about one hundred miles southeast of Berlin in what is now Poland. Once settled into the camp, he discovered that, while the food was short and barely edible, and the living conditions were one small step above the barest of primitive, there was both a well-stocked library and a system where he could obtain nearly any book that he desired. With that, Harsh decided that he could tolerate imprisonment for however long it might take, happily consumed with reading to his heart's content.

As fate would have it, or as Harsh would say, "another little joke the gods had in store," his reputation as a murderer and long-term chain gang prisoner soon spread to the "right" people, those British officers running the "X Organization," the escape committee present in every camp. One of his fellow inmates, Flight Lieutenant Wally Floody, approached Harsh a few months after the Georgian had attempted a rather improbable escape from the camp, telling him of the elaborate plans to break out the entire population of six hundred plus prisoners, and recruiting him to join the effort. Harsh reluctantly agreed to join the effort, assuming he would play some low-level role. In due course, presumably when he had been thoroughly checked out and vetted by British intelligence (who had an effective communications network within the POW camps), he was introduced to Group Captain H. M. Massey, Wing Commander Harry Day, and Squadron Leader Roger Joyce Bushell, the heads of the escape committee at Stalag Luft II, otherwise known as "Big X." Bushell had already made two attempts to escape, the second leading to an intense torturing at the hands of the Gestapo. Harsh was ordered by the committee to take charge of security for the entire escape project, at the head of two hundred picked men, the three leaders confirming that they needed a man like Harsh whom they could trust, protecting their backs as they worked underground. Floody humorously told Harsh that he was "probably the only man in the world that got a job

George Harsh in Stalag Luft III, taken before the "Great Escape"
COURTESY OF THE IMPERIAL WAR MUSEUM, LONDON, IMAGE HU 1602

because he was an ex-con." Harsh made it clear in his memoirs that he found the position and the plan to be less than humorous.

The escape plan was massive and elaborate, featuring not one but three long tunnels dug from underneath the barracks to outside the wire in the tree line, called Tom, Dick, and Harry. Harsh claimed the three tunnels were originally nicknamed Father, Son, and Holy Ghost, but Bushell nixed those, fearing any divine wrath against what was already a high-risk and improbable operation. The plan was to use all three tunnels to completely empty out the camp in one night, causing massive disruptions to normal German operations and the need for a huge search and recapture effort. No one had any real illusions about most getting back to England or some other friendly or neutral country. Bushell was very straightforward about this point in his first meeting with Harsh, "None of us in this room are stupid—how many people do we really think we're going to get back to England? Damned few ... we all know that. ... And the whole damn lot of us may die in the attempt, but by God, we'll die as men."

Begun in the spring of 1943, each tunnel progressed very slowly under the direct control of Floody, the "Tunnel King," due to the very soft, sandy soil that had to be shored up and the need for an elaborate ventilation and soil removal system. Harsh was indeed a good man for his security position, and maintained an effective lookout system that warned of German guards and protected the dispersal of soil removed from the tunnels, against the best efforts of both the Luftwaffe security service and the Gestapo, who suspected such an operation was ongoing. In September 1943, "Tom" was discovered, basically by the accident of a German guard stumbling across its opening, and construction on "Dick" was suspended when an expansion of the camp pushed the wire past its planned exit. "Harry" was completed in March 1944, but by then the Germans were not only convinced of its existence, but also had a pretty good idea of who some of the key players in its construction were. Without warning, on February 28, 1944, Harsh, Floody, and eighteen other prisoners, all members of the X organization, were suddenly transferred to another camp near Belaria, about five miles away.

The final construction of "Harry" progressed without these critical men, finishing up in mid-March. On the night of March 24, 1944, over two hundred men prepared to escape, but the attempt was aborted when a guard observed the seventy-sixth escapee exiting the tunnel, which had inadvertently come out in the open ground between the wire and tree line. Their sudden transfer had spared Floody and Harsh's lives; all but three of the escapees were soon recaptured, and on Hitler's direct and explicit order, fifty of them were murdered by the Gestapo.

The tale of this breakout attempt was told, in typical somewhat-truthful, somewhat-fictional Hollywood style, in the 1963 movie, *The Great Escape*, based on the excellent 1950 book of the same name. Harsh, incidentally, wrote the foreword to the book, but was renamed "George McDonald" in the movie, portrayed by Gordon Jackson, his murderous reputation still fresh even so many years later. Wally Floody was renamed Danny Velinski, and portrayed by Charles Bronson.

His transfer had saved his life, but Harsh had yet one more adventure left in his wartime experiences. In January 1945, with the Soviet army prepared to overrun the easternmost POW camps, the Germans moved him and all the other remaining prisoners out of Belaria, moving due west toward the advancing American and British armies. Stating that they were doing this on behalf of the Allied officers, to "protect them from the Russians," it was in fact the Luftwaffe officers and men who were trying to protect their own necks, knowing full well what would happen if they were captured by the enraged Soviets. This forced march lasted well over a month, covering roughly one hundred and twenty miles, before the advancing Red Army overran the column of prisoners temporarily housed in a camp near Luckenwalde, south of Berlin. Harsh's war was finally over.

Harsh seems to have led a remarkably charmed life, even despite all the tragedy he caused and endured, but would have been quick to agree that he had been a "jerk" in his Atlanta years, for which he spent all his remaining life trying to compensate, even if he never managed to produce a full confession of his many crimes in the city. He drifted from job to job after the war, writing his memoir *Lonesome Road* (which some historians familiar with his story consider mostly concocted and self-excusing, especially about his Atlanta years), selling books, farming trees, and marrying and divorcing twice, but he had great difficulty overcoming the brutal hardships he had endured in the Georgia chain gang and during the war. All this culminated in a failed suicide attempt on Christmas Eve of 1974, for which he was briefly hospitalized. He suffered a crippling stroke shortly afterward; his old friend from Stalag Luft III, Wally Floody, took him into his home to care for him. At Harsh's own insistence, he left Flood's home to enter long-term care in 1977 in the Veteran's Wing at the Sunnybrook Medical Centre in Toronto, where he died on January 25, 1980, free at last of the demons that had so long tormented him.

CHAPTER 14

John S. Williams:
Peonage Master and Mass Murderer

Sometimes history has a way of pointing out that what we think happened in the past did not in fact happen, at least the way we believe it did. Armchair and cocktail party historians delight in pointing out that people in Columbus's time did not, in fact, widely believe that the earth was flat; that the Pilgrims did not land on Plymouth Rock; that George Washington never actually chopped down a cherry tree, nor did he throw a dollar across the Potomac, and he was not in fact the first president of the United States; that Paul Revere did not ride all night warning Massachusetts Minutemen that "the British are coming!"; that Lincoln never freed a single slave, at least directly; and that President Millard Fillmore did not introduce the bathtub to the White House, nor did President William Howard Taft get stuck in one. However, when a war that took over 652,000 American lives resulted in the passage of a Constitutional amendment outlawing the practice of slavery, one might be excused for thinking that slavery in America ended in 1865. To the contrary, in some parts of the South, including central Georgia, the inhumane institution endured well over fifty years after the Civil War. One Jasper County plantation owner, John S. Williams, was even willing to commit mass murder in order to keep the dark secret of slavery's continued existence hidden.

Slavery as an American phenomenon began in 1619, when a small load of African slaves was brought into the Jamestown settlement by a Dutch merchantman, but the practice itself dates back many millennia, well before the era of recorded history. Throughout most of history, though, including what is mentioned in the Bible, slavery was a very different establishment than what it became in America. Slaves of the ancient world were usually the product of wars, what we would refer to as prisoners of war today, though the chance they would ever be repatriated to their home-lands was slim. Others were more like bondservants or indentured servants, serving for a period to repay debts or simply to provide for an otherwise unobtainable income. In America, the practice revolved around "chattel slavery," people bought and sold as com-mercial products, and wholly owned by the purchaser, with few, if any, rights of their own. Every American British colony had slaves before the Revolutionary War, but soon afterward, the majority remained confined primarily to the Deep South, where the large plantations made slavery affordable. Slaves were not exactly free labor, given that their average purchase price was roughly equiva-lent to what a new car would cost today. Despite the myriad horror stories that came out of that era, slaves also had to be provided with at least basic housing, clothing, food, and medical care.

While Lincoln's 1863 Emancipation Proclamation did not directly free any slaves (it only declared that slaves "in states cur-rently in rebellion" were freed, which of course was ignored by the Confederate government), it did change the focus of the Civil War from simply preserving the Union to freeing the slaves from their bondage. Ex-Confederate states were forced to ratify the 1865 Thirteenth Amendment, which outlawed slavery, as a condition for readmission to the Union following the war. However, the practice of using very low cost, subdued, and even brutalized workforces to man the fields across the South did not end with the Civil War. One result of the deeply corrupt presidential election of 1876 was that Republicans in Congress agreed to end the Reconstruction military occupation of the South in exchange for Southern Demo-crats allowing the Republican candidate to win in the deadlocked voting. The immediate result of this was that "black codes" were quickly passed and enforced in all the former Confederate states, reimposing many of the conditions of servitude on poor black fami-lies. "Separate but equal" schools and public areas were legalized by the 1896 *Plessy v. Ferguson* Supreme Court decision, while the "convict lease system" allowed states to rent out prisoners to land-owners, initially almost exclusively the black prisoners, to work in nearly exactly the same conditions they had endured in servitude, until this system was at last abolished in 1928. These and other legal and aboveboard actions helped keep alive at least the flavor and spirit of slavery, but three other less well advertised systems kept it alive in fact, as well.

Sharecropping grew out of the failure of Reconstruction-era governments to impose any workable plan for reconfiguring the labor system across the South. Over the next hundred years it nearly defined Southern crop production, with poor and landless blacks and whites in roughly equal numbers working landowners' fields in exchange for a share of the crop profits. From the very beginning it was a widely and deeply corrupt system, with the poor farmers never managing to make enough from each harvest to pay off the debt they owed the landowners. Often having no other resources, sharecroppers had to borrow on credit the seed, tools, and other essentials they needed from the landowners, who charged sky-high prices for these supplies and frequently employed "creative" bookkeeping come settlement time. A parallel system, more utilized by poor white families, existed with tenant farms, where farmers would rent land from a large landowner in exchange for a fixed fee, either in crops or in cash, come harvest time. It, too, was a system notorious for corruption and bad dealings.

A third system, practiced almost exclusively with the poorest of blacks, was peonage, debt bondage. Those who had been jailed for not paying taxes or who had court-imposed fines and could not pay them, even debts as minor as five dollars, could be forced to "work off" their debt to landowners who had paid the taxes or fines for them and bailed them out of jail, sometimes without the knowledge or consent of the debtor prisoner. As with other such systems, corruption was widespread, bookkeeping was shoddy, and quite frequently the debt was never quite paid off, resulting in the "peon" being forced to work a lifetime in conditions identical to slavery. Although a federal law in 1867 had technically abolished the practice, there was no serious effort to stamp it out in practical terms, and it was allowed to flourish, albeit quietly and largely unspoken of in polite society. It flourished so well, in fact, that a Justice Department investigator estimated that as many as one-third of all the large plantation owners in the South engaged in the practice by 1907. While the sharecropping system endured into the 1970s, and even today there are still a relative handful of tenant farmers across the region, the peonage system died a well-deserved and quick death, after a single Georgia plantation owner showed that he was willing to commit mass murder, or at the very least direct it to be committed on his behalf, in order to cover up the practice on his own property.

John Sims Williams was possibly born in Meriwether County (other sources state in Jasper County) on October 11, 1866, to William Sims and Sophronia (or Surfronia) Elizabeth Williams. His father had served during the Civil War, as a corporal in Company C, First Battalion, Georgia Sharpshooters, in the famed Confederate Army of Tennessee, before returning to Georgia to resume farming. By 1870 his family had moved to the Lane and Fears District of Jasper County, where his father owned and worked a farm. The few available records have sparse details about most of his early adult life. He married Lucy Alice Lane in 1890, when she was nineteen, and they lived for at least a short time in Forsyth, a few miles north of Macon, Georgia, where one report claimed his plantation home and all the outbuildings had been destroyed in a fire. Around 1894 he either purchased or took over from another family a large (for the area) plantation in the Martin and Burney District of Jasper County, midway between Covington and Monticello, near the Newton County line. Various sources list it as being between 2,000 and 2,700 acres in size, large enough to sustain a moderate-size population of workers, but not quite in league with the massive, many tens of thousands of acres plantations owned by wealthy planters farther to the south in the state. Even so, Williams owned one of the largest plantations in the area, probably the largest in Jasper County, and comported himself as a wealthy planter in the best antebellum tradition. News reports note that

John Williams's grave in Monticello, Georgia
PHOTO BY JOHN MCKAY

he was a physically imposing man, over six feet tall, always impeccably groomed, clean shaven with a neatly trimmed mustache, and possessed of a self-assured air. His large plantation house and three cars in their individual garages transmitted his wealth and power to all who happened by. He and Lucy had twelve children (one source stated six of them were adopted), the last born in 1918. According to multiple reports, Williams was a prominent, politically influential, and well-respected man, not only in Jasper County, but also across the state of Georgia.

The forerunner of the Federal Bureau of Investigation had been organized in 1908 as the Department of Justice Bureau of Investigation (BOI), and had slowly acquired various oversight duties against crimes that could fall under the general heading of interstate commerce. By late 1920, agents in the BOI's Atlanta office were fielding as many as fifty complaints a year directly related to serious abuses of the still-tolerated peonage system, and performing at least perfunctory investigations into many of them. Part of the problem was that residents of the state in general were highly reluctant to talk to federal agents about pretty much anything, much less something as shameful yet deeply institutionalized as peonage. Another problem was that some of the people that the BOI would normally have expected to help them, local law enforcement officials, were just as reluctant to do so as any ordinary citizen; the sheriff of Jasper County himself was under indictment for peonage in 1921. While the complaints came from across the state, and at least some appeared to be attempts at revenge against political or community enemies instead of honest outrage at this illegal enslavement, some of the reports centered on numerous plantations in Jasper County, and John Williams's name specifically cropped up in more than one complaint. Still, little was done until an "escapee" from Williams's plantation, Gus Chapman, showed up at the Atlanta BOI office, wanting to tell his story.

Chapman had been arrested a year earlier for loitering in Atlanta, and unable to pay the five-dollar fine, had been locked up in the Fulton Tower, the Atlanta penitentiary. One of Williams's sons, Huland, was involved in peonage, and he soon showed up at the Atlanta jail, offering to pay Chapman's fine and get him released, in exchange for working off the amount as a laborer on his farm. Seeing farm work as the better of the two possible situations, Chapman agreed and left with Huland. He ended up as part of the peonage crew, literally locked up in a barracks after hours on the main Williams plantation, where the reality of his situation did not take very long at all to become clear. Other peons told him of the immense cruelty demonstrated by Williams and his sons, including frequent individual or group whippings (with leather buggy whips, plow line, or rubber strips taken off old automobile tires) as punishment for minor infractions (e.g., when the black cook failed to have dinner ready in time, or "just to suit [Williams]"). According to several accounts, Williams usually would not "dirty his hands" with administering these whippings, but would order his overseers to do them while he observed.

Stories later told to reporters and in court included claims that Williams and at least one of his sons also frequently shot at or pistol whipped workers—both peon and "free" laborers—for equally minor offenses.

Before Chapman arrived, Williams's peons learned first-hand that attempting to escape from the plantation resulted in worse punishments, including whipping to the point of death, followed by a terminal gunshot to the head. These were not just frightening stories, either; several sources confirm that at least one escaped peon who had made it a whole week off the plantation before being brought back, Nathaniel Wade, nicknamed Blackstrap, was executed in just such a manner. Another peon, only known as Iron John, was similarly executed for not unrolling a reel of wire in a manner acceptable to Williams. The effect on the other peons was exactly what Williams sought: By and large, they quietly assented to the workload and nighttime incarceration in exchange for food, a small amount of pay (thirty-five cents a year in Chapman's case, but as much as twenty dollars a month for the black overseers) and clothing that was of somewhat better quality than what the slaves of earlier generations had been given. In his book about Williams's crimes, *Lay This Body Down*, Gregory Freeman commented that these minor details were the difference between maintaining slaves and "hiring" peons in Williams's mind.

On a moonless night in early September 1920, with some help from one of Williams's trusted black overseers, Clyde Manning, Chapman slipped out of the locked bunkhouse with little more than the twenty-five cents in pay he had earned in his pocket, and headed south, with no real destination in mind other than getting away from the Williams plantation. When his escape was uncovered the next morning, Manning made up a story and told Williams that Chapman had tried to rape his wife, and then fought with him before running off through the woods. Manning knew that if he told Williams the truth, it would absolutely end with his own tortured death. Chapman had little more chance of escape than slaves in the antebellum plantations of the area; almost every worker on the farm, except the "foreign" peons, had grown up there and rarely, if ever, traveled so much as a mile from its gates. There was no system of friendly farm workers to help him out; rather, the white farmers and plantation owners would be quick to call the law on any "vagrant" black man spotted walking down their roads.

Much to Chapman's great dismay, his freedom was short-lived. Less than two days later Williams and two of his sons, along with Manning and some of the other peons, tracked him down to a stand of woods near Shady Dale, just a few miles from their plantation. Chapman was tied up and hauled back to what the black workers called the "whipping barn," where Williams cursed and debated what to do with him, threatening, "If you won't work and won't stay on the farm, maybe it's best if I just get rid of you right now." Chapman pled for his life, and Williams was sufficiently moved to "just" viciously whip and beat him, joined by his two sons, instead of killing him outright. He did threaten, though, that if Chapman ever tried to escape again, he would simply kill him "like [he] was a snake."

Three months later, a week after Thanksgiving in November 1920, Chapman escaped again, once more with some help from overseer Clyde Manning. This time he only had the additional ten cents in his pocket that he had earned for work over that period, but moved quickly north and encountered some friendly black farm workers who helped him get all the way to Atlanta. Once there, he was urged to go talk to the federal authorities, the only law enforcement officials likely to have anything to do with an escaped peon. Two months later, he finally entered the Atlanta offices of the Department of Justice's Bureau of Investigation, and told his story to two investigators, George W. Brown and A. J. Wismer. Unbeknownst to Chapman, the two investigators had already spoken with another "escapee" from the Williams plantation a few weeks before, James Strickland, and both men's stories closely paralleled each other.

While not making it a priority, Brown and Wismer traveled to Williams's plantation on February 18, 1921, while on other federal business in the area, to investigate the validity of Chapman's and Strickland's claims. Williams and his sons were away on business, but the two agents spoke with Clyde Manning, the lead overseer present on the farm. Manning denied anything was out of line on the farm, offering to show them around and prove such to the agents. As they toured the houses and fields, the agents asked Manning if a peon named Chapman had ever escaped from the farm. He told them yes, but that he had voluntarily come back to the farm without a pursuit. During the tour, Williams came driving up, and after introductions, offered the same openness to the agents that Manning had displayed, further offering to take them to his sons' farms five miles away, to prove to them the same acceptable conditions also existed there. During their discussions, Williams asked what he was being accused of, and when told "practicing illegal peonage," he asked the agents for a definition of what that was. Brown responded, "If you pay a nigger's fine or go on his bond and you work him on your place, you're guilty of peonage." Reinforcing the fact that the federal agents were no less enlightened about race relations than Williams, Wismer then told Williams that they were also "most alarmed" by the fact that they saw the black overseer Manning openly carrying a pistol as he went about his duties.

Williams did not address Manning's armed status, but told the agents that if their definition of peonage was true, "me and most of the people who have done anything of the sort were guilty of peonage," while laughing at what he considered the absurdity of it all. He and the agents discussed this legal issue for a few more minutes, while Williams protested that he did not understand the law, but would fully cooperate with it as soon as he did. This seemed to satisfy the agents, who made ready to drive back to Atlanta, asking one more question as they did. "By the way, have you ever worked a nigger by the name of Gus Chapman?" Williams said he did, and when Brown asked if he ever escaped, confirmed that he had, the previous September. "Did you take some nigger laborers and bring him back?" Yes, Williams replied, he had, explaining the tale Manning had told him of the attempted rape. Both agents knew that either Manning or Williams was lying, or more likely both of them to some degree, and had already agreed with each other that it was clear that most of the workers were terribly afraid to talk with them, and none had told them the truth about what was going on. They had also noted that the "bunkhouses" for the peons had fittings to chain-lock and bolt the doors, and that all the windows locked from the outside. One other small detail that they noted, which later was a key piece of evidence, was that one farm worker was busy making shoes out of worn-out tires from Williams's three cars, creating the unusual footwear that all the peons and farmhands were wearing. Despite all this, they told Williams that they had found evidence of illegal peonage going on, but that all his black workers seemed well fed and well dressed, and that they appreciated his openness and cooperation. As they started their car to drive back to Atlanta, Brown told him, "I don't think you need to have any fear of any case before the federal jury."

Despite the agent's assurances, Williams was worried. Jasper County Sheriff Persons, one of Williams's cousins, himself was under indictment for conspiracy to commit peonage, scheduled for an April 1921 federal trial, and rumor had it that the federal grand jury was preparing to indict several Jasper County farmers for the practice. Worried that he stood to lose his freedom, land, business, reputation, and power—and, worst of all, that his own sons might also be convicted and jailed—Williams decided to eliminate any traces of evidence that he had engaged in the latter-day slavery practice. The very next morning, he arose at his usual early hour, ate a hearty breakfast with his wife Lucy and several of their youngest children, and headed out to find his overseer Manning. They had some hard work to plan out. First, though, he visited the farms of three of his oldest sons, Huland, Leroy, and Marvin, telling them to immediately leave the county and to not come back until he sent for them.

According to Manning's later sworn testimony, Williams ordered him to "do away" with their peons, what he called the "stockade niggers." When Manning made it clear, though unspoken, that he was loath to carry out the plantation owner's dire order, Williams made it clear he would have little choice but to obey. "Well, by God, if you don't want to do it, that's all right. But it's your neck or theirs." Two days later, the killings began. Williams took Manning out to one field where a peon named Johnnie Williams (a namesake but not related) was working. On his order, Manning murdered the black farmhand with multiple blows from a heavy axe, and then he and Williams dragged the body over to a washout gully and covered it up with the loose red clay. The next day, it was John Will "Big John" Gaither's turn, killed by a pickaxe blow to the side of his head while he dug what he thought was a well, as Williams watched nearby. It served instead as the victim's own grave.

The remaining nine peons posed a disposal problem, though. Williams did not seem to mind having an unmarked grave or two on his property, and had already allegedly dumped the body of another peon who had tried to escape some years before in the large pond on his property, but if multiple graves were uncovered by further federal agent searches, he would have some uncomfortable explaining to do. On Friday, February 25, 1921, Williams walked into the stockade, announced that he had decided to release all the men from their peonage who wanted release, and asked who wanted to go free that night. John "Big Red" Brown and Johnny "Little Bit" Benson were the first to speak up. Williams said to follow him, along with Manning and another overseer named Charlie Chisolm, and he would drive them to the railroad station. Instead, they were taken several miles away to Water's Bridge over the Alcovy River, trussed up with chains, weighted down with hundreds of pounds of iron bars and wheels, and thrown alive into the dark, deep waters. Manning later said that he heard their terrified screams as they hit the water every night in his dreams, for the rest of his life. The following night it was Lindsey Peterson and

Willie Preston's turn, each trussed up with wire and chains and weighted down with iron bars, horseshoes, and rocks before being tossed alive off Allen's Bridge on the Yellow River, followed later that same night by Harry Price, who said a short prayer and let out only a sigh of despair when Manning and Chisholm threw him off Mann's Bridge over the South River.

Williams saw no need for the Sabbath to interrupt his plans to protect himself and his sons from federal prosecution. Sunday morning, February 27, 1921, he ordered Manning to kill Johnny Green with blows from an ax as he worked out in one of the fields. A few minutes later, Williams summoned another peon, Willie Givens, to walk with him and Manning on the pretext that they were going to walk down to a local store. Instead, they went to the spot where Green's mutilated body lay in the grass, where Manning struck him in the neck with the same axe, nearly decapitating the black worker with a single blow. Manning buried both bodies where they lay later that night. A week later, it was Chisholm's turn. Fearing that he would spill the beans to any federal agent who happened by, Williams drove him and Manning back out to the Water's Bridge, weighted the black worker down with wire and rocks, and tossed him off the bridge. Knowing from the beginning of the trip what was coming, Manning later said that Chisholm never pled for his life, even as he was being tossed off the bridge to his death. As they drove away, Williams warned Manning that he would kill him with a shotgun if he ever spoke of what they both had done.

The killing was not over. Later in the week, Williams walked out into his son Huland's fields, carrying a double-barreled shotgun. Clyde Manning was there, leading a work crew, when Williams walked up and ordered all of them to leave except Manning and the last peon left on his farm, Fletcher Smith. Manning was told to go fetch some tools, and as he was on the way back, he later reported that he heard a single shotgun blast, and then found Williams standing over Smith's lifeless body. Manning was ordered to dig a shallow grave, bury Smith, and then run a plow team over the grave, to eliminate any easily visible traces of it.

It took less than ten days for Williams's cunning plan to fall apart. Agents Brown and Wismer had decided not to pursue any peonage case against him, feeling that they had a lack of evidence for any of the violent acts and murders that agents Chapman and Strickland had already reported as connected to Williams. Other agents forwarded them a news clipping, though, that reported the discovery of bodies in the Alcovy, South, and Yellow Rivers in Newton County, bordering Jasper County. The weights that had been sufficient to drown the six black workers turned out to be insufficient to keep their bodies hidden. The first victim, who turned out to be Willie Preston, was discovered by two young men from Newton County, Carl Wheeler and Randall Parker, who were walking across Allen's Bridge one morning when they spotted a foot sticking out of the water. Newton County Sheriff B. L. Johnson launched an investigation, which soon dredged up the five other bodies. That someone was "getting rid" of the workers was obvious; the question was who was doing it.

Yet another black worker, Eberhardt Crawford, who lived just across the river from Williams, provided that last bit of the puzzle. He made his way to the BOI office in Atlanta, where he related to Brown and Wismer the rumors he had heard about the murders from other field hands, and what he had personally witnessed. He had been present when two of the bodies were being examined by the Newton County authorities, and at the agent's prodding, told them about their general appearance, including the fact both bodies he saw had on "rubber tire shoes," the same kind the agents had seen being made on Williams's plantation. He told the agents that he had mentioned to the Newton County authorities that the bodies might have come from Williams's plantation. Williams's discovery of this report prompted him to make a nighttime "visit" to Crawford's home soon afterward, warning his neighbor never to speak his name again. Possibly coincidentally, but probably not, that same night Crawford's house was shot up by a "carload of white people."

Both federal agents were convinced by these details that the bodies were from Williams's plantation, and based on the earlier rumors and testimony they had heard, that he was either the solitary culprit in their deaths or at least involved in them. The problem was that they had no jurisdiction over this case, murder being a state, not federal, crime and quasi-constitutional federal statutes allowing them jurisdiction over "violations of civil rights" in such cases were still several decades away. Knowing that it would be less than useless to try to work with the local authorities, the agents took the highly unusual move of approaching Georgia Governor Hugh Dorsey, bringing Crawford along to bolster their request for his direct intervention. To the agents, this must have seemed like a desperate long shot at best, particularly as Dorsey had been the crusading Atlanta solicitor general who tried Leo Frank for the murder of young Mary Phagan in his factory eight years previously, which eventually led to Frank's lynching death after a sentence commutation. It was this highly emotional prosecution of the doomed Jew that brought Dorsey to statewide prominence and national recognition, and won him the governor's seat two years later. Dorsey's case was widely recognized afterward to have no basis; it was all moonshine, smoke, and mirrors, with Frank's religion being tried in place of the evidentiary facts.

Dorsey had been the sort of "finger in the wind" politician who would be highly unlikely to intervene in this sort of case. After all, the only real evidence against Williams that the agents could offer him was the testimony of a handful of black farmhands, and no white man in Georgia had ever been convicted of a capital crime based solely on the testimony of a black man. However, the governor was in the twilight of his political career, and had in the latter years been promoting an antilynching campaign. After taking some time to consider all the ramifications of the case, and after a second visit with the federal agents, Governor Dorsey agreed to use his office and influence to promote the case as best he could.

A grand jury was soon convened in Newton County, where the first three bodies had been pulled out of the rivers, and subpoenas were issued for Williams, Manning, and another black overseer named Claude Freeman (who had been involved with the killings), as well as three of Williams's sons and a list of peonage workers signed out to his plantation. Sheriff Johnson and the two federal agents arrested Williams, Manning, and Freeman on his farm, but could not find the three sons or any of the listed workers.

Freeman, Manning, and yet another identified "escapee" found living in Covington, Frank Dozier, all provided details of the murders, albeit very reluctantly at first, in what the agents later described as "vigorous examination." Manning and Freeman accompanied the sheriff and federal agents back to the farm, pointing out where the bodies they had helped kill were buried. They and other workers later testified to the grand jury all that had occurred, including their own involvement and details of widespread abuse, evidenced by many of them partially disrobing to display their scars. Several testified about other murders that had also occurred on the farm, but had never even been suspected, much less investigated. Williams, on the other hand, proudly and aloofly told the grand jury during his own testimony that it was "all a lie," that he had never done any of the things of which he was being accused, and neither had any of his sons. The grand jury did not buy his story, handing down indictments that same afternoon against Williams and Manning, charging them with the murders of Lindsey Peterson, Willie Preston, and Harry Price.

Following his arrest, Williams heatedly denied to reporters that he had any involvement with mistreatment of his farmhands, much less murdering or having them murdered. He insisted that his legal troubles arose from a feud between himself and the neighboring farm family, Mrs. Mary Leverett and her three sons. He elaborated that the feud began with disputes over property lines and ownership of some livestock, but accelerated when the Leverett boys complained that Williams's own sons had reported their illicit still to the sheriff. During the trial, Williams's defense team also tried to claim that his prosecution was the result of a conspiracy by Georgia Governor Hugh Dorsey, the Bureau of Investigation, and wealthy liberals from Atlanta who wanted to "stir up the blacks" in middle Georgia.

Williams might have thought that he was safe in being tried and judged by a jury of his true peers, the very farmers, bankers, merchants, and others in whose society he had such prominence and good repute, but this belief was dashed even before the trial began. Details of the murders appeared in newspapers across the nation, and several Northern papers sent reporters to Covington to cover the trial firsthand. With the knowing arrogance of provincial Yankees covering Southern events, each immediately set off to gather as many bigoted and racist remarks as possible from residents of the rural Newton County community, obviously hoping to score yet another strike against the "backwards and ignorant South." To their obvious and published surprise, each found little, if any, of the institutionalized racism they all expected, and more than a little anger directed toward Williams and his terrible cruelty toward his black workers.

One *New York World* reporter, Rowland Thompson, was moved to report that, "every decent white man and woman in Georgia, which means at least 90 per cent of the state's white population, is as deeply outraged and indignant over the recent revelations as the people of any other part of the country can be." This could be excused as protectionist Southerners hiding the truth of their opinions from Northern reporters, but the remarks of Rev. J. M. Winburn, Williams's own pastor, published in the *Atlanta Constitution*, should have convinced him that he had badly miscalculated the opinions of his neighbors:

> *I wish to make myself perfectly understood. I am Johnnie [John S.] Williams's pastor. I am Johnnie Williams's friend. It has been my privilege to be entertained many times in his home. I have been permitted to baptize and receive into the church four of his children.*
>
> *I have prayed and will continue to pray for him, but let me say this with emphasis, I am not engaged in his defense. If he is guilty of the atrocious crimes with which he has been charged, then let justice be done—and the heart and soul of Jasper County speaks through my pen.*

Williams's trial began on Tuesday, April 5, 1921, and lasted until Saturday, April 9. After just a few hours of deliberations, the jury found him guilty, but recommended mercy, meaning he would receive a life sentence instead of the death penalty. For the first time in Georgia's long history, a white man had been convicted of murder based solely on the testimony of black people. Members of the jury later said that their only real deliberation had been whether to request a sentence of death or not, given that the evidence against him was overwhelming. Manning's trial began in the same Covington courthouse on May 30, lasting just two days, with the same result and sentence. Huland, Marvin, and Leroy Williams were all arrested and indicted by 1927, when they finally returned to Georgia, but were never prosecuted for their parts in the murders. Manning died in prison of tuberculosis while still on the hard labor chain gang in 1927. Williams was killed in 1932 while trying to prevent an escape at the Milledgeville state penitentiary. He is buried in his family plot in Monticello, with no mention of anything connected to the peonage case on his tombstone. Manning's burial location is unknown.

This case caused much distress far removed from the crimes committed and subsequent courtroom dramas. The South has a number of legacies, legends, and reputations across the region and nationally, some true, some with various levels of truth, and others simply made up by those who do not know and love the area. One of the reactions to this case was a profound sense of shock and horror at how far this peonage system could go, and how it could corrupt the wealthy, powerful, and influential just as it could the common working folk. This sense of betrayal, shame, and embarrassment over the actions of one admittedly violent and arrogant man resulted in the one thing that Williams himself would have found most distressing: He has been nearly completely forgotten, even shunned in his grave. There is no mention of him, his extensive plantation, or even his war-hero son Gus—who to all accounts was an honorable and upright man who had no knowledge of or connection to his father's crimes—nor of any of the other extensive Williams clan in any of the accessed official and unofficial histories and genealogies of Jasper County. His former plantation northwest of Monticello bears no historical marker or other sign that it ever existed, the former property simply surrounded by a high privacy fence. Other than his tombstone, bearing the epitaph, "May the resurrection find thee, On the bosom of thy God," there is almost no hard physical evidence that John Sims Williams existed in the very community where he was once widely admired and respected.

Even with all of the publicity and fallout as a result of Williams's excesses and trial, the peonage system of modern slavery did not completely die. Accusations of peonage-like conditions in migrant worker camps in Florida cropped up as late as 1969, but the last formal trial and conviction for outright slavery took place in 1954. Two brothers of a very wealthy and prosperous west Alabama plantation family, Fred and Oscar Dial, were convicted on May 14 of holding several black men in peonage for alleged debts. One of those men, Hubert Thompson, died as the result of a sustained and vicious beating the Dial brothers ordered eight other workers to administer, after he was caught trying to escape from their farm near Boyd, in Sumter County. Both brothers served eighteen-month sentences for the crimes.

CHAPTER 15

John Wallace:
Perpetrator of the Famous
"Murder in Coweta County"

The lore of the South is full of stories of rogue lawmen, "county bosses" who ruled their small part of the state just as any medieval lord ruled his serf workers. Film culture helps to spread, expand, and perpetuate this darker part of the Old South, with films such as *Smokey and the Bandit*, *Macon County Line*, *O Brother Where Art Thou?*, and *White Lightning*—along with a whole host of television shows and commercials ("You in a whole heap o' trouble now, boy!")—portraying the typical Southern sheriff as an overweight, mirrored-sunglasses-wearing, foul-mouthed, violent bully whose only law is the one he makes up himself.

The painful part about this entire mythological perpetuation for Southerners is that it is partly based on fact. Theophilus Eugene "Bull" Connor was the public safety chief for Birmingham, Alabama, during the height of the modern civil rights movement, and his highly aggressive, over-the-top treatment of protestors not only nearly defined this category of redneck sheriff, but was also broadcast on TV news nightly during the 1960s civil rights protests in his city, to the shock of the entire world. However, the worst part about the mythology of the "county boss" is that they were very real, highly effective, and rarely lowered themselves to take such a position as sheriff or other lawman, and even more rarely seriously moved in political circles.

These men (and they were, to all accounts, exclusively male) were the wealthy in political influence, land, or financial power, who were the kingmakers of those in more public roles. Everyone who lived in the county knew and feared these men, and had to either support or at least acknowledge them in nearly every facet of life. County bosses also were usually centrally involved in nearly every criminal and underground enterprise present in their area, suffering no opposition in their own quest for more money, power, and influence. Most were like the wealthy plantation owner John S. Williams, discussed in the previous chapter, who usually hired or directed other men to do his dirty work; but others were by no means reluctant to personally deal with anyone who had crossed them, even to the point of murder. At the same time, these men were widely, deeply, and to all appearances, sincerely admired throughout their area of influence, even by many people who had no overt reason to publicly support them, and, perhaps most surprisingly of all, by many who had great reason to fear them. These powerful men could usually be counted on to lend aid to the poor and supported many charitable organizations, almost always including at least one of the local churches, which their supporters would invariably point out as being key to their "true nature." One of the best examples of this type of violent yet philanthropic "boss" was the ruler of "The Kingdom" in Meriwether County near Pine Mountain: John Walton Wallace.

Wallace was born on June 12, 1896, into a wealthy and powerful family in Glass, Chambers County, Alabama, just west of the Chattahoochee River and the Georgia state line. Although his parents, Thomas "Welsey" and Myrtie Strickland Wallace, owned one of the largest estates in that part of Alabama, they kept their house plain and unpainted on the outside, in the country fashion. The family's wealth was also tied to the land instead of bank accounts, their ancestral holdings in monetary wealth and slaves had been wiped out by the Civil War, and in this agricultural setting, their true fiscal status was absolutely beholden to the variations in crop yields. When the young Wallace turned six, he joined his older sister Jean in attending a local whites-only, one-room private school, Bryson Academy. The elder Wallace turned his attention to local politics, soon moving easily in the ranks of the swells and movers and shakers of Alabama politics, while his farm continued operating, albeit at a much lower pace of production than it had previously. Five years later Welsey died suddenly, probably of appendicitis, leaving his family with a large debt and the crops to pay it off still growing in the fields. After a three-year struggle to pay off the debts, including not only farm-related and medical bills but also significant credit debt owed to several department stores in nearby West Point, Georgia, Myrtie was forced to sell the remaining bits of the farm and its assets and move in with a nearby family friend, LaFayette Lanier, and his own large family.

It was during this difficult period that Wallace began to show another side of his personality. Before the death of his father, he had been known as a sweet, kind, and generous soul, but afterward began displaying a fiery temper, frequently fighting with other students at Bryson, and coming to the unwelcome attention of the local sheriff. Myrtie was advised to take young John out of the school and out of the area before he got into some real trouble. With the final bits of their bankrupted estate settled, in 1912 Myrtie took her children east into Georgia and moved into her own parents' home in the White Sulphur Springs community of Meriwether County. She never remarried, but her brother, Mozart Strickland, became a substitute father for the Wallace children. John stayed in the area for only a year before enrolling in the Gordon Military Academy in Atlanta, later known as Woodward Academy. He was there just one year before moving on and enrolling at Young Harris College in far north Georgia, where he stayed for two years but did not graduate. He apparently did quite well at Young Harris and was popular with other students, and he mentioned his time there frequently for the rest of his life. Wallace left Young Harris in 1916 and moved back to Meriwether County, into a new house down the street from his grandparent's estate. He had a prosperous life for the next two years, allegedly through farming cotton, even though cotton prices were terribly depressed at the time. More than one source mentions that he most likely had learned the moonshining trade by then, which allowed him to turn a tremendous profit with relatively little "seed money" or physical labor involved.

With the entry of the United States into World War I in 1918 came the first military draft since the Civil War. Wallace was called up on September 4, and reported into a training program at Alabama Polytechnic Institute (now Auburn University) on October 1. He was there for less than three weeks before contracting the Spanish flu, which was then tearing across the world in a lethal pandemic. While some of his fellow soldiers were sick but able to get home to recover, Wallace was severely ill and moved to the army's Fort Meade Hospital in Baltimore. He was not well enough to be discharged from there until June 4, 1919, nearly seven months after the war had ended, and was honorably discharged from the army the same day. Although almost the entirety of his nine-month-long army service was spent in the hospital, and he was on active duty barely long enough to break in a single uniform, he would proudly mention his military veteran's status later in life, as part of his honest and honorable personal heritage. Many of his friends, though, later remarked that he came back to Georgia a very changed man, with one friend expressing belief that the disease "messed up his brain."

Wallace apparently picked right back up where he had left off when he returned to Georgia. Aside from his relatively small farm operation and some minor fruit production from some land his mother had purchased in Texas, he seemed to have no visible means of support. This did not stop him, however, from almost immediately buying up various lots of real estate around the northern end of Meriwether County, putting together what he would eventually call his "Empire," as well as a warehouse business in the small town of Chipley, later known as Pine Mountain. His real income came from his semisecret and enormous illegal moonshining and bootlegging operation he ran with his uncle Mozart. With the passage of the Eighteenth Amendment in 1920, banning the manufacture, sale, or transportation of alcoholic beverages, Wallace quickly became widely known in west Georgia and east Alabama as the go-to person for those who "took a drink." Allegedly, his operation grew so large that he and his uncle loaded train cars at the local rail station, taking his booze up to Chicago to be sold in the illegal speakeasies there. Unsurprisingly, an operation of this size soon attracted the attention of federal authorities, despite local lawmen being "on the payroll" at one level or another to protect the operation. Wallace and his uncle were arrested in both 1926 and 1928 for violations of the Prohibition Act, convicted in 1928 in the federal court at Columbus, and each sentenced to two years in the Fulton Tower, the Atlanta penitentiary.

Their term was cut short and both men were released after Wallace "turned in" some of his competing moonshiners to the federal authorities. He again picked back up where he had left off, both with his moonshining operation and with his carefully crafted public demeanor. To most people in and around Chipley— white people that is—he was a friendly, gregarious, and even jovial person who could be counted on to donate whatever was needed to local churches or when someone respected in the community was down on their luck. On the other hand, he also had a well-known reputation for a quick and fiery temper against anyone who crossed him, his family, or his many friends, and especially against the blacks he employed to do all the work around his farm. Even now, sixty years after his death, people in this small west Georgia town who knew him speak only very cautiously about him, invariably mentioning his many acts of friendly charity and his warm public nature.

Even his defenders mention his temper, though, and the exceptionally violent ways he dealt with both the white and black sharecroppers and tenant farmers who worked for him. According to several accounts (not directly backed up by police or court records), Wallace even shot and killed a black man in broad daylight on the main street of Chipley, casually tossing a throw-away knife on the dying man and proclaiming to onlookers that the act was in "self-defense." The man had owed one of Wallace's friends some money, and that friend had just mentioned to Wallace that he was having a hard time collecting it. Wallace later told a law enforcement official about beating a black farmhand to death with

Motto placed by a friend on John Wallace's grave in Pine Mountain
PHOTO BY JOHN MCKAY

a shovel (another crime for which he was never charged) for failing to work hard enough to suit him. This heartless admission, oddly enough, was his attempt to explain how he could not be guilty of the murder that eventually got him executed, as the way it was described as happening simply wasn't his style of violence. He also allegedly told a relatively casual business acquaintance about drowning another black sharecropper, but did not explain why.

Wallace's grandiose ways and complete failure to adequately hide his illegal moonshining operation soon got him in trouble with the federal authorities again. In 1934 he was handed a three-year sentence for his second conviction of making untaxed alcohol, a sentence that was reprieved twice, and eventually reduced to just nine months back in the Fulton Tower. On his release, he decided at long last that he might just need to lay off the illegal still operations, at least for awhile, and turned to dairy farming, a field he had learned about while incarcerated, to support his simple but lavish philanthropic lifestyle. By 1945 he had additionally started up and closed a small milk production business in Chipley, and then settled back down on his farm, satisfied with just shipping his dairy cows' production to a distributor in Columbus, and restarting his still operation when the mood struck him. Some time during that year a poor white man named William Turner came onto his farm, asking for work.

Turner was allegedly AWOL from the US Army, and according to one source, was using his brother's name, Wilson, to avoid being picked up on those charges. At the time this same source claimed Turner was working as a driver for a lumber operation out of nearby Carroll County, when he asked Wallace for a "day job" (meaning he would be basically a hired hand for very low wages), and then was given a sharecropper's position on the dairy farm several months later. He may have also worked in a cotton mill at one point, was a tenant farmer for another landowner, and was married to Julia Windham, but his wife did not know his true first name. All of this is conjecture, cannot be confirmed by any available records, and primarily comes from a single source, but the known and documented facts concerning Turner are that he was working for Wallace in some capacity between 1945 and 1948, and got in a dispute with him about some missing cows. This theft was reported to Meriwether County Sheriff Hardy Collier on April 12, 1948, and Turner was arrested on a charge of theft by Carrollton Chief of Police E. Rada Threadgill on April 18, when he was caught with one of Wallace's registered cows in Carroll County. He was transferred to the Meriwether County jail in Greenville on either April 18 or 19, and for some reason his truck was transported to the facility, presumably by a deputy, as well.

Both Wallace, in a lengthy 1949 letter to the Georgia Board of Pardons and Parole, and one of Wallace's lawyers, Allen Lumpkin Henson, in a subsequent book, paint a very bad portrait of Turner. Wallace claimed he knew that Turner was a fugitive from Carroll County for moonshining, and that he had paid his fine for him to get him out of that trouble, a claim that bears some very uncomfortable reminders of the vicious peonage system, considering what subsequently happened between the two men. He said that Turner did well in his farming, asked for more land to farm, to which Wallace agreed, and then used some of his income to buy a car, "which was his undoing." Wallace also claimed that Turner, unbeknownst to him, had started making illegal untaxed whiskey again, but claimed that he only warned him to stop. He further claimed that Turner used some of Wallace's black sharecroppers in his own operations, which Wallace warned him to stop doing, and when he persisted, personally called the federal revenue authorities and showed them where Turner's operations were. Wallace claimed that as a result of all this illegal operation, he turned Turner over to the courts and then threw him off his property. Turner was given a suspended sentence of twelve months and a fine of two thousand dollars. Wallace also claimed that Turner swore revenge on him, and that he turned to Sheriff Collier for protection. Henson recounted most of this in his book, adding that Turner was a well-known cattle thief who had never served in the military (though Turner himself claimed in court that he was AWOL from the army!), taking his deceased brother's medical exemption form to avoid being drafted.

Wallace had never stopped producing moonshine, and allegedly had increased the scope of his operation, which probably included Turner. He did, however, have a healthy fear of being discovered again by federal revenuers; another sentence from producing untaxed whiskey would probably result in a life sentence in the Fulton Tower. A likely if undocumented scenario of what happened on his farm in 1948 was that he discovered that federal investigators were looking at his operations again, probably tipped off by his friend Sheriff Collier, and decided to use Turner as a handy scapegoat. He fired Turner, refusing to pay him his share of the cotton crop produced, turned him, his wife, and one-year-old son John William out of their house, and informed both law enforcement agencies that any and all moonshining operations found on his land were Turner's, not his. When he was released by the Meriwether Court on bond to finish his harvest, to be able to pay his fine, Turner had nothing in fact to harvest, and instead took two of Wallace's cattle as payment in kind. Five months later he was caught with one of these cows in Carroll County.

Meriwether County Sheriff Hardy Collier was lock, stock, and barrel under Wallace's control, and acted more like one of his employees than as the elected head of the county law enforcement establishment. He held Turner in jail until told to release him by Wallace, who had already drained most of the sharecropper's gas from his truck, so he couldn't escape Wallace's wrath. Despite Wallace's later written protests that he "feared" Turner's alleged wrath, it was clear that Wallace himself was the wrathful one, and was not about to allow some poor "white trash" like Turner to take anything from him, especially his pride. Wallace's plan was to intercept Turner as soon as he left the jail, probably to kill him on the street of Greenville's town square as an "escapee." Turner was released from the jail a bit earlier than expected, just before noon on April 20, before Wallace was present in front of the jail. One account said it was more like Turner was tossed from the jail to the wolves waiting for him, and immediately got in his truck to try to escape from the county. Another part of this story that remains undisputed by any of the involved parties is that Turner raced up the Moreland road toward Newnan in Coweta County, pursued by Wallace and a group of other men. His depleted truck ran out of gas just over the Coweta County line, slowing to a halt in the courtyard of the Sunset Tourist Camp, a small restaurant and motel by the side of the road south of the small town of Moreland. Turner leaped from his truck and raced toward the restaurant's door, closely pursued by Wallace—who had a sawed-off shotgun in hand and a large frame revolver stuck in his belt—and his friend Herring Sivell. Sivell had his own pearl-handled revolver in hand when he caught Turner just before he could get into the building. Both men beat Turner with the butt and stock of their weapons, which brought a sharp retort from Sunset owner Steve Smith.

"What the hell's going on here?" demanded Smith. Wallace responded, "We're officers, this man's an escaped prisoner. Dangerous. Wanted for murder." As the two men continued to beat Turner, and attempted to shove him in their car, Smith called after them, "Why don't you handcuff him, then?" Wallace did not respond, but tiring of the struggle, hit Turner forcefully on the top of his head with either the stock of his shotgun or the butt of his pistol. The firearm might have discharged at that time—accounts vary on that point—but Turner did go limp, and the two men were able to shove him into the back seat of their car. They immediately took off south back into Meriwether County. Turner was never seen alive again. Smith called Coweta County Sheriff Lamar Potts, the twelve-year veteran sheriff who already had a widely recognized reputation for integrity and conscientiousness. Smith reported to him that he thought a murder had just occurred in front of his restaurant.

The facts presented in court by the prosecuting attorney and the defense differ from this point on. Sivell said in a formal disposition that Turner did not die at the Sunset motel, that he was just stunned, with a cut on his head where Wallace had struck him. He further testified that shortly after getting back into Meriwether County, his car had a flat tire, and Wallace and Turner got into another car that had been following them, with Wallace's brother Tom Strickland and his friend Henry Mobley. Wallace claimed in his 1949 letter that Sheriff Collier had told him that he needed to get Turner to confess to taking the cattle before he could be prosecuted, as there was little evidence connecting him to the theft. He claimed that Mobley drove them to an outlying parcel on Wallace's farm, where he took Turner over to an old abandoned well, "anxious to get the details about his operations . . . and had no intention to take his life . . . " Wallace claimed that he was just threatening Turner with his pistol, "when the gun accidently fired, I did not know that he had been struck until I turned around and found him dead." He then said that the three men pushed Turner's body off into the well, and that he later contacted Sheriff Collier, who simply told him to "forget that I ever had seen Turner."

When Coweta County Sheriff Potts responded to the Sunset motel scene, he spoke to at least eight direct eyewitnesses to the scene, all of whom had more or less the same descriptions of what had happened. At least one of them had recognized Wallace and Sivell, while another had gotten a partial license plate number from Sivell's car, along with an accurate description of its make and model. Turner's wife Julia filed a missing persons report the next day, and a massive search for his body began under Pott's command on April 27. At least twice Potts spoke to Sheriff Collier, who deflected all of his questions, maintaining he did not know anything so far as William Turner was concerned, obviously covering for Wallace. Over two hundred lawmen from across the region, along with state revenuers and Georgia State Troopers, combed the woods and farms of southern Coweta and Meriwether counties. While the search was ongoing, Potts contacted Wallace, asking him and Sivell to come up to Newnan to answer some questions. When they arrived, with attorney Gus Huddleston in tow, Potts arrested both of them, charging them with kidnapping. Without Turner's body, a legal demand known as *corpus delicti,* he could not properly charge them with murder.

After arresting Wallace, Potts went to his house in White Sulphur Springs to search for any evidence that could connect him to Turner's death. He found a set of massively bloodstained clothing in the dirty laundry hamper, which a Fulton County medical examiner confirmed was human blood, though they had no way to match it to Turner. A still-unidentified confidential informant told Potts about a large fire at one of Wallace's still sites, and told him that two of his black sharecroppers, Albert Brooks and Robert Lee Gates, had helped him dispose of a body in that fire. When Potts questioned the two, they admitted helping Wallace find Turner's body, using a grappling hook to search the many old wells around the property until they found it, and then burning it up in the fire and dumping the ashes in a creek. One source claimed that this informant was in fact Tom Strickland, who "broke" after being arrested as an accessory and spilled the beans to Potts while in jail. A further search of the nearby area uncovered some small bone fragments in the nearby creek, which were presumed to belong to Turner. In 1948, there was no way to forensically prove whose they were.

A grand jury indicted Wallace for kidnapping and murder, along with Sheriff Collier, Strickland, Sivell, and Mobley as accessories to the kidnapping and murder. Wallace's trial began on June 14, 1948. He already had Huddleston as a lawyer, but since this was a capital case, was convinced to hire another, more experienced "city lawyer" to help in his defense, and was pointed toward Henson, of the Atlanta law firm Harris, Henson, Spence, and Gower. Two of the Sunset motel witnesses testified as to what they saw, two expert witnesses confirmed that Turner probably received a killing blow at that location from the butt of Wallace's weapon, and the two sharecroppers, Brooks and Gates, who had been hidden away in the Columbus jail, were brought in as surprise witnesses, to tell how they had helped Wallace find and dispose of Turner's body.

The next witness exposed another particularity of rural Georgia, Alabama, and Wallace personally. Mayhayley Lancaster (invariably referred to as Mayhayley by all who knew of her) was a lawyer, full-time eccentric, sometimes school teacher, and political activist who dabbled in numbers running and lived in nearby Heard County. She was very widely recognized as a "seer," sometimes referred to as a fortune teller (though she violently rejected this label), whom many people from across the region came to see when faced with a problem or dilemma. The long-time famed columnist of the *Atlanta Constitution*, Celestine Sibley, who covered the trial and was the only reporter to find and interview Julia Turner, once remarked that Mayhayley was "an astute businesswoman and the closest thing to a genuine, old-fashioned witch that I ever saw." Mayhayley referred to herself at least once as "The Oracle of the Ages," admittedly in a setting where she might have simply been displaying her propensity for outrageously dramatic acting out. Wallace had visited Mayhayley for many years, asking her for advice and guidance on many problems and situations, and even considered her his friend. He had come to her once more after the crime, asking her about where he could find Turner's body, admitting the whole story to her, as he had forgotten in his rage where he had dumped it and assumed that, as his friend, she would keep their conversation confidential.

He assumed incorrectly. Mayhayley, for all her eccentricities, still considered herself both an honorable person and an officer of the court, and in short order relayed to Sheriff Potts everything Wallace had told her about the murder. In a rambling, typically eccentric style, she told the court everything Wallace had related to her, and then briefly sparred with the Atlanta defense attorney Henson. It was an unequal battle, to say the least. Henson asked her, "Did the Deity equip you with these supernatural powers before you were born or did it leak in afterwards?" Henson later said in his book that she responded in a most intimidating manner, "'Look-a-here,' she almost screamed, leaning forward to drill me with crazed eyes, 'if you go to tryin' any of these here tricks and lawyer smartness on me, they'll find you in a well, 'n' it might be the same one they throwed Turner in!'" Henson, wisely, refrained from continuing to cross-examine her.

Wallace's primary contention in his defense, carried out by his courtroom lawyers, was not to deny that he had killed or at least had a hand in the death of William Turner, but that the sharecropper's death had not happened exactly in the manner outlined in court papers, and it had not occurred in the jurisdiction where it was being tried, Coweta County. Although he admitted that he was responsible for Turner's death, the fact that it did not happen in Coweta County, as the prosecutor's case maintained, made all the difference in both the strict letter of the law and his mind. It did, in fact, although just not in an overt manner: Wallace "owned" Meriwether County politics and law, and it would have been highly doubtful that he would ever have been indicted there for the crime, much less stood trial or been convicted of the murder. In the end though, his only witnesses, Strickland, Mobley, and Sivell, all refused to testify on his behalf in court. Left with literally no defense case, his lawyers allowed Wallace to speak on his own behalf, a major error to say the least. He gave a long, rambling, and mostly irrelevant speech, seven hours long, giving most of the details of his life. When it came to Turner's death, he only remarked that he did shoot him, but by accident and on his own property in Meriwether County, and that afterward his mind "just went blank" and he could not recall any further details.

With nothing left to present, Wallace's defense team rested after this solitary attempt in his own defense. Closing arguments ended on Friday, June 19, and the judge took about a half hour to charge the jury afterward. The jury took just seventy minutes to carefully consider all the evidence, and returned with a guilty verdict on the same afternoon that they were charged with the case. Judge Samuel Boykin pronounced his sentence to be execution by the electric chair, to be carried out on July 30 of that year. Wallace responded by tipping back in his seat, and nonchalantly popping a stick of chewing gum in his mouth, arrogantly confident that the sentence would never be carried out. On Monday, June 21, Sivell, Mobley, and Strickland all pled guilty to their parts in the case in Judge Boykin's courtroom, and all received life sentences. During the September term of the Superior Court, Brooks and Gates were tried as accessories to murder, but found not guilty. Sheriff Collier was scheduled to be tried on the same charge during that term, but died of a heart attack before the court session began.

A number of lower-level appeals failed, as did a last-minute petition effort in Meriwether County to have Wallace's sentence commuted to life imprisonment. In his subsequent Georgia Supreme Court appeal, though, Wallace's lawyers argued that his sentence should be commuted and his conviction set aside, because of a number of errors in his trial. Most arguments were of the usual lawyerly bluster, insisting that newspapers (from distant Atlanta) had inflamed the jury pool, who had known of Wallace and his reputation all their lives; that Sheriff Potts had engaged in witness tampering by offering rewards for information leading to the conviction of whomever killed Turner; that the sheriff had also improperly acted in the state's role of prosecutor during the investigation and trial by some of his actions, and so on. One specific set of points that did seem to have some serious merit, though the state Supremes did not appear to think so, centered around prosecution witnesses Gates and Brooks: The two men were completely unknown to the defense team (the first time that any defense counsel had met them was when they were testifying in court); the deal they cut with the prosecutors had elements that could have led them to concoct a false testimony for their own benefit; and their testimony was by their own admission scripted and rehearsed. This was all to no avail; Wallace's verdict and sentence was reconfirmed on February 13, 1950, with any chance for additional appeals denied a month later.

In one of his last media interviews, Wallace told *Atlanta Constitution* reporter Celestine Sibley that the death sentence against him would never be carried out. "I'm not going to die for a murder I didn't commit, don't you think a man would know inside if he was facing death?" He also claimed to have found the Lord: "Besides, I've been studying the Bible a good deal since I've been in here. I got religion now. You know, religion is a good thing to have in these parts. People really set store by it."

Margaret Ann Barnes, in her best-selling 1976 book about this case, *Murder in Coweta County* (later made into a TV movie starring Johnny Cash as Sheriff Potts and Andy Griffith as Wallace), related a most remarkable exchange between Potts and Wallace. The two men spoke regularly during the year Wallace spent in the Coweta County jail, awaiting his date with the executioner. He was outraged about what he called "this persistent prejudice against [him]," and on one occasion spoke openly with the sheriff about it. "I simply can't understand it," Wallace said, according to Barnes, "I am *not* a violent man. I'm fifty-three years old and I've only killed four men." Potts directly challenged him about the "only" statement, and then about each of these self-confessed murders, while Wallace insisted all of them were justifiable killings. In the end, Barnes wrapped up the case she and the courts separately built against Wallace by relating Potts's thoughts about this conversation:

Sheriff Potts studied Wallace's implacable face. The appalling fact was that Wallace believed what he said. Over the years, the undeterred progression and escalation of evil deeds and illegal acts had stripped him of all humanity. In his mind, the law, as applied to ordinary men, did not apply to him. Always allowed his own discretion, it had become his right to execute whatever judgment he made.

Insisting to literally the last minute that he was innocent of the specific charges for which he was convicted, Wallace was executed in Georgia's electric chair at 11:00 a.m., on November 3, 1950.

Wallace's influence remains visible even today: The road off Georgia Highway 18 heading toward his old home place is still called Wallace Road (the signs used to say John Wallace Road, but the locals got tired of curious tourists after *Murder in Coweta County* was released), and the drive leading up to his former home is still called Kingdom Lane. His influence continues today in the still-raging online and public debates over his true nature, the circumstances surrounding the death of Turner, and the motivations, integrity, and historical accuracy of Barnes and several other authors who have written books and magazine articles about Wallace and this case.

Wallace's lasting influence has extended even to his grave, where his isolated, individual plot in the old Chipley Cemetery in Pine Mountain bears an additional monument marker on top of the main slab, placed years after his burial by some unknown friend or relative, bearing the inscription, "I kept the pleasant memory; Just rest in peace. J. L. W." Wallace was not buried in his family plot, but far away on the north side of the graveyard, closest to the church where his funeral had been preached. Every photo located showing his grave revealed a flower arrangement at its head; a large and fresh arrangement was even present in December 2011, sixty-one years after his death.

Bibliography

General Sources:

Ancestry.com

Atlanta Constitution newspaper

Atlanta Journal newspaper

Genealogy.com

Georgia Department of Archives & History

The National Archives & Records Administration

The New Georgia Encyclopedia

New York Times newspaper

Chapter 1: Edward Teach

Cordingly, David. *Under the Black Flag: The Romance and the Reality of Life among the Pirates.* New York: Random House, 1996.

Johnson, Captain Charles. *A General History of the Robberies and Murders of the Most Notorious Pirates,* 2nd ed. London: T Warner, 1724.

Parry, Dan. *Blackbeard: The Real Pirate of the Caribbean.* New York: Thunder's Mouth Press, 2006.

Public Record Office, Great Britain. *Calendar of State Papers: Colonial Series: America and West Indies.* London: British Government Publication, 1728–1729.

Vanstory, Burnette. *Georgia's Land of the Golden Isles.* Athens, GA: The University of Georgia Press, 1956.

Woodard, Colin. *The Republic of Pirates: Being the True and Surprising Story of the Caribbean Pirates and the Man Who Brought Them Down.* Orlando, FL: Harcourt, 2007.

Chapter 2: John Wesley

Ahlstrom, Sydney E. *A Religious History of the American People.* New Haven, CT: Yale University Press, 1972.

Brown, Kenneth O. "Wesleys in America: What Went Wrong?" *Christian History*, Issue 69.

Conner, Judson J. *Muskets, Knives and Bloody Marshes: The Fight for Colonial Georgia.* Kearney, NE: Morris Publishing, 2001.

Crutchfield, James A. *It Happened in Georgia.* Guilford, CT: TwoDot, 2007.

Fries, Adelaide L. *The Moravians in Georgia, 1735–1740.* Raleigh, NC: Edwards and Broughton, 1905.

McCain, James R. *Georgia as a Proprietary Province: The Execution of a Trust.* Boston: Richard G. Badger, 1917.

Nelson, James. "John Wesley and the Georgia Moravians." *Transactions of the Moravian Historical Society*, vol. XXIII, no. 3 & 4 (1984), pp. 17–46.

Petry, Janine. "The Matchmakers," *Christian History*, Issue 69.

Queen, Edward L. III, et al. *The Encyclopedia of American Religious History, Volumes I & II.* New York: Facts On File, Inc., 1996.

Wesley, John. *The Journal of John Wesley.* Chicago: Moody Press, 1951.

Chapter 3: Thomas Brown

Alderman, Pat. *One Heroic Hour at King's Mountain.* Johnson City, TN: Overmountain Press, 1968.

Callahan, North. *Royal Raiders: The Tories of the American Revolution.* Indianapolis: Bobbs-Merrill, 1963.

Cashin, Edward J. *The King's Ranger: Thomas Brown and the American Revolution on the Southern Frontier.* Athens, GA: University of Georgia Press, 1989.

Davis, Robert S. "The Cherokee Village at Long Swamp Creek," *A North Georgia Journal of History, Volume I.* Woodstock, GA: Legacy Communications, 1989.

Edgar, Walter. *Partisans & Redcoats: The Southern Conflict That Turned the Tide of the American Revolution.* New York: Harper Collins, 2001.

Jones, Charles C. Jr. *The Dead Towns of Georgia.* Savannah, GA: Morning News Steam Printing House, 1878.

Killion, Ronald G., and Charles T. Waller. *Georgia and the Revolution.* Atlanta, GA: Cherokee Publishing, 1975.

The On-Line Institute for Advanced Loyalist Studies, www.royalprovincial.com.

Scruggs, Carroll P. *Georgia During the Revolution.* Norcross, GA: Bay Tree Grove Publishers, 1975.

Starr, J. Barton. *Tories, Dons & Rebels: The American Revolution in British West Florida.* Gainesville, FL: University Presses of Florida, 1976.

Ward, Harry M. *Between the Lines: Banditti of the American Revolution.* Westport, CT: Praeger, 2002.

Chapter 4: Major Ridge

Davis, Robert S. Jr. "The Cherokee Village at Long Swamp Creek," *A North Georgia Journal of History, Volume I.* Woodstock, GA: Legacy Communications, 1989.

———. "The Indians of Pickens County," *A North Georgia Journal of History, Volume I.* Woodstock, GA: Legacy Communications, 1989.

Day, Charmaine. "Andrew Jackson's Dilemma," *Georgia Backroads,* vol. 9, no. 1, Spring, 2010, pp. 11–15.

Head, Sylvia, and Elizabeth W. Etheridge. *The Neighborhood Mint: Dahlonega in the Age of Jackson.* Macon, GA: Mercer University Press, 1986.

Hemperley, Marion. "The Assassination of Chief William McIntosh," *Moonshine, Murder & Mayhem in Georgia*. Roswell, GA: Legacy Communications, 2003.

Jackson, Olin. "The Murder and Burial of Cherokee Chief James Vann," *A North Georgia Journal of History, Volume I*. Woodstock, GA: Legacy Communications, 1989.

Mooney, James. *James Mooney's History, Myths & Sacred Formulas of the Cherokee*. Fairview, NC: Bright Mountain Books, 1992.

Roper, Daniel M. "The Battle of Hightower Town," *A North Georgia Journal of History, Volume III*. Roswell, GA: Legacy Communications, 1995.

Wilkins, Thurman. *Cherokee Tragedy: The Ridge Family and the Decimation of a People*, 2nd ed. Norman, OK: University of Oklahoma Press, 1986.

Williams, David. *The Georgia Gold Rush: Twenty-Niners, Cherokees, and Gold Fever*. Columbia, SC: University of South Carolina Press, 1993.

Chapter 5: Harrison W. Riley

Cain, Andrew W. *History of Lumpkin County for the First Hundred Years, 1832–1932*. Atlanta: Stein Printing Company, 1932.

Cole, J. Timothy. "Axe Murders in North Georgia: The Baxter Slayings," *Georgia Backroads*, Spring 2002, pp. 36–42.

Head, Sylvia, and Elizabeth W. Etheridge. *The Neighborhood Mint: Dahlonega in the Age of Jackson*. Macon, GA: Mercer University Press, 1986.

Kinsland, William S. "The Life & Times of Gen. Harrison W. Riley," *A North Georgia Journal of History, Volume I*. Woodstock, GA: Legacy Communications, 1989.

Williams, David. *The Georgia Gold Rush: Twenty-Niners, Cherokees, and Gold Fever*. Columbia, SC: University of South Carolina Press, 1993.

Chapter 6: John P. Gatewood

Battey, George M. Jr. *A History of Rome and Floyd County: Including Numerous Incidents of More Than Local Interest: 1540–1922, Volume I.* Atlanta: Webb and Vary, 1922.

Bohannon, Keith S. "Guerrilla Warfare during the Civil War." *The New Georgia Encyclopedia.* www.georgiaencyclopedia.org.

Davis, Robert S. "The Civil War Comes to Pickens County," *A North Georgia Journal of History, Volume I.* Woodstock, GA: Legacy Communications, 1989.

———. "Civil War Guerilla Fighter John P. Gatewood," *North Georgia Journal,* Autumn 2000, pp. 56–58.

———. "A Union Soldier P.O.W. and a Civil War Adventure," *A North Georgia Journal of History, Volume I.* Woodstock, GA: Legacy Communications, 1989.

———, and William S. Kinsland. "Forgotten Union Guerillas of the N. Georgia Mountains," *North Georgia Journal,* Summer 1988, pp. 30–40.

Fisher, Noel C. *War at Every Door: Partisan Politics and Guerrilla Violence in East Tennessee, 1860–1869.* Chapel Hill, NC: University of North Carolina Press, 1997.

Hale, Will T. *A History of Tennessee and Tennesseans: The Leaders and Representative Men in Commerce, Industry and Modern Activities.* Chicago: Lewis Publishing, 1913.

Jackson, Olin, ed. "Guerilla Fighter John Gatewood and a Notorious Livestock Theft," *Moonshine, Murder & Mayhem in Georgia.* Roswell, GA: Legacy Communications, 2003.

Kinsland, William S. "The Civil War Comes to Lumpkin County," *A North Georgia Journal of History, Volume I.* Woodstock, GA: Legacy Communications, 1989.

———. "Murder or Execution? A Tale of Two Counties," *North Georgia Journal,* vol. 1, no. 2, 1984, pp. 13–30.

Sarris, Jonathan D. "Anatomy of an Atrocity: The Madden Branch Massacre and Guerilla Warfare in North Georgia, 1861–1865," *The Georgia Historical Quarterly*, vol. LXXVII, no. 4, Winter 1993, pp. 679–710.

Sartain, James A. *History of Walker County, Georgia, Volume I.* Dalton, GA: A. J. Showalter, 1932.

Chapter 7: William T. Sherman

Battey, George M. Jr. *A History of Rome and Floyd County: Including Numerous Incidents of More Than Local Interest: 1540–1922, Volume I.* Atlanta: Webb and Vary, 1922.

Ewing, Joseph H. "The New Sherman Letters," *American Heritage,* vol. 38, no. 5, July/August 1987.

Hart, B. H. Liddell. *Sherman: Soldier, Realist, American.* Cambridge, MA: Da Capo Press, 1993.

Hirshson, Stanley P. *The White Tecumseh: A Biography of General William T. Sherman.* Hoboken, NJ: Wiley, 1998.

Jones, Archer. *Civil War Command & Strategy: The Process of Victory and Defeat.* New York: Macmillan, 1992.

Marszalek, John F. "Sherman, William Tecumseh," *Encyclopedia of the American Civil War: A Political, Social and Military History, Volume 4.* Santa Barbara, CA: ABC-CLIO, 2000, pp. 1764–1769.

McKay, John E. "William Tecumseh Sherman," *Insiders' Guide to Civil War Sites in the Southern States.* Helena, MT: Falcon Publishing, 2000, pp. 134–135.

Sherman, W. T. *Memoirs of General W. T. Sherman.* New York: Library of America, 1990.

Wheeler, Richard. *Sherman's March.* New York: Thomas Y. Crowell, 1978.

Wortman, Marc. *The Bonfire: The Siege and Burning of Atlanta.* New York: PublicAffairs, 2009.

Chapter 8: John Bell Hood

Bailey, Anne J. *The Chessboard of War: Sherman and Hood in the Autumn Campaigns of 1864.* Lincoln, NE: University of Nebraska Press, 2000.

Castel, Albert. *Decision in the West: The Atlanta Campaign of 1864.* Lawrence, KS: University Press of Kansas, 1992.

Davis, Steve. "John Bell Hood's 'Addictions' in Civil War Literature," *Blue & Gray,* vol. XVI, issue 1, October 1998, pp. 28–31.

Freeman, Douglas S. *Lee's Lieutenants: A Study in Command.* New York: Charles Scribner's Sons, 1972.

Hay, Thomas R. "Davis, Bragg, and Johnston in the Atlanta Campaign," *The Georgia Historical Quarterly,* vol. 8, no. 1 (March, 1924), pp. 38–48.

———. "The Davis-Hood-Johnston Controversy of 1864," *The Mississippi Valley Historical Review*, vol. 11, no. 1 (June, 1924), pp. 54–84.

Hood, John B. *Advance and Retreat: Personal Experiences in the United States and Confederate Armies.* Philadelphia: Burk & M'Petrdige, 1880.

The John Bell Hood Historical Society, www.johnbellhood.org.

Johnson, Robert U., and Clarence C. Buel, eds. *Battles and Leaders of the Civil War.* 4 Vols. New York: The Century Company, 1887–88.

McWhiney, Grady, and Perry D. Jamieson. *Attack and Die: Civil War Military Tactics and the Southern Heritage.* Tuscaloosa, AL: University of Alabama Press, 1982.

Meredith, James. "Hood, John Bell," *Encyclopedia of the American Civil War: A Political, Social and Military History, Volume 2.* Santa Barbara, CA: ABC-CLIO, 2000, pp. 995–998.

Sorrell, Moxley G. *Recollections of a Confederate Staff Officer.* New York: Bantam, 1992.

Watkins, Sam R. *Company Aytch: Maury Grays, First Tennessee Regiment, or A Side Show of the Big Show.* Nashville, TN: Cumberland Presbyterian Publishing House, 1882.

Chapter 9: Henry Wirz

Ambrose, Stephen E., ed. *A Wisconsin Boy in Dixie: Civil War Letters of James K. Newton.* Madison, WI: University of Wisconsin Press, 1961.

Jones, James Pickett. *Yankee Blitzkrieg: Wilson's Raid Through Alabama and Georgia.* Athens, GA: University of Georgia Press, 1976.

Joslyn, Mauriel. "Who Caused Andersonville?" *Journal of Confederate History*, Murfreesboro, TN: Southern Heritage Press, vol. 8 (1995) pp. 181–191.

McKay, John E. *Brave Men in Desperate Times: The Lives of Civil War Soldiers.* Guilford, CT: Globe Pequot Press, 2006.

Ransom, John L. *John Ransom's Diary.* New York: Paul Erikson, 1963.

Speer, Lonnie R. *Portals to Hell: Military Prisons of the Civil War.* Mechanicsburg, PA: Stackpole Books, 1997.

Chapter 10: Charles B. Blacker

Dabney, Joseph E. *More Mountain Spirits: The Continuing Chronicle of Moonshine Life and Corn Whiskey, Wines, Ciders & Beers in America's Appalachians.* Fairview, NC: Bright Mountain Books, 1980.

———. *Mountain Spirits: A Chronicle of Corn Whiskey from King James' Ulster Plantation to America's Appalachians and the Moonshine Life.* Ashville, NC: Bright Mountain Books, 1974.

Miller, Wilbur R. *Revenuers and Moonshiners: Enforcing Federal Liquor Law in the Mountain South, 1865–1900.* Chapel Hill, NC: University of North Carolina Press, 1991.

Stewart, Bruce E. *Moonshiners and Prohibitionists: The Battle Over Alcohol in Southern Appalachia.* Lexington, KY: University Press of Kentucky, 2011.

Chapter 11: Tom Woolfolk

Coulter, E. Merton. *The Toombs Oak, the Tree That Owned Itself, and Other Chapters of Georgia.* Athens, GA: University of Georgia Press, 1966.

DeLoach, Carolyn. *Shadow Chasers: The Woolfolk Tragedy Revisited.* Newnan, GA: Eagles Publishing, 2000.

———. *The Woolfolk Tragedy: The Murders, the Trials, the Hanging, and Now, Finally, the Truth!* Douglasville, GA: Anneewakee River Press, 1996.

Moore, John H. *Carnival of Blood: Dueling, Lynching, and Murder in South Carolina, 1880–1920.* Columbia, SC: University of South Carolina Press, 2006.

Wilkes Jr., Donald E. "Remains of Mass Murder House Found," *Flagpole Magazine*, February 12, 1997, p. 6.

Chapter 12: Thomas Watson

Brown, Walter J. *J. J. Brown and Thomas E. Watson: Georgia Politics 1912–1928.* Macon, GA: Mercer University Press, 2009.

Pierannunzi, Carol. "Thomas E. Watson (1856–1922)." *The New Georgia Encyclopedia.* www.georgiaencyclopedia.org.

Shaw, Barton C. *The Wool-Hat Boys: Georgia's Populist Party.* Baton Rouge, LA: Louisiana State University Press, 1984.

Woodward, C. Vann. *Tom Watson: Agrarian Rebel.* Savannah, GA: Beehive Press, 1973.

Chapter 13: George R. Harsh

Brickhill, Paul. *The Great Escape.* London: Faber & Faber, 1951.

Carroll, Tim. *The Great Escape from Stalag Luft III: The Full Story of How 76 Allied Officers Carried Out World War II's Most Remarkable Mass Escape.* New York: Simon & Schuster, Inc., 2004.

"Collegian on Trial as 'Thrill' Bandit-Slayer," *Elmira Star-Gazette,* Elmira, NY, January 17, 1929, p. 2.

Currey, Josiah Seymour. *History of Milwaukee, City and County, Volume 2.* Chicago: S. J. Clark Publishing Co., 1922.

Davis, Rob. "The Great Escape, Stalag Luft III, Sagan, March 24/ 25th, 1944," www.elsham.pwp.blueyonder.co.uk/gt_esc/index .html.

"Halifax W7824 Information," *Lost Bombers,* www.lostbombers .co.uk/bomber.php?id=9546.

Halliday, Hugh. "Flyboys in the Great Escape: Air Force, Part 22," *Legion Magazine,* July 1, 2007.

Harsh, George. *Lonesome Road.* New York: W. W. Norton & Co., 1971.

"Nab Rich Student as 'Thrill Slayer,'" *Milwaukee Journal,* Milwaukee, WI, October 28, 1929, p. 1.

"Prisoner of War," *The Pegasus Archive,* www.pegasusarchive.org/ pow/frames.htm.

Chapter 14: John S. Williams

Carnes, Marcia H. *History of Jasper County, Georgia: Compiled and Sponsored by the Jasper County Historical Foundation, Inc.* Roswell, GA: W. H. Wolfe Associates, 1984.

Cooper, Len. "The Damned: Slavery Did Not End with the Civil War. One Man's Odyssey into a Nation's Secret Shame," *Washington Post*, 16 June 1996, p. F1.

Daniel, Pete. *The Shadow of Slavery: Peonage in the South, 1901–1969*. Chicago: University of Illinois Press, 1990.

———. "We Are Going to Do Away with These Boys . . . ," *American Heritage*, vol. 23, no. 3, 1972.

Dittmer, John. *Black Georgia in the Progressive Era, 1900–1920*. Chicago: University of Illinois Press, 1980.

Fishback, Price V. "Debt Peonage in Postbellum Georgia," *Explorations in Economic History 26*, 1989, pp. 219–236.

Freeman, Gregory A. *Lay This Body Down: The 1921 Murders of Eleven Plantation Slaves*. Chicago: Lawrence Hill Books/ Chicago Review Press, 1999.

Howe, William Wirt. "The Peonage Cases," *Columbia Law Review*, vol. 4, no. 4 (April 1904), pp. 279–286.

"Six More Bodies of Negroes Found on Georgia Plantation," *New York Tribune,* March 27, 1921, vol. LXXX, no. 27,160, p. 1.

Chapter 15: John Wallace

Barnes, Margaret Anne. *Murder in Coweta County*. New York: Reader's Digest Press, 1976.

Franklin, Harry. "Sister Says Turner Was Told to Leave Farm," *Columbus Ledger-Enquirer*, June 18, 1998.

Henson, Alan Lumpkin. *Confessions of a Criminal Lawyer*. New York: Vantage, 1959.

Moore, Dot. *No Remorse: The Rise and Fall of John Wallace.* Montgomery, AL: NewSouth Books, 2011.

———. *Oracle of the Ages: Reflections on the Curious Life of Fortune Teller Mayhayley Lancaster*. Montgomery, AL: NewSouth Books, 2007.

Nance, Ivey. *From the Farm to the Electric Chair: The John Wallace Story*. CreateSpace (self-published), 2011.

Sibley, Celestine. "Rich Man's Murder Trial Memorable," *Atlanta Journal-Constitution*, October 5, 1995.

South, Glovis Gore. "The Story of Mayhayley Lancaster," *A North Georgia Journal of History, Volume III*. Roswell, GA: Legacy Communications, 1996.

Wallace v. Foster, Sheriff. 16924, 206 Ga. 561, 57 SE2d 920, 1950.

Index

About the Author

John McKay is a near-native of Atlanta, growing up in the Brookhaven area near Buckhead and Lenox Square, and has rarely left the area since. He is a historian specializing in military subjects, especially the Western Theater of the American Civil War, and a high school history and government teacher. He is a veteran of the US Army and Georgia Army National Guard, worked for many years as a paramedic and firefighter in and around Atlanta, and lives in the northern suburbs with his wife, Bonnie, a nurse, professionally trained chef, and recovering debutante.